I0225300

The Great Persian Saga Continues

King of Lands, King of Peoples,
King of Kings
Book IV Movement IV

Pray to the Wind
Armageddon

By Dr. Jeffrey Donner

Copyright 2018 by Dr. Jeffrey Donner
All rights Reserved.

No part of this book may be used or reproduced by any means, graphic, electronic, or mechanical, including photocopying, recording, taping or by any information storage retrieval system without the written permission of the author except in the case of brief quotations embodied in articles and review.

978-1-7320143-4-3

Table of Contents

The Players

The Persians

Major Persian Players

Xerxes- The King of Kings and ruler of the Empire

Penish- known as the Executioner-bodyguard of the King

Darius the Great- Xerxes' father (deceased)

Ho of Sebennytos- Xerxes stepmother

Hamas great warrior-Xerxes teacher- killed by Leonidas at Delphi.

Artemisia- The Warrior Queen of Halicarnassus

Adon- Phoenician bodyguard of Artemisia

Ningizzida- renegade priest-enemy of Xerxes

Demaratus- ex-Spartan King- turncoat- one of Xerxes generals

Smerdomences- General of the Elite 10,000 Immortals

Cypercant- Moon woman- witch

Minor Persian Players

Datis- disgraced Persian general from Marathon

Mardonius- Xerxes uncle- general in the army

Persian Generals

Masistes

Gergis

Tritantacechmes

Persian Admirals

Zephan

Ariabignes

Prxaspes

Matten- Phoenician King

Vashti- Xerxes' wife

Volesmo- Xerxes concubine

Hadassah-Xerxes Jewish concubine

Golnar- Lector priestess- Xerxes confidant

Magi to the King

Assim- the great one

Balthasar-the war advisor

Asanaladace- Great Persian Engineer

Amon- Egyptian Engineer

Hailama- Phoenician Engineer

Harpalus- Macedonian Engineer

The Greeks

Major Greek Players

Themistocles- father of the Demos

Eudox- second under Themistocles

Thantos- explorer- adventurer – sea captain

Leonidas- Spartan King

Sakarbaal- Phoenician turncoat- sailor

Lasiandra-blind Pythia

Ptea- pirate- ally of Thantos

Eurybiadas- Spartan Admiral

Skyllias of Skione- pearl diver

Aristides- "the just" political adversary of Themistocles

Minor Greek Players

Eudocia- Greek Spy

Lason- Aegean Diplomat

Gelon- Dictator of Syracuse in Sicily

Lycomedes- first Greek to take a Persian ship intact

Paramonos- organizer for evacuation of Athens

Eudoxia- Athenian woman evacuated from city

Eudoxia's Children

Nikon

Zoe

Damianos- Priest at Athena Temple in Athens

Ephialtes- traitor of Leonidas at Thermopylae

The Gods

Athena- Goddess of foresight

Bubo- wise owl of Athena

Poseidon- God of the Oceans

Zeus- Father of all Gods

Apollo-God of the Sun and the Oracle at Delphi

Anemoi- God of the wind

Notus- God of Storms

Ares- God of fear and terror

Ahuramazda- Persian God

Other Things of Interest

Phecontalis- Thantos' second in command- killed by Persian general

Smerdomences

Simeron- Lioness- pet of Xerxes

Pythia- Priestess of the Delphic Oracle- merges with the God Apollo

Solon- Great Athenian thinker

Anthousa- female form Athena took during evacuation of Athens

Chapter I – The Executioner

The chariot had pure gold posts and a fashioned façade in the shape a shield, but rather than the customary bronze, it too, was also pure gold. On each of its side rails sat the bust of a great lion with it mane made of horse hair. The lion was sculptured with its mouth open and one could almost hear its roar as the wind passed through it. This Persian scythed chariot had a yoke with four large, white, Nisaean horses leading the way. On its axles spinning with the wheels, sat two razor sharped scythes that could cut through armor. It was believed that no army could survive a coordinated direct assault from these attack chariots. The scythes could cut through men as easily as a hot knife through butter. Under the gold shield that stood protectively on its front, was an image of the Egyptian dwarf God BE, the protective deity that the Persian King had introduced from their Egyptian satrap. After all, the Persian King was also the Pharaoh of that ancient civilization, having declared himself such during the conquest of Egypt. The Egyptian satrap had rebelled against the young Persian monarch. Xerxes took his army and quickly crushed the Egyptian priests that orchestrated the uprising. And he did so in brutal but efficient fashion. He was dramatic in his execution of the leaders, and high-minded in declaring himself the new pharaoh.

The Nisaean horses that pulled these powerful and fearless chariots were the most imposing animals that this enormous Empire could breed. The Persian Empire was the most powerful and wealthiest Kingdom in all known history. It stretched from the Indus River in the east, to the Black Sea in the north, to Macedonia on the European continent, and south to Egypt on the Dark Continent. It stretched at its width over 2500 miles, and, although was it run by governors and minor Kings, they all answered to the King of Peoples, King of Lands, King of Kings, Xerxes the Great.

The Nisaean horses were powerful animals with large heads and small necks. Their saddle cloths were brightly colored and heavily embroidered with geometric designs and scalloped edges. Their leather bridles were dyed red and their metal bits were bronze. As impressive as the Persian scythed chariots were, this lead chariot was slightly larger and embossed with gold and pearls throughout. On its sides, two large purple flags blew gently in the wind. On the flags was the other image of the protector of the realm, the male lion.

It was a very warm day with the early sun beating down on the water starved land. The sky had not opened with water for months. The royal chariot created its own dust storm as it flew over the dry earth. When one watched it move, it was easy to tell that this spectacular vehicle was different from the others. More embroidered and embellished than the others, it displayed a regal image and moved across the ground with the sound and fury of an earthquake kept purposely noisy. It was either impressive or terrifying, depending on where you stood.

Riding on the chariot were three men. The elite charioteer was the most decorated of the drivers in this immense Empire. He was chosen from among hundreds of successful soldiers, not only for his skill and bravery, but for his loyalty to the throne. His devotion to the young monarch was beyond reproach. His name was Penish, but he was known in the inner circle of the Empire, as 'The Executioner'. Of all the warriors in the Empire, Penish was arguably one of the most dependable protectors of the dynasty. He was omnipresent, always on the outskirts, always protecting his sovereign. Penish was not only a fierce combatant, but had twice saved his King from assassination attempts. This had forever fused the two men and led to Xerxes referring to him as The Executioner.

Penish was tall for a Persian. He was in fact, a Mead, and hailed from the same tribal group as the King himself. His face was cold and focused, often frozen in a grim stare with vacant eyes. As he rode, his alertness was apparent. He took his job as body guard to the King of Kings very seriously and was always on watch. His life was meaningless, and he would gladly sacrifice it for protection of his monarch. His only purpose was to safely carry out the King's orders and protect the throne from its many enemies.

As the chariot made its way, any unlikely movement got The Executioner's attention. He was not afraid to stop the procession if he felt there was something unusual. Penish was a hard man. It was rumored that he felt no pain. Penish's parents were murdered by marauding neighboring tribes when he was only five. He was taken as a slave, tortured and beaten, until he escaped his bondage by murdering his captive in the middle of the night. The young Penish was taken in by Darius the Great, Xerxes' father. Treated with respect, the young Penish became radicalized and completely devoted. His King, this unique King, was his life.

The Empire was familiar with assassination attempts. When a single ruler holds such great power, the ability to control every aspect of his subject's lives, attempts at revenge were not uncommon. The most dramatic attempt on this young King's life occurred in Babylonia before he ascended the throne, when Xerxes was attacked by the society of killers called the Sand Dancers. The Sand Dancers were a brotherhood of assassins willing to sell their services to the highest bidders. These men were experts in their field, trained from a very early age to be proficient in their tasks. Their reputation as silent murderers was legendary throughout the Empire. Usually it was the King of the Empire that utilized their services, but their contracts were for sale, and reimbursement spoke louder than loyalty. It was their peculiar religion.

On that momentous day, Penish was on a routine mission bringing a message to the young prince of the Empire. When he had entered the temple, he had a sense that something was amiss and hurried his walk. There was an eerie quiet as Penish made his way through the halls. What he eventually saw shocked and surprised him as he noticed blood flowing from behind a pillar. For a heartbeat, Penish stared at the red ooze slowly flowing from behind the column. He could feel his neck muscles tighten and his hands close into a fist. Investigating, Penish found the guards butchered in quite a gory fashion. It was not just a killing, it was a butchering. At first glance, it did not appear as though the guards had put up a fight, as their weapons remained in their place. Penish reacted immediately and burst open the doors of the King's chamber. He feared the King had already been assassinated. He found Xerxes surrounded by five men dressed in black with their heads covered in sand colored masks. The would-be-King had his own sword drawn and the assassins were circling him, slowly backing him into a corner. Penish caught Xerxes' eye for a moment and was impressed that he saw no fear, only determination.

In a split second, Penish realized that Xerxes was expertly fending off the men almost to a standoff. But even so, he was backing up and would soon be in an inescapable position. Penish flew into the antechamber, rushing straight at the men surrounding the King. As he approached he yelled, then slid to his knees. In the process, he adroitly took out two of the attackers, slashing at their legs. Xerxes immediately responded as well, going on the offensive against the other men. As the would-be King impaled one of the attackers, Penish felled a third with a sword in the spine. With four of his comrade's dead beside him, the last assassin fell to his knees, eventually ending his own life because of his failure. This experience bonded Penish to the young prince.

Penish also was the warrior that captured the rebellious priest, Ningizzida, who was the sworn enemy of the Archimedean monarch. Ningizzida, the renegade priest from Babylonia was one of the most hatred and wanted men within the royal court. When the young King took over the leadership of the Empire after his father was poisoned, he went to Babylonia to perform a sacred religious observance. During that ceremony, Ningizzida embarrassed and assaulted the young King, knocking Xerxes unconscious in front of the parishioners. The priest escaped, but Penish finally tracked him down hiding in a cave in the desert. He was brought back to Susa and caged in a subterranean pit. Xerxes enjoyed watching the priest's life slowly drain from his body. The King wanted the priest to suffer both physically and spiritually, before he was allowed the release of death. The young King would often come to the dungeon and urinate into the hole in which the priest was imprisoned. Miraculously, Ningizzida escaped a second time, and to this date was still at lodge. After his escape, the priest had staged his own death, but Xerxes saw through the rouse. Through co-conspirators, the renegade priest had also engineered an unsuccessful rebellion of Babylonia. Xerxes was harsh in his retaliation, destroying the lovely city of Babylonia and melting the gold statue of its God to be brought back to Susa.

Now, the executioner's stellar service had vaulted him to the young King's personal bodyguard. The King of Kings was rarely seen in public without the vigilant eyes of Penish on him. Penish was a harsh man and single-minded in his devotion. Raised in poverty he fought his way up through the military ranks. In many ways he was similar to the King, emotionless and cold. Whereas Penish was a better warrior than the young monarch, Xerxes was much smarter. Penish knew his life was sacrificed for Xerxes. He would not hesitate to martyr himself in that protection.

Behind Penish on the chariot on a large throne, sat Xerxes, The King of Lands, the King of Peoples and the King of Kings. He was magnificent in his regalia and his stare was emotionless, icy, and unwavering. His makeup was impeccable, red eyelids with a dark outline. His beard was braided into a square design, with not a single hair out of place. His hair was long and reached down to the center of his back. His body was muscled, and every morning was oiled by three slaves. Although not a womanizer, Xerxes was vain. He frequently wore only a short Egyptian kilt made of cotton imported from India. He was proud of his upper body and this sparse outfit showed off his arms and chest. But today the wind was blowing, so the great King wore a Kalasiris outfit. This ritual outfit was also very symbolic for the young King. The Kalasiris was a tight fitting, sleeveless garment made from different pieces and colors of linen. A leopard skin hung around his shoulders, and a lion tail hung from his belt. It was the tail of the lion that the King had slain in his coming of age ceremony. On his head, Xerxes wore a Nemes, a favorite of his since declaring himself pharaoh. The Nemes covered his entire head with two large flaps behind his ears reaching down to the front of his shoulders. It was gold and blue striped. On the front of the Nemes was the image Uraeus, the reared body of the Egyptian cobra. This had special relevance for Xerxes, as the Uraeus was the representation of the Wadjet Cult in Egypt. Its followers were called Buto priests. Wadjet was the ancient Egyptian Goddess that protected lower Egypt. It was the Buto priests that fermented the rebellion that Xerxes crushed. Xerxes wore this outfit to symbolize his defeat of Wadjet and to express his supremacy over the ancient traditions.

In contrast to this impeccably dressed monarch, behind him on the chair sat a mostly naked slave (save for his sandals). This nameless person had only one life purpose. His only duty was to remind the great King of his hatred for the Greeks. Xerxes did not want his resolve for the destruction of Greece and Athens in part to waiver. He wanted his hatred of that inferior race to boil within his veins. Twice a day the slave was instructed to lean over the King's back shoulder and say, "Remember Marathon". Every time that hated word was uttered, Xerxes could feel bile accumulate in his chest. This was the third slave to assume this post. The person who held the post of telling the revengeful King about the most embarrassing defeat in Persian history, did not have a long lifetime. For the word Marathon could spark an uncontrollable rage within the young sovereign.

Marathon was the battle where the King's father, Darius, sent a large expeditionary force to punish the Greeks for their instigation and support of an Ionian rebellion in the Empire's Western frontier. When the Persians arrived on the plain of Marathon, their general Datis, was manipulated by an Athenian conspirator to believe that the city of Athens was open for the taking. Thinking that he was seizing the moment, Datis took his navy and cavalry south to Athens, leaving his troops unprotected on the Marathon plain. The Greeks, led by a military genius named Militates, immediately noticed the Persian mistake. He surprised the superior Persian force by taking the aggressive initiative, ultimately destroying the much larger force. The Greek Hoplites pushed the Persian soldiers into the swamp that backed up their position. The troops either drowned or were slaughtered. It was the most humiliating defeat in recorded Persian history and one that still burned in Xerxes' belly. The general, Datis, who was responsible for this travesty, became an unspoken word in the Empire. Xerxes father Darius was so incensed by the stupidity of his general that he almost beheaded him in person. To call someone Datis was the worst curse one could make.

Marathon left such a bad taste in the Persian mouth that it consumed Darius. He took it as a personal defeat. The usually pleasant Darius had become moody since the Marathon defeat, at times spending days alone ruminating. With the change in the King's personality, the palace became a different place. The man who was the most progressive monarch in history, became tyrannical and obsessed.

Darius had taken a second wife while in Egypt. Her name was Ho of Sebennytos and she was considered a prophet of God in her ancient land. Ho was versed in the papyrus of Ani or the Egyptian Book of the Dead, and it was rumored that she could speak directly with the spirits. In his despair and anguish, Darius visited his wife who had taken up residence in caves outside of the royal palace. She had refused to live in the palace.

Like all others who visited her caves, Darius was placed in a lavishly decorated area to wait for Ho. No matter what their status, all waited for Ho. Darius sat with his elbows on his knees and his hands on his head. When Ho entered and saw this, she walked straight to the King and slapped him in the head.

"You are King of the greatest Empire that the world has known,"

She screamed. *"Why to sit and whine like a child?"*

Darius looked at his wife with surprise. He was more embarrassed than angry.

"Have you seen my future?" the King questioned.

"I have, my love. Your father has spoken to me."

"And what was said?"

"I am sorry, my King, but your future is your future and revealing it will change what is prophesized."

Darius stood, took a step forward and kissed her forehead. He knew what his wife's response meant. His life was reaching its end and there was nothing he could do to influence fate.

Then one afternoon, not long after his visit, Darius was walking the gardens with two advisors. While passing a small reddish bush, the King turned to the right and grabbed his stomach. Darius fell to his knees dry heaving. As the advisors stared, Darius turned around back and began talking to the sky. His eyes rolled back in his head and the King began seizing. It was eventually concluded that Darius was poisoned. The entire kitchen staff died for that execution. Xerxes was immediately vaulted into the limelight and inherited the blood vendetta against the Greeks and Athens. His blood boiled for revenge. And after the word Datis, Athens was the second most abhorrent sound.

The gold chariot carrying Xerxes, now King, was surrounded by one of the units of 10,000 Immortals, the most feared and well-trained soldiers in the Achaemenid Empire. They were disciplined and their appearance on a battlefield brought terror to the enemy. They surrounded and protected their King with their lives. In legend they were called, Ausiya.

In the field, the Ausiya were easy to recognize. Under their robes they wore scale armor. They carried wicker and leather shields. As they marched, they wore their dress robes. These were elaborately designed garments. They wore large gold-hoop earrings. The Ausiya were separate from the other army squadrons. They had their own food, their own tents, and their own concubines. This squadron was led by the most ruthless and cold hearted general that Xerxes had. His name was Smerdomences.

This general had many successes in his bloody resume, not the least of which was when Smerdomences and his elite troops had captured three Greek spies infiltrating the Empire to measure the strength of the Persian army. They destroyed the ship that was hidden in a small cove, waiting to carry the spies back to Athens. In that process, Smerdomences had personally murdered the man left in charge of protecting the vessel. He still carried the gold-plated scabbard that he took off the man in his death throes. The man happened to be the compatriot of one of the spies. Phecontalis, the man that Smerdomences killed, was the closest thing that the captain, Thantos, had to a brother. When Thantos saw the specialized scabbard that Smerdomences carried, he knew that the general had murdered his friend. At that time he had to be restrained to save his life, from the general's wrath.

Of the three spies captured, only two lived to reach Susa and the King. Xerxes himself murdered one during a dinner and came close to slaying the other. The lone survivor's name was Thantos, and unbeknownst to the Persian King, was a very close associate of the Greek politician, and de facto leader of his hated Athens, Themistocles. Xerxes surprised his military commanders by showing Thantos the entire Persian force. In this unusual move, The King authorized that Thantos be led through the assembled forces, with the hope of impressing upon him the tremendous army that he was gathering to march on Athens. He then sent the Greek saboteur back to Athens to report the immense strength of the army and navy opposing them. Xerxes was not naïve. If he could convince the Greeks that their defense of their country was hopeless, it would give his army an edge in the field.

When he realized the unorthodox scheme being employed by the young monarch, Smerdomences was duly impressed by the psychological strategy. Like Penish, Smerdomences was one of the great King's most trusted advisors. Although ruthless and sadistic, Smerdomences was devoted to the young monarch. A true psychopath, Smerdomences was charming when he needed to be, but sensitivity and empathy were not natural in his makeup. Every one of the Immortals under his guidance would need to be lying in their own blood before an enemy would be allowed to touch Xerxes.

Directly behind the royal chariot was a wagon with a single wooden cage on it. The cage housed Simeron, the King's pet lioness. This beast had been captured and raised from a cub by Xerxes. The lion was the symbolic representation of the Persian Empire. When Xerxes and his troops put down the Egyptian uprising, he had left Simeron home, and even though the army proved successful, Xerxes himself missed the company of his pet. He would often sit in meditation near the feline, talking quietly to her when he needed guidance. He also knew that Simeron's presence intimidated foreign dignitaries who visited the palace. When heads of state visited the palace, Simeron was placed between Xerxes and the dignitaries. Xerxes pledged to the Gods that Simeron would travel with his master and observe the destruction of the Greek city states.

Since his coronation, Xerxes had led the army to Egypt to squelch the rebellion that rose from sects of the Egyptian priesthood. It was Median tradition that the King would lead his troops, proving his worthiness. Until he did, Xerxes knew that the nobles would have questions about his leadership skills. The Egyptian campaign was a revelation for the young King because he lost some confidence in his own troops. It was at the end of this campaign, after securing the Egyptian capital of Memphis, Xerxes declared himself Pharaoh. Xerxes alleged that he had a familial connection to the Egyptian throne, as his step-mother, Ho, was of Egyptian decent.

But the Greek campaign would be a completely different matter than reconquering Egypt from a group of monks and vigilantes. Xerxes had taken only certain elements of the army to Egypt. Greece was another story. The decision to bring an enormous army such a distance to satisfy revenge was not an easy one for the young King. Many of his advisors warned against it. Although the bile burned in his throat, up until the last minute, Xerxes questioned his decision to bring this mass of people and equipment such a distance. He had tried to buy off the young Greek democracy to no avail. Both Athens and Sparta not only refused the King's offers, but murdered the men sent to deliver them.

But now that he was King, Xerxes knew that the satisfaction of revenge couldn't be the only driving factor in the invasion. He needed to guide his passions with reason. He knew that this expedition to Greece could bankrupt the Empire. He also worried that some of the remaining satrap's would attempt to gain advantage and rebel as the army left Asia. In his young tenure as the leader of this great Empire, Xerxes had already put down two revolutions, one in Egypt, and the second led by the renegade priest, Ningizzida, in Babylonia. Even thinking that cursed cleric's name brought dark and hostile thoughts to the King's mind. But it was the strategic issue of the Greek invasion that gave the young King sleepless nights, not the rebel priest. Bringing such a large army and their cohorts such a distance, had never been attempted before.

It took years of preparation and wavering indecision by the young King, but the time had arrived to seek vengeance again the hated Athenians. The task of bringing his army over 3000 miles was a mammoth undertaking. As the young King wrestled with the pros and cons of the undertaking, eventually his deep-seated loathing and vengeance won out over financial responsibility and reason. Besides, he reasoned, it was the Persian destiny to rule the known world. This initiative could ruin the Empire and Xerxes' advisors were split on the advisability of taking this step. In fact, the man that he trusted most, the man that he called, 'the teacher' had warned the young monarch of the danger of this undertaking.

Hamas had been the juvenile boy's mentor. He had trained him in strength and reason. Not a day had gone by in the young man's life that Hamas was not teaching him about the ways of the Persian, the ways of a warrior, and most importantly, the ways of a leader. Xerxes himself was an exceptional student. He was stronger, more cunning, and swifter than most. And most importantly, he had total self-confidence and little, if any, fear. He was resolute in his purpose.

Hamas was never as sure of these traits as when he watched the young man successfully complete his last rite of passage. It was an old Median custom that a King had to defeat a male lion to prove his supremacy. It was a tradition that was rarely attempted because of the inherent danger of the exercise. But Xerxes, in the exuberance of his youth, insisted on the rite.

"It will show my people my true heart," he had reasoned.

To make the task more daunting, the room where the confrontation was to take place was in darkness, and the soon to be King had to use his instincts to outwit the animal. The lion's ability to hunt in darkness gave it a distinct advantage in the confrontation. When Hamas protested that the ritual was too dangerous even for an accomplished warrior, Xerxes turned to him with fire in his eyes and in a reassuring voice, said, *"I am Khashayarshah, the lion King. I will rule with strength. Even my Hebrew slaves call me Achavhverosh, the Great Warrior, the Lion Warrior."*

The young soon to be monarch defeated the lion, but not without scars that he proudly displayed to this day.

Xerxes had been told that there was one last chance of securing peace without war. The Greeks were willing to speak with representatives of the Empire at the great Oracle at Delphi. Strangely, Xerxes had sent Hamas, 'the teacher' in the delegation, to the great Oracle at Delphi seeking wisdom and endorsement of his upcoming invasion. It was a strange delegation that included Artemisia, the great Warrior Queen. She was the least diplomatic person that the King knew. By this time, Xerxes obviously knew that peace or submission was a distant dream. Therefore, including the Warrior Queen was almost a provocation. It was almost as if the King wanted Artemisia to start the fight. Behind the scenes, Xerxes was lining up Greek cities to stand with the Empire against the Greek alliance of Sparta and Athens. He already had the assurances of almost 60 cities. Each had agreed for a different price, some happy just to receive the offer.

Xerxes knew that the Greeks were sending two delegations to Delphi. For over 1000 years, Kings and commoners had been depending upon the great Oracle at Delphi for direction and insight. The priestess, called the Pythia, spoke directly to the God, Apollo, and relayed his answers to those who asked. The Oracle was miraculously accurate in its reading of the imminent. Both the Spartans and the Athenians were sending delegations to ask the God Apollo about the future. The King had sent secret delegations to the Athenians again to measure their interest in a diplomatic solution to their conflict. Through the underground channels, came the answer:

"Meet us at Delphi!"

Xerxes had mulled over this decision to send a delegation to the Oracle for some time. He had no misconceptions about the Greek agenda. Either they were going to try to convince him with some deceit that they wanted peace, or they would try to convince him not to invade. Xerxes knew that the Greeks were greedy and could be bought. But still, why send a delegation for what he knew was a scam? It eventually boiled down to curiosity.

Hamas and the Warrior Queen had both protested their involvement in this diplomatic mission to the great Oracle. But the young King wanted Hamas, his most trusted confidant, to evaluate the Greek spirit and resolve. Unfortunately while at Delphi, Hamas forced a confrontation with the Spartan King, Leonidas, who was also visiting the great Oracle. After a dramatic and pitched fight, Hamas was killed by the Spartan King. When Xerxes heard of the murder of his teacher, he was sent into a hurricane proportion fury. The death of his friend and counselor was unfathomable to the young King. His rage at the death of his mentor was the final straw that tilted the King in favor of invasion. But now it wasn't just for conquest. He wanted destruction and annihilation, not just defeat. It was no longer a feud guided by his father and Marathon, it was now personal, and Greek blood was the only way to heal this wound.

This impending war was a very serious burden for the young King and for the vast Empire in general. His ancestors called to him nightly in his dreams, demanding vengeance and placing the burden of the revenge directly on his shoulders. The young King would wake sweaty and anxious, shivering even when the night's heat was high. The dead were reaching out to him and he could not evade their chants.

Xerxes claimed heritage to the ancient Elamic powers, backed as well by a strong Persian heritage. But more importantly, he believed the great God anointed him to this position, as he had done with his father, Darius. He was not just a ruler, he was the chosen one, the one of destiny. All history was written to converge on this space and at this time. Ahuramazda, the God of creation had chosen Xerxes to spread his glory. To Xerxes, the Greek belief in a pantheon of Gods was a mistaken and delusional conviction. They were followers of the lie and needed to be destroyed for it.

Xerxes father, Darius, had practiced religious tolerance, allowing subjugated people to believe and worship whatever they chose, as long as their earthly loyalty was to the Empire. He felt that challenging long held beliefs were ways to ferment rebellion. But his son Xerxes was of a different mind. Tolerance was not one of his strengths. Everyone had to understand the genuineness of belief in the true God, Ahuramazda. Only through belief and deference could salvation be reached. He further felt that if he could convert people to the truth, it would cement the Empire and eliminate traditional intra tribal hatreds. It sounded easy to the young mind of the King, very black and white. But as Hamas had warned:

"The truth of conviction does not guarantee success. Belief does not sway to the might of armies. Wars are won by preparation and strategy, not by faith and hope."

Because the Greeks could not understand monotheism and the beauty of the one God, was all the more reason for their destruction. They were inferior in body as well as in spirit. They clung to their ancient beliefs and outdated rituals. It was time that the truth overcame the lie. Xerxes was the hand of the almighty. He could feel it. In his meditations, the young King could clearly see the blood of his ancestors rushing through his veins like water through a bamboo pipe. It was the Persian destiny to rule the known world, and it was time to fulfill the scriptures. No other result would satisfy Ahuramazda.

In his short ascent to the head of the Empire, Xerxes had already reconquered Egypt and put down Babylonia. But these were both satraps, provinces of his Empire. Greece was a foreign power whose leaders foolishly intervened in Persian affairs. Interestingly, most of the Greek city states had already formed submissive relationships with the great King. He had sent envoys to seek earth and water subservience from most of the Greek cities. It was the Persian way to ask for earth and water from adversaries. If given, these two foundations of life, would symbolically tie the peoples to Xerxes. Two thirds of the Greek cities and territories had already pledged subservience to the great King. Only Athens, Sparta, and twenty-eight other cities resisted the inevitable decision to submit to the superior power of the Empire. In doing so they were purposely defying Persian destiny and would be branded with the mark of infidels. They also sealed their fates with their stubbornness. But even the most determined of these cities wavered in their resistance. Xerxes was still confident that they could be brought under the whip.

Xerxes did not completely understand the resolve of the Spartans and Athenians. He believed that every conviction of infidels, everything they dedicated their life to could be altered for a price. Most of the Greek cities that held out would be irrelevant to the eventual outcome. He wanted Sparta and Athens, and he wanted them to burn. When emissaries from the Empire arrived in many Greek cities, they were treated with respect from the existing governments. But not in Athens and Sparta, where the emissaries were brutally murdered. In Sparta they were thrown in a deep ditch and urinated on until they died of exposure and hunger. It is one thing to reject an offer, but this lack of respect had to be answered and countered with blood. Xerxes would spit on their bodies, burn their temples, use their woman, and enslave all the children.

Next to the gold chariot of the King of Kings rode another similar looking chariot. But this one only held a slave as it charioteer. For in this chariot rode the God Ahuramazda. He would accompany the great King to Attica and be there when the fire of destruction rained down on the Greek Peninsula.

Xerxes left his castle in Susa at the beginning of April with the goal of bringing his vast army to Sardis on the western edge of the Empire before winter came. This was, in and of itself, not an easy trek, as it was almost 2,000 miles. He would pass Babylonia, Assyria, Cilicia and hundreds of other smaller cities. It was in Sardis that the King would winter until his crossing into The European continent the next spring.

Xerxes had assembled the largest and most imposing army in history, destined to cross into Europe and punish the Greeks. The numbers were beyond belief. Over a million soldiers were from Asia, and almost 300,000 from European allies. When servants, attendants, magi, slaves, and concubines were included, the number of people that were making this incredible journey reached a million and a half to two million souls. They were accompanied by 1200 trireme warships with over double that in transport vessels.

Xerxes had planned this invasion well, planting large stores of grain, feed and water along the royal road in anticipation of this march. But even so, a collection of so many animals and people needed endless sustenance. The route was planned to pass rivers that could be used to replenish the men and animals. Many of these estuaries would be drunk dry to satisfy the traveling masses.

It was the eighth day of April and the King's entourage stopped in Assyria by the shores of the Tigris. This area was well known to Xerxes, as he had served as Viceroy in Babylon, not far from this place where they now rested. Although he would never admit it, this area created a large degree of bitterness in the throat of the young King. For it was in that cursed city of Babylonia that the King, not long after his ascension to the throne, suffered his greatest insult. During a religious ceremony honoring the Babylonian God, Xerxes was rendered unconscious by a turncoat priest named Ningizzida. Xerxes sent his minions out and dragged the priest back to his dungeon in his palace at Susa. But then, under the nose of his guards, Ningizzida was rescued from his certain death by some of his followers, a situation which infuriated the young King and cost the lives of many guards. Xerxes eventually leveled Babylon when the city rebelled against his rule. But he could still feel tightening in his neck and chest muscles when he thought that this hated man, this turncoat priest, still walked free.

It took hours for Xerxes' slaves to set up his large, sumptuous tent. Fifty slaves of Assyrian descent accompanied the army with the sole purpose of erecting and taking down the royal tent and the living quarters of his entourage. It was a daunting task that required precision and exactitude. The young King was not a patient man, and he could become outraged if he found something amiss with his accommodations. He had once killed five slave girls who had difficulty with his morning makeup.

****

The owl flew high above the clouds. Although in perfect synchronicity with the wind, there was something about the path that seemed unusual, out of place. This owl was one of the most graceful of flyers, but today its flight was irregular. It was as if it was attempting to fight the wind and the natural flow of nature with its gyrations.

Beneath the owl sat a green-eyed beauty. As she heard the screeching she slowly glanced upward, not surprised by unusual scene that she was witnessing. This woman knew this bird very well. In fact, its spirit and soul were forever connected with hers, and would be forever. As she stared into the sky, her face appeared dysphoric. As she gazed her eyes began to water, an unusual emotional response for this woman.

The Goddess Athena had fought many battles. She found, as she began losing her Godly powers, that her emotions were becoming more uncontrolled. It was unfamiliar to her, this weakness. For millennium this Goddess controlled fates. She successfully transformed the wild furies, turning those three haunting spirits into positive forces. She stole the beautiful city on the Aegean, her beloved Athens, away from her uncle, Poseidon. No other God or Goddess was able to stand up to the almighty Zeus, but many times Athena forced him to back down. Unlike most of the Gods who considered the human experience to be beneath their attention, Athena frequently intervened to effect mortal history. She would take the shape of humans, or of familiars, gently nudging people in the direction she desired. She spoke often to Odysseus during the long Trojan conflict. More recently she had intervened as a lover of a local engineer who was responsible for finding the silver that provided the funds to build the Athenian navy. Many events in human history were not simply coincidence, Athena, the Goddess of foresight, nudged events to their favor. Athena even intervened when fellow God, Apollo, sent a pessimistic message to the Athenians at Delphi. The Delphic Oracle had been the direct connection between the peoples of Attica and Apollo for over a thousand years. Whenever there was a crisis, the people would visit Delphi and speak to the God through the high priestess called the Pythia. The Oracle offered divination in many ways, some clear and concise, some obtuse. When asked by a King what was the best course of life, the Oracle responded, "know thyself". But when the Athenians asked about the Persian invasion, the Oracle was gloomy and harsh, *"Flee to the ends of the earth, leave your homes and the heights of your city...miserable things are on the way."*

In hearing this proclamation, the Goddess intervened again, directly with Apollo. Even the God, Apollo, did not have the fortitude to stand up to a direct confrontation with Athena.

"Give them hope," She demanded, *"Or I will wink and the mountains will swallow your Oracle forever."*

Apollo headed this warning and called back the Athenian delegation for a second proclamation.

But the greatest power that Athena could bestow was not insight into the future, it was metis. Metis was a skill that very few humans possessed, and when given, it was a powerful ability. It was a combination of foresight, intuitive reasoning, charisma, and the skill to formulate creative solutions to unsolvable problems. At a very early age, the Goddess had given this skill to the Greek politician, Themistocles. Metis was the bridge between being and becoming.

But to Athena' dismay, humans were turning away from her influence. For thousands of years they had sought advice when their world became troubling. But things had abruptly changed. They were now developing a fledgling democracy, making their own rules, abandoning divine guidance in favor of their own ministrations. Such harsh payback was hard to imagine for the green-eyed Goddess.

Athena watched Bubo glide overhead. She knew that the owl sensed the sadness of the time. She imagined that Bubo was flying so erratically from the knowledge that her time was nearly spent. More tears flowed down her beautiful face. Then, as if shocked by a bolt from her father Zeus, Athena turned her attention away from her own burdens and refocused on the happenings on earth. She watched the great army being assembled in Persia and its purpose, and was partially aware of the outcome. This was another troubling happening for the Goddess. She had always seen future events clearly. Sometimes small insignificant aspects of history eluded her, but now her visions were clouded, shrouded in mist. It was unsettling for her to watch her skills and abilities fade into uselessness. A hard pill to swallow.

As she watched the Persian armies advance, Athena decided that she would not fade from the memories of the people without further impact. She would hold onto whatever small trace of influence that she had. She would muster all her remaining powers to help her fledgling democracy grow to adulthood. Ironic, she mused, *"I am the fire by which my own destruction burns"*.

Athena smiled to herself realizing that some influence remained. Even though weakened, she still had some command over the elements. She felt an inward surge when she realized she could also still walk among her people in their time of need. The Goddess shook herself. She had never backed off a challenge and she would hold true to her nature now. She lifted her arm. Bubo flew down and landed on her, and the Goddess spoke, *"My love- I know you grow tired, but our duty is not over. Regain your strength, my dear, for we have more to do."* A horrifying screech from the bird, filled the air.

✳✳✳✳✳✳✳✳✳✳✳✳✳✳✳✳✳✳✳✳

The great King relaxed on his pillows as he waited. He could hear the heavy breathing of Simeron lying on the floor by his bed. Instinctively he reached down and began stroking the lioness' neck. She purred in response to the King's touch. The King had summoned his generals and admirals to a tactical meeting. Xerxes was planning on staying for five days in this location outside of Babylonia to make sure that the strategic approach to Greece was in order. He was skeptical of all his generals, each for a different reason. Before Hamas was murdered at Delphi, Xerxes had spent many hours with his teacher, talking strategy about the upcoming war. He knew that Hamas was not in favor of this conflict because he didn't like fighting a war based on someone else's hatred. He vividly remembered their discussion on the subject.

"This was your father's war, my young prince. Not yours. You've reconquered both Egypt and Babylonia and righted their rebellious ways. You have nothing left to prove."

"But I do!" Shouted Xerxes as he jumped from his chair *"I do!" My ancestors call out in the night for vengeance! I can hear their cries in the wind."*

Hamas smiled and carefully responded, *"Don't mistake the storms of the mountains or the dreams of our fears as a need for revenge."*

Xerxes listened to his "teacher", but his pacing and irritation increased, betraying his apprehension. He was emotionally committed to invasion and he knew it. But how could he avoid the advice of the one man that he trusted over all others. No other man could talk to the great King this way. If they tried, it would mean having their skin peeled off their bones. Xerxes knew that others never really spoke their true opinions in fear of his wrath. So the words of his teacher became that much more precious. Finally, the young King stopped and quickly walked over to Hamas. He grabbed the smaller man by his shoulders. *"I am going to Greece! They built a monument in celebration of their victory at Marathon. I cannot have such an insult remain. They will realize that their victory was only a harbinger of their evil destiny. Their tears and their blood will soak the earth. They will succumb to the glory of Persia. "*

He stopped and almost shouted at his teacher, *"I am bearing our disgrace Hamas, our shame. I am going to Greece, Hamas; I must burn that city down to restore the natural order. They will bow to me. I have been anointed by Ahuramazda himself. This disgrace is like a choke forever surrounding my neck, strangling me with every breath."*

He took two steps backwards and turned away from his friend. In a faint voice, almost with a begging tone, he said, *"Help me Hamas. I need your strength. I understand your objections, but help me."*

The teacher bowed, and said *"I am yours my prince. Your word is the only one I hear. Please forgive my insolence. You are heaven and I will follow."*

In remembering this discussion, Xerxes silently cried. Even more than his father Darius, he loved Hamas. He now had further reason to take the army to Greece. He now had his own vengeance. Xerxes prayed every night to the God, Ahuramazda, that he would let the Spartan King, Leonidas, the man who murdered Hamas, live long enough to come under his sword. In his daydream the young monarch could taste the revenge in his throat. He could feel his heart beat faster at the thought. A low growl was heard as Simeron responded to the increased tension.

Xerxes was released from his daydream as a slave entered and begged his attention. As they entered the room, every man blew kisses to the great King, a sign of their love and allegiance.

The slave bowed with his head touching the floor. Xerxes could let a man stay in that prone position for long minutes until he acknowledged their presence. Finally, the young King spoke: *"I wait for your message."*

"Thank you, lord, your generals and admirals await your word."

With a wave of his hand, Xerxes shooed the slave from his presence. As he left he said, *"Send in each one, but wait five minutes between each entrance."*

Xerxes sat back on his bed awaiting their individual arrival. The first man that entered was an uncle named Mardonius. The young King had mixed feelings about his uncle. Mardonius' father, Gorbryas, was a skilled assassin. Gorbryas assisted Xerxes' father, Darius to gain the throne of the Empire. Mardonius was considered an excellent, but inconsistent general. He was more efficient as a ground general than a sea tactician, but even then, he was not a good defensive general. Mardonius had argued heavily in favor of attacking Greece. The argument didn't influence the young monarch, but he knew Mardonius had gained perceived favor by Xerxes' ultimate decision. For this occasion, Mardonius was dressed in his finest outfit as he walked slowly into the chamber. As he approached, it was his obvious arrogance that irritated the young King. Leaning on his bed, the King smiled and said;

"Welcome' uncle, I hope your family is well."

Mardonius threw kisses then bowed deeply. Xerxes smiled again but didn't move. His eyes bore down on the man standing in front of him. Expecting more verbiage, Mardonius rose and stood at attention. As he stood, Xerxes rose and slowly walked to his relative. *"You argued for this course, uncle. It is in your corner. Will your troops perform better than they did in Egypt?"*

"You will be proud of us, my King."

Silently, the King gently nodded his head.

The next two generals that entered were mostly nondescript. Neither of these two generals would spearhead the attack. Both would be used to control the rear and the flanks. Both Masistes and Gergis blew their kisses and sublimely bowed to the King of Kings. Xerxes disliked Masistes because of his sexual preferences. It disgusted the great King when he thought of Masistes with young boys. If it wasn't for his aggressive military skills, the King would have left him behind. Gergis was also a solid military tactician, but unlike Masistes, his poison was wine. Xerxes did not like weak men, and although tolerable generals, he considered them both inadequate.

Demaratus was the next man that entered the room. Out of all the men in the King's presence, this man stood the straightest and looked the most confident. He walked unhurriedly into the chamber, slowly turning his head from side to side, instantly evaluating the situation. He made no eye contact. This man had been a King in his own right. Unlike the other generals, Demaratus wore full armor. He did not blow a kiss to the young King or offer him his sword. He walked slowly towards Xerxes, stopping within a few feet of the monarch. He bowed his head in deference.

Demaratus was an ex-Spartan King, exiled in the Persian Empire. He proved his superior military skills in Egypt. He and his self-trained troops embarrassed the almighty Immortals in the reconquest of Egypt. But there were hateful rumors that ran through the Empire like blood through the veins. As much as he trusted this man, Xerxes had only limited faith in a non-Persian. Only three days before, Xerxes had heard from a spy that Demaratus might have secretly contacted the King of Sparta, Leonidas. The evidence was very sketchy, and the King of Kings spent hours trying not only to understand it, but whether to believe it. The spy's name was Elonquire. Xerxes had never heard the name before the man reported to him.

"Lord," Speak Elonquire *"Lord, I intercepted a man who claimed to be returning from the city of Sparta. I befriended this man lord, and*

after we drank a few bottles of date wine he began bragging about his voyage."

It was evident to the King of Kings that Elonquire was anxious in his rendition of the events. Elonquire knew that his life was on the line with his report. *"As* he bragged, h*e said that he was hired by a local King in the Empire to bring a message to the King of Sparta, Leonidas. He was given a blank tablet and told to bring it to the Spartan King."*

Xerxes' eye twitched as he surprisingly said, *"A blank tablet?"*

"Yes, lord, that's what he said, A blank tablet."

Xerxes lunged toward the man. He grabbed him by the throat with burning eyes. *"What does that mean, a blank tablet? Why would a fool send a blank tablet?"*

The man struggled to speak, as the air was pulled from his throat.

The Spartan King, Leonidas, was just as confused as the Persian Emperor when he received a blank tablet. He was told it was a secretive message. But what kind of message was a blank tablet? Leonidas' wife eventually figured out the dilemma. The tablet was covered with a wax that had to be burned off to reveal the message. This stopped snooping eyes from reading the secret until it reached its destination. It was an old Spartan trick.

This information that this spy had brought put the King of Kings in a dilemma. Should he consider that one of his best generals might be a turncoat? But beside his strategic skill, Demaratus also knew the potential Greek strategy better than anyone he had in his service. Even though Demaratus survived a confrontation from the King by offering his life, Xerxes still didn't trust him.

The ex-Spartan King was a very proud man, and unlike the other generals, hesitated for a moment before beginning his bow. His eyes even contacted the King as he started towards bended knee. Xerxes could feel his teeth grind as he watched the entrance.

The last general to enter the room was Smerdomences. Unlike any of the other entrances, Xerxes himself rose when his friend and protector entered the room. The bow was immediate from the general. But unlike the others, Smerdomences laid his scabbard on the ground, a gesture suggesting he was willing to lay down his life for his King. Xerxes walked over to him as he knelt and placed his hands on the general's shoulders as he rose. Surprisingly though, the King of Kings did not utter a word, but just returned to his bed.

After all the generals lined to the right of the King, the three Admirals entered together. All three were relatives to the great King. Their names were Zephan, Ariabigues, and Prxaspes. The Persians were not sailors. But control of the shipping lanes to support the ground advance was essential to a Persian victory in the far away peninsula. The Persian navy was a diverse group made up of ships and sailors from many areas of the Empire. But above all, the Phoenician allies were the most proficient sailors. Success would depend on their skill which Xerxes knew, for if the troops couldn't be supplied, the army would rot in place. As strong and powerful as the land army was, success would depend on controlling the sea. And the most successful Phoenician general was the great Warrior Queen, Artemisia. Coming not from Phoenicia itself, Artemisia was from Halicarnassus, a small island in the Aegean. But the Phoenicians considered her their Queen, and to a man would die defending her.

Artemisia was an aggressive oceanic warrior. Her skills in hand to hand combat were almost as legendary as her sailing abilities. She was an extremely attractive, statuesque woman, reminding Greeks of the Goddess, Athena. It was one of the reasons that Xerxes had sent her in the entourage to Delphi to consult the great Oracle. Artemisia had made a bold statement at Delphi by murdering the Pythia in her temple and fleeing the country with her Phoenician entourage. The

God, Apollo, spoke through the Pythia. Murdering her in the Oracle chamber brought both fear and amusement to the great King. The monarch had heard only extraordinary things about the great Oracle, and Xerxes feared insulting it. And yet he didn't believe in the God Apollo, and he thought it amusing that 'the God' would not protect his human voice. After all, the Pythia was supposed to be the personification of the God. He pondered that inconsistency for days without reaching resolution. But as he did, he secretly admired the fearlessness of the Warrior Queen in her actions. After he heard of the audacious act, Xerxes said to an advisor, *"Artemisia has no fear. She spits at the Greek Gods in their own temple and they waivered in their response. She is a tigress that one."* Xerxes chuckled at the thought.

The general staff was now assembled before him. The men that would control the fate of the Persian Empire. Only Artemisia was missing. She was still in northern Greece and would join the navy soon. Xerxes slowly paced in front of his general staff. Finally he spoke, *"There is no turning back."*

He looked each of the men in the eye after making the statement.

"Is there any man in this room who questions this action?"

There was silence in the tent. Behind his back, Xerxes had heard rumors that there were men who questioned going to Greece. Why not? He himself had. But now, when the decision had been made, there could be no hesitancy. Xerxes waited. Would any of the men who were diffident stand up to the monarch? Would any dare place their lives in jeopardy?

Finally, after long moments, Masistes took a step forward. Xerxes had his back to the generals, but he immediately sensed the movement. It confirmed the rumors that he heard. Masistes stood silently, a few steps in front of the other generals. Without turning to face him, Xerxes said, *"General, you have concerns?"*

"My King, with all due respect. Taking such a large army across such a distance does not seem pragmatic to me. Wouldn't it be better to?"

Before he could finish his thought, the King of Kings turned and glared at him malevolently. The action seemed to pull all the air from the tent. Masistes immediately dropped to his knees, recognizing the life-threatening situation he was in. He tried backtracking, but his words came out only as a blurred stutter. Xerxes turned away from the bent general and slowly walked toward the farthest part of the tent. When he reached the wall of the enclosure he turned quickly and flung a dagger toward Masistes. The dagger hit the man directly in the forehead, and was thrown with such force that it sunk halfway into his brain. Remarkably, Masistes did not die, but just fell to the ground in agonizing pain. Xerxes looked at Smerdomences and nodded his head. The general of the 10,000 Immortals drew his sword and swung, cutting the man's arm mostly off. As the general continued screaming, Smerdomences slowly walked behind him. The sword swung again, this time cutting the generals other arm from his body. Xerxes had turned away from the massacre. Smerdomences took out the gold-plated dagger that he had liberated from a Greek spy and cut the generals neck. The King of Kings turned to a slave and demanded, *"Bring me, Tritantacechmes. He will replace this piece of shit."*

A second slave asked, *"Lord, should I clean the remains?"*

"No," barked the King of Kings.

"I want the remains of this traitor mounted on spears and placed along this road as we move west. Every soldier will view his remains and be reminded about the importance of loyalty."

****

Chapter II – Cypencant

There was not a hair out of place. She sat on a large wooden stool in the main palace of the Thessalion King, Thorax. Artemisia and her Phoenician guards had ridden for days after escaping from Delphi. In an audacious action, the Warrior Queen slayed the sitting Pythia, daring the Greek God, Apollo, to exterminate her in retaliation. In the millennium that Apollo had spoken through the Oracle at Delphi, no siting Pythia had died from the sword. Then again, Delphi had never seen a combatant like Artemisia. Many of the Delphic priestesses had perished because of the intense experience of merging with the great God. Some of the priestesses had seized during their rapture with the God, with their blood leaving their bodies through their eyes and hair. One had even taken her own life by ingesting a very lethal poison after one of the merging ecstasies.

The Pythia was the priestess who was chosen to communicate with the God. This priestess was chosen because of her superior insight and religious sensitivity. By murdering the Pythia, Artemisia had challenged the Greek Gods to retaliate against her insolence. When no response came, she laughed and spit on the shrine as the Pythia lay bleeding by her feet. She confirmed in her mind that the Greek Gods were false prophets, just illusions of a weak people. The Warrior Queen herself was not spiritual. She had no use for what she considered a misguided trust in a supreme being. Adon, Artemisia's personal Phoenician protector guarded the entrance to the Delphic temple while the Warrior Queen was inside with the Pythia. Adon sensed his Queen's intentions and it was his job to secure their escape from Greece, a job which he had little trouble carrying through.

Adon was a large stoic man. He wore a long beard and had strong imposing shoulders. Adon never backed down from a confrontation. He would place himself in the face of any adversary, especially to protect his ward. He was an intimidating presence with his broad shoulders and jet-black eyes. Eyes that seemed endless, like staring into a galaxias void. And when teamed with the antagonistic Warrior Queen, they were a lethal pair.

Thessaly was in northern Greece and one of the first Greek areas to side with the Persians. The Queen of Halicarnassus had now been in this capital city of Dium for weeks and was getting restless. Artemisia was not the kind of woman who relaxed or sat still. Her mind was always moving, almost in an agitated frantic fashion. And yet outwardly, an observer would not perceive that persistent internal activity. Other people saw a stoic woman who seemed indifferent and aloof. But Artemisia silently observed, registered, and analyzed everything. Artemisia had learned how to hide her thoughts of anger and anxiety.

The Warrior Queen was an enigma to everyone in Thessaly. She was a female warrior of such renown, that her reputation was more esteemed than almost any man since the great Greek warrior, Achilles. Her superior strategic ability and seafaring skill made her a dangerous enemy. Adding to this, her utter fearlessness in combat only enhanced her deadliness.

Artemisia had heard the Persian army was on the move and her inactivity still only annoyed her more. She had protested to the great King of King of his decision to send her to Delphi with the Persian delegation. She was not a diplomat, she was a warrior, a combatant, not a negotiator. She did not seek reconciliation with the Greeks, she sought blood. And yet, the King was deaf to her protests, and here she sat, stewing in her own annoyance. The world was on the move and the Warrior Queen sat on her hands. Artemisia knew that the gravity of the earth was changing and the conversion would be born in the fire of death. And of all the portals that destiny had used, it had chosen the Warrior Queen to be the final catalyst.

Artemisia's only distraction was the slave girl, Agatha, who Artemisia became enchanted with during the ceremony that led to her murdering the Pythia at the Delphi temple. The slave girl spent every night in the Warrior Queen's bed. But even such a sweet diversion could not satisfy her lust for the sea or her desire to bloody her weapons. Her sword tasted blood at the Oracle and it remained hungry. It also needed to be satisfied.

As she sat musing over her current predicament, in the corner of her line of sight, Artemisia noticed that her bodyguard, Adon, had entered her chamber. Adon was a large man. His long-braided hair and beard were hard to ignore. But even with his size, his walk was not heavy.

"My Queen, Thorax, the King of Thessaly, and our current benefactor, wishes your presence at his supper table."

Artemisia had rejected, or more accurately, ignored the previous invitations. She quickly flicked her head away from Adon in disgust.

"My Queen, we owe Thorax. We were supposed to go farther north to Macedonia. But it is much more convenient to stay here. He has asked many times, my Queen, and been very patient."

The Queen replied with some annoyance. *"It is Thorax who owes us, Adon. He is a sniveling mouse. He lives because of the great King's generosity. Besides we still must travel east to meet the navy. This is only a temporary respite."*

"My Queen, protocol."

Artemisia acted deaf to the words. But like a spoiled child, eventually the Warrior Queen nodded her head, reluctantly approving. Adon knew not to press his luck further with the obstinate woman. He bowed and backed his way out of the room. After he left, the pacing began. Although the Queen was alone in the room, she began to quietly rant.

"Thorax! I am more of a man than he is!"

She spit on the ground at the thought of having to smile at the effeminate monarch.

"Plus, I must put up with his two idiot brothers, Eurypylus and Thrasydaeus."

She laughed to herself at the thought that Thorax was the most competent of the three.

Two hours later the Warrior Queen slowly strode into the very grand area that was the main dining area of the palace. Her face did not betray either appreciation at being invited or her repulsion as having to attend. She was surprised by the amount of people sitting around the large table. Upon her entrance, everyone at the table stood in respect. She stopped and looked over the gathered people, imperceptibly gazing her eyes in recognition. Her eyes then met Adon and he unnoticeably touched his right shoulder, then his elbow. The

Phoenicians had a very complex unspoken language. They secretly communicated with each other with surreptitious gestures and expressions. His left hand then went again to his elbow, then to his left eyelid.

After watching Adon, the Queen immediately turned her attention to a strange looking woman sitting at the end of the table. There was nothing unusual about her dress nor her face; it was her eyes that stood out and gained the Queen's notice. They seemed to burn, as their blue sheen appeared as though light was emerging from them. And yet, as the stare glared ahead there was a distance about them as well. Artemisia immediately looked past her, but out of the corner of her eye noticed that Adon made a jerking motion with his right wrist. So within a short period of time, the Queen had identified a potentially troubling situation. As she hesitated, Thorax bowed and then began to speak:

"We are all honored by your presence, Queen Artemisia."

Artemisia slightly turned her head toward the Thessalion King and gave him a half smile. Thorax, appearing buoyed by that minor recognition, continued: *"It is not since the great warrior, Achilles, and the adventurer, Jason, that we've been blessed with such illustrious company."*

He bowed again as the Queen walked to her seat.

"Let me introduce you to the gathered guests."

Thorax went around the large table introducing the Queen to the assembled royalty, but she paid little attention until he arrived at the woman that caught her primary attention. Even then, nobody at the table would have noticed the heightened attention that the Warrior Queen paid to this introduction. Thorax raised his arm pointing to the woman sitting at the end of the table.

"This is another guest with us tonight. May I introduce Cypencant. Cypencant is a moon woman."

Even though she had heard the designation before, Artemisia turned and acted as if the words had never touched her ears. Thorax smiled and continued.

"A moon woman is.... how can I say......a medicine woman? She is fluent in spells and incantations. Cypencant is quite famous in our corner of Greece. Her powers have received considerable attention."

"A moon woman?" Artemisia said in a low, ominous voice. She looked straight at Cypencant with her face contorting and said in an accusatory tone, *"Spells and incantations, you mean she is a witch!"*

Now it was the Warrior Queen's eyes that blackened. Cypencant smiled as she captured the stare of the Warrior Queen. It was obvious from her demeanor that she was not intimidated by this woman with a warrior reputation. Now it was Cypencants turn to speak, *"That term holds bad fortune."*

Slowly, Cypencant began to rise. As she did, Artemisia's hand indiscernibly went to the hilt of her sword. But Cypencant noticed, and a small smirking smile touched the corners of her mouth, as if the motion itself was a silent victory, an acceptance of her power.

"I am a child of the moon."

Cypencant was now halfway around the table and all eyes turned to follow her movement. She continued, *"Media, visited our land a millennium ago and dispersed holy herbs. These magic plants took root in our rich soil. Media taught some special women to use these herbs. They were called moon woman. Some of us still know how to mix these prescriptions to aid man in many ways."*

Cypencant approached the window in the great hall. She pulled back the elaborate covering and the full moon shown through, illuminating the table with an eerie light. There was a gasp from many of the nobles around the table. As Cypencant stood, holding the fabric away from the window, the Queen from Halicarnassus also arose from her place. Another pant rang through the chamber, but this was more obvious and had a tinge of panic in it. She spoke,

"Well, witch, show us some of your capability. I am quite bored and would like to see a display of this power that you inherited from an ancient Goddess"

Cypencant laughed out loud, throwing her head backwards. Her long flowing white hair seemed to spread across half the room. As her head returned to face the group, she revealed a small glass jar which housed a cerulean potion. *"This innocuous potion allows me to control others. It is a very special mixture, quite rare. But for this occasion, I will show off its potency."*

Cypencant walked over to Eurypylus, Thorax's younger brother, and the fear radiated from the young man's eyes. He visibly began shaking, unable to control his racing heart. Cypencant demanded him to hold out his hand. He quickly looked at Thorax, silently begging for his brother's intervention to stop this experiment. But Thorax remained mesmerized by the moon woman, ignoring his brothers pleading eyes.

"Hold out your hand," the moon woman commanded. With his muscles tight and his body quivering, Eurypylus held out his hand. Cypencant dripped a few of the blue drops of liquid on it. The color seemed to migrate up the man's arm as his eyes seemed to bulge out of his skull watching the progression. Suddenly he dropped to his knees. The witch approached him and bent down next to him. *"I especially like controlling men,"* she remarked, with a faint smile on her lips. It reminded one of the pleasures a predator gets in playing with its pray before eating.

She cackled again as she lovingly stroked Eurypylus' blond hair.

"Now, my dear, stick out your tongue," the Moon Woman demanded, this time in a seductive tone. Eurypylus hesitated as his eyes dripped with tears. But the witch tightened her grip on his hair and the man immediately obeyed. It was becoming evident that he was losing voluntary control of his actions.

"You have no need for such a big tongue. Bite off the tip with your own teeth."

Tears now began streaming down Eurypylus' beet red face as his teeth closed on his tongue.

"Keep going, you have not completed your task."

She continued to stroke his hair. Blood began dripping down the young man's cheek as his mouth closed on his own tongue.

"More, more" the enchantress cried out, urging the young man on. Then, in a state of panic, Thorax jumped up and shouted, *"Stop this!*

But before he could finish his plea, Artemisia had jumped out of her chair, drew her sword, and leaped across the table to the fallen man. Adon was close behind his Queen. Almost before any breath could be expelled, the Queen had her sword under the chin of the Moon Woman. She glared into the eyes of Cypencant, and with an unearthly scowl demanded, *"You have proven your magic. Release the spell, or lose your head"*

The witch's hand tightened on Eurypylus' hair and with a frustrated moan, let go of the young man's head, pushing it down. Eurypylus fell to the floor screaming, holding his mouth as the blood drenched the floor by his knees. Thorax waved his arm and two slaves appeared and dragged Eurypylus out of the chamber. Artemisia reset her sword with its point now touching the chest of the witch. *"You are not out of danger yet, witch."*

Artemisia looked at Thorax and said, *"Give the word and we will drink the blood of this woman for our supper."*

Thorax raised his arm and the Queen backed away. Throughout all of this, the expression on Cypencants face barely changed. She showed no fear, no anxiety at the assault. The Queen and her guard began walking to the table when the witch said, *"What about you?"* looking and pointing at Artemisia. *"Would you like to experience the power of my potions?"*

Artemisia stared back at her and stepped forward. Thorax pleaded, *"Enough drama for today!"*

But Artemisia ignored his pleas, continuing to move toward the witch. When she arrived at the woman's chest, with her eyes glaring, piercing through the sorceress, she held out her hand. Again, a smile crossed the Moon Woman's face and she took out her potion.

"Enough, I said," Thorax demanded. But the two women were now mesmerized by this dangerous game that not yet played out. The Warrior Queen held her hand up in a stopping motion. Adon was also gesturing. But the die was cast, and once the Warrior Queen decided on an action, changing her mind was like stopping the sun from rising in the desert.

"I await your evil brew, witch." The Warrior Queen but an emphasis on that last word!

As if in slow motion, Cypencant lifted the vial and removed the top. She hesitated as if asking the Queen if she should continue. Artemisia did not move an inch and the witch sprinkled a few drops on the Queen's outstretched hand. As with Eurypylus, the blue color spread up the Queen's wrist and arm. Artemisia took two steps backward and her face appeared to flush. The Moon Woman spoke, *"I have always wondered what it would be like to have a Queen bow before me. Now you are your knees, Queen."*

The people around the table seemed to hold their breath as the Queen's knees appeared to buckle. But even though they initially seemed to falter, it was clear that she was straining to maintain her stature. She was now shaking, but she remained upright. Surprisingly, the Queen began to slowly move her hand and place it on her sword.

"Leave the sword in its scabbard," the sorceress demanded, in a heightened worrisome voice. But remarkably, the Queen's arm continued to move toward her sword. Artemisia struggled with her control, but she slowly kept moving. As she strained, it was becoming evident that Artemisia was beginning to win her battle against the potion. And then, as if in slow motion, she reached her sword and drew it out. As surprised as she could be at the astounding resolve and strength of this adversary, Cypencants voice shook as she spoke, *"I am astonished. No person has ever stood up to the effect of the herbs."*

The Warrior Queen continued with her measured approach to the Moon Woman. When she was not more than five inches from her face, she spoke in a low voice, *"It is easy to control simple and undisciplined minds. Controlling the heart of the warrior is a tougher undertaking."*

Artemisia thrust her sword into the ground and patted the witch on the cheek. She bent forward, and in a low tone said, *"Prepare yourself. Put your potions and magic in a box, for you will travel with me. Your power is stronger than any magi I have encountered. You will use it in my behalf."*

The Queen turned and pointed at the Thessalion King. *"Prepare yourself, Thorax of Thessaly. The King of Kings will soon arrive on your shores. You will either impress him with your loyalty and your hospitality, or you will forfeit your realm."*

With that Artemisia turned and walked from the room.

Chapter III- Duplicity

It was a difficult mission but an easy decision. His King, Matten, demanded that he had to carry out this final mission. He was a dedicated devotee of the monarchy that governed Phoenicia. Matten was a very compelling ruler, he was quite ingenious in his deceptions and his political strategy. Matten knew that his ally, the King of Kings of Persia, was planning to attack the Greek cities. He recognized the odds, but he also knew the lessons of history. Like most rulers, Matten was shocked by the battle at Marathon. When the much smaller Greek army surprised and defeated the considerably larger Persian contingent, Matten took notice. Not only did he take notice, but it changed his evaluation of the parties involved. Could it happen again? He had no doubt of the possibility. Of course, he revealed his misgivings to nobody, not even his closest advisors. Matten also knew that the King of Kings had ears throughout his vast Empire. He was very aware of what it meant to be an ally of the most powerful man on the planet, even if he did question his competence. It was an all or nothing arrangement, or so others thought.

At one-point Matten decided he had to strategically hedge his bet. Matten had always been an aggressive and astute man. He depended on his foresight. He sent his ships from their home port in Tyre to all corners of the known world, not only for exploration and trade, but for information. The colony of Carthage, on the north African coast, had grown from the Phoenician egg and now had become a strong ally. When Xerxes was to attack Greece, he wanted to block any possibility of retreat. The Persian King's plan was to have the Carthaginians attack the Greek colony at Sicily, freezing the ability of the Sicilian army to reinforce the Greek cities. It was a brilliant strategy devised by the young, King. Matten knew that Xerxes was sending the largest land and sea force ever created to destroy the Greek cities. But even so, Matten was surprised that both Athens and Sparta declined the invitation to ally with the Persian King. Yes, it meant subservience, but it was better than seeing your city burn to ground. There was no question in Matten's mind that the King of Kings would rain vengeance on the Greek cities, Athens in particular. These Greeks were noble people, but proud to the point of foolishness, concluded the Phoenician King. Matten knew that they would end up choking on their pride. He had seen the force of the young King's will when Xerxes took his armies to Egypt. But then again, the Immortals, the elite Persian units, the praised Ausiya, had been usurped by the unit led by Demaratus, the ex-Spartan King. Matten had placed men in each of the Persian's armies to report progress. Matten's Phoenician navy efficiently supported the Persian troops during the Egyptian hostilities, but the Persian elite ground troops were weaker than advertised. This increased the skepticism of the Phoenician King. But even with his uncertainty, the size of the Persian army was undeniable. The Persian would outnumber the Greek forces by at least 10 to 1. The Navy was at least three times as large as what was expected from the Greek cities. So even if they were less than competent, by force of numbers alone, they should still persevere.

But Matten was still unsure, even with the overwhelming numbers. Matten concocted a bold plan but he needed just the right man. He had to be daring, be an exceptional sailor, and have strong organizational ability. But mostly he had to be loyal, able to risk his life and his family for the court. The man he chose also had to speak Greek. Matten picked one of his most experienced, but least well-known men he could find. His name was Sakarbaal.

Sakarbaal was an experienced and brave sailor. He had proven over the course of his life that he would take any step to support his King. Through back channels, the Phoenician King had sent the message to the Greek city of Athens that the Phoenicians were willing to negotiate with them. It would not be a military negotiation, but one centering on trade and economics. A favorable response came back and Matten sent a vessel with four men to conduct the discussion. Sakarbaal was the captain of the ship named Baal. Two of the men, Yutpan and Baido, were both diplomats. The fourth man was a spy who had been included in the entourage. Unbeknownst to any of the other three, the spy's task was to find and eliminate the leader of the fledgling Greek democracy, Themistocles. Unfortunately for Matten, the spy was tracked and murdered by a Greek counterinsurgent.

During the discussions with the Greeks, Themistocles proposed an exchange with the visiting Phoenician emissaries. He would agree to a trade agreement with Phoenicia in exchange for Sakarbaal's personal services. The Phoenicians knew that Athens needed to build and train a navy. That Themistocles asked for Sakarbaal to work for the Greeks was a stroke of uncanny luck for the Phoenician monarch. His plan was to have Sakarbaal return to Athens after meeting Themistocles. He was to ask for asylum, thus placing a spy near the Greek leader. But now, because of the Gods and fortune, not only was Sakarbaal among the Greeks, but he was given the task of building and training the new navy. Beyond providence, this could only be an intervention from Yamm, the God of the Seafarer.

Unfortunately, Sakarbaal fell in love with Athens. He also was fond of Themistocles. Sakarbaal took his job very seriously (like he did everything else). He was very proud to oversee the construction of over 200 ships. He named each of them and could tell the subtle differences between each vessel. Then the word came. His King wanted him to complete his nefarious mission. He was to murder Themistocles. He certainly would have the opportunity, but could he do it?

This task involved many mixed emotions for Sakarbaal. He was never an assassin, never thought of himself in that vein. He was a sailor and a shipbuilder.

Sakarbaal sat on the docks at Peiraieus, the new Greek navy yard. This facility was built after Themistocles ordered the abandonment of the old yards at Phaleron Bay. It was beautiful to the sailor's eyes. This day, Sakarbaal sat in his place at Sdea. It was a beautiful day, the clouds moved slowly across the sky mesmerizing the old sailor. The Aegean stretched out before his eyes as Sakarbaal's thoughts drifted aimlessly. He felt an arm on his shoulder and jerked his head around. He immediately recognized Themistocles standing slightly to his right. As he began to rise he noticed that behind Themistocles stood Thantos.

Thantos was one of Themistocles' closest associates. He was a sailor, a spy and an adventurer. Before he became associated with the Greek politician, Thantos had been a very successful trader and black-market broker. He was a very wealthy man in his own right. Thantos was one of the spies sent to the Persian Empire to scout the strength of the military that was being prepared to invade Greece. Of the four men who were sent to the Empire, Thantos was the only man to return. Xerxes had captured the spies and sent Thantos on a grand tour of both his army and navy. Xerxes wanted the Greeks to become aware of the enormity of the challenge that faced them. He believed it would undermine their confidence and their will to see the overwhelming destructive power of the enemy.

Themistocles began the discussion.

"My friend, you look in deep thought."

It didn't go unnoticed that Sakarbaal was not smiling when he recognized his friend. Thantos and Sakarbaal did not trust each other. They had a history of disagreement, often vying for Themistocles' attention and approval. Thantos couldn't imagine how a Phoenician could help the Greeks plan and build a navy to sail against his home fleet. He couldn't get over the mistrust and the betrayal of his native land. He had spoken to Themistocles about his concerns, but the politician pointed to the new fleet and the work that Sakarbaal had done. The last time Thantos had voiced his concerns, Themistocles had looked at his friend and while walking away said, *"I am old enough to not be naïve. Everyone has a purpose. Trust that I know how to use others."*

On this day Sakarbaal looked distant, and the emotional state did not escape the astute Greek.

"Your mind is in other places, perhaps far away? Are you thinking of home?'

This last comment seemed to awaken the Phoenician. He looked up and smiled.

"This is my home now, you know that"

"Yes, I know what you have said in the past, but your land of the beautiful trees and purple gowns cannot always be far from your mind."

Sakarbaal knew that his friend had begun fishing for information with his questions. He had seen this approach before with others. He decided to take a chance. *"I've always wondered if you doubted my loyalty."*

In the background, Thantos grunted.

"Loyalty?" questioned Themistocles, *"I ask you about your home and you take it as questioning your allegiance? If I didn't know better, I would conclude that you were having second thoughts about your decision to stay with us"*.

Sakarbaal rose and Thantos stiffened. But when he stood, he slowly bowed to the Greek politician. He pointed to the bay full of beautiful ships.

"I have built you a strong navy, trained your farmers and tradesmen to be sailors. Is this a sign of disloyalty?'

"Of course, it is not. But the wind is impetuous and always changes direction. It would blow from the west for days, then change to south. The oceans calm and tranquil, can quickly become dangerous and life threatening"

And with this last comment, Themistocles was staring directly into the Phoenician's eyes. Putting on his most humble face, the Phoenician said, *"I am not the wind nor the ocean. I am a slave to both."*

He swallowed and said, *"and to Athens"*

Themistocles smiled, tapped him on the shoulder, and turned to leave. Thantos waited another two heartbeats facing the Phoenician sailor then followed his mentor. There was mistrust in his eyes and both men knew it. As Sakarbaal watched the two men leave, he felt as though he had betrayed his real feelings. He shook slightly, now not as assured of his position as he was when the sun rose this morning. Themistocles smiled to himself as he walked away.

"The truth cannot hide long behind the dark clouds of deception," he thought, and continued *to* walk.

****

The woman leaned on the pillows with a smug look on her face. Slaves surrounded her as she demanded, shooed them away, and raised her voice to each one in turn. At one point she vaulted out of her reclining position and slapped a young slave in the face, knocking her to the floor. With the girl prone in front of her, the woman reached down and grabbed a full handful of hair lifting the woman off the floor. She called another slave over and ordered her to hold the young woman up. The woman walked over to the end of the tent, picked up a large stick, and started to hit the woman in the face until the floor showed puddles of blood that stretched feet around the spot where she stood. One could see the young girl's life drain from her body. The slave girl's crime-she brought the wrong kind of wine to the prima donna.

Although beautiful and alluring, Vashti was spoiled and short tempered, but the foulest trait she had was her underlying sadistic nature. It was legendary. There were many rumors of the joy she got watching others in pain. Vashti had no children. People had seen her pregnant and yet after it was assumed, she gave birth, the children seemed to disappear. The gossip was that Vashti, not really wanting children, sacrificed them in a dark religious service. Of course, if witnessed, sacrificing a child would mean instant death from her husband, Xerxes. It was a capital crime in the Empire.

Vashti had no compassion for others; they existed for her benefit. And if they did not meet her immediate needs, she could be cruel and unforgiving. She was vain to the point of narcissism. What Vashti did know was that her husband, the King of Kings, held the real power. She was careful how and when she pushed. He too could be brutal when angered. She had caught small smiles on his face when he punished others. Vashti was spoiled but knew her limitations. At least she hoped she did. There had been times when she pushed too far and had to deal with her husband's retribution. It was not pleasant for this pampered child of a woman. Sex was also something Vashti used. Other than manipulation, she really had no use for it. Yes, there was some pleasure, but the effort outweighed the result. She had to act, moan and groan, and tell her husband how perfect he was.

Vashti was especially irritated now because her husband forced her to join the army and march to Greece. When the King informed her through a personal slave that she would be accompanying him, she threw a monumental tantrum. It was interrupted when the King stormed into her chamber and lifted her up by the throat and held her up until she succumbed to his demands. He threw her down on the ground and glared at her, daring her to protest. Vashti gave no response, but inside the King smiled. He almost wanted her to protest, so he could pull his sword and rid himself of this problem. Xerxes had long ago grown tired of her quickly changing moods and the drama that she created in the court. Her beauty was no longer a reason to keep her around. He knew the demand of accompanying the army to Greece would irritate her, so much the better. Xerxes was tired of her spoiled childish behavior. She spread rumors, gossiped and made up stories about her and others. Vashti had accused people of hideous behavior. It took Xerxes a year after their marriage to realize that most of her complaints about others were just a figment of her paranoid personality. While she lay on the floor the King of Kings stared at her. He spoke, *"Do you understand that you have no rights. No say in what you do?"*

Vashti seemed to growl as she looked up at him. Her face then quickly softened, and she crawled over to the King, grabbing his leg.

She slowly rubbed his calf, making purring noises. The King allowed the behavior for a while then kicked his wife away. She sprawled over the floor with her hair now disheveled.

"You don't like it when you get hurt, yet you quickly hurt others."

"I hurt no one," Vashti protested.

"You hurt no one? Lying is another one of your traits."

"I am a Queen," Vashti protested

"And who made you a Queen?" the King of Kings reminded her. And with that he left her chamber. Since that time, Vashti had sulked, brooded, and plotted.

To make matters worse, Xerxes decided to bring his two concubines along with the army to Greece. He decided this in part to irritate his wife, plus he preferred his concubines in the bedroom. The first women's name was Volesmo. She had been a very poor woman who Xerxes took a liking to while passing through her village. At the time, Xerxes was the Viceroy of

Babylonia. When he ascended the throne, she came along with other slaves. His second concubine also came from the Babylonia area. She was different than Volesmo. Although Volesmo was very alluring, Hadassah was stunning. Her uncle, with whom she lived, had since become a lower level advisor to the royal court. A man of patient emotional response, Xerxes was stunned when he met Hadassah, taken aback, as if struck by a storm. Others around him had never seen the King of Kings pay attention to a woman, no less give her a second take. Hadassah immediately became his favorite and Vashti's sworn nemesis. To complicate the situation, Hadassah was Jewish. Vashti hatred minorities, especially the Jews. She believed that her Persian blood made her superior to all other races. She seethed when she heard that the other women would also make the journey to Greece. Although angry, Vashti knew better than to express her indignation to her husband. She smiled an insidious smile when she heard the news. Many slaves would suffer for the King's decision. Besides, it would be a long journey, and many accidents could befall an unsuspecting concubine.

****

Chapter IV- Eclipse

It was predicted by his astronomers, so the King was not completely surprised by the unearthly occurrence. His throne was taken outside of the tent so the King of King could watch the spectacle in comfort. But also, Xerxes wanted heaven to see that he was not afraid of either the sun, nor the moon. He also wanted them to see that he was appreciative of their dance. As he sat with his eyes to the sky, Xerxes was surrounded by his advisors and his two most important Magi, Assim- the "great one" and Balthasur the "war advisor," but directly behind him stood Golnar, an Egyptian born Persian woman. Golnar was an Egyptian priestess of renown.

Although it was very uncommon for a woman, Golnar was a lector priest. The lector priests were able to read the ancient magical books. She was a psychic healer and went through many rituals to make sure the King of Kings was safe from evil. Golnar prayed to both Sekhmet and Ra. Sekhmet was the Goddess of the plague and Ra the sun God. Golnar carried a magical amulet, in which she had ultimate faith. Although Xerxes was not a true believer in Egyptian magic and spells, his stepmother, Ho of Sebennytos, convinced him of Golnar's considerable abilities.

Ho had been married to Xerxes' father Darius. She was considered a profit of God in Egypt, and she had personally trained Golnar. When he became confused, Xerxes retreated to her cave which was outside of the palace at Susa. She refused to go to court because she believed that there was more truth in the desert than in any palace. During her rituals, in which Xerxes would consume hallucinogenic potions, she was able to unite him to his ancestors. Xerxes would seek advice from his ancestors in the mind-expanding rituals that Ho put him through. This experience was so powerful for him that it convinced him to trust in another Egyptian priestess, Golnar. Golnar came to the royal court with an impressive resume. She was the most honored of the Egyptian priestesses (after Ho), and Xerxes anticipated her insight would be helpful with his quest to destroy Greece. While not as powerful or as celebrated as Ho, Golnar was a powerful force. Ho had predicted the death of two of Xerxes' advisors. One she said would die a hideous death at the hands of a wild beast. The man had been kicked in the head by one of the many horses that would travel with the army. Golnar predicted that the second man would die at supper. Golnar had arranged this death by putting poison in the man's soup. She had also predicted the upcoming heavenly event, which Xerxes now sat ready to witness. But in truth she had heard others discussing it. She made sure she was first to reveal to the King that the heavens were dancing that night.

As the moon began to slowly devour the sun, Xerxes leaned forward in anticipation. He was warned by Golnar not to look directly at the event, as Ra, the sun God, could render him blind to punish his insolence. Although the King protested the warning, pushing out his chest in defiance, he was now heading the warning. At last, the moon fully covered the sun and total darkness descended on the royal entourage. At the height of the darkness, when for an instant, one could wonder whether the sun would return to its glory, Xerxes jumped off his chair and held his magical amulet, which he called "the Answerer", over his head, pointing it at the moon.

"I am Xerxes- King of men- King of all lands- King of Kings. Return to your true nature. You do not scare us with your evil dances."

Again, he pointed the Answerer at the moon as it began its decline away from the sun. *"I am the sun- and my power will overcome your desire to rule the sky. Go back to your lair. You do not belong here. Go back to the night where you belong."*

He yelled, *"Be gone, evil omen"*

And with that the King turned his back on the celestial wonder. After he returned to his palatial tent, the King of Kings called his magi to his side. They entered and immediately bowed low in front of the monarch. All three knew why they were summoned. The great King wanted to know the meaning of the eclipse. Xerxes rose to face the three bodies each on one knee in front of him. Words were not necessary. Xerxes made a motion demanding that the three rise. Silence overcame the enclosure hanging over the meeting like a storm cloud.

Finally, Assam began to speak.

"My lord, the heavens have bowed to your greatness."

The magi spoke. *"You are the most powerful ruler in both heaven and earth."*

It was now Balthazar's time to speak. Xerxes had a habit of staring through people. It was meant to intimidate others. Balthazar was used to the treatment and gently switched his gaze to the floor and began to speak. *"My lord, the heavens are yielding to your supremacy. This is a sign of your domination. The Greeks have tried to cover the light from your Empire and have failed. I am now more convinced than ever that Greece will burn under your feet."*

With this, Balthazar lowered his head in deference to his lord.

Finally, the King walked slowly to Golnar. But as he did the other two magi glanced at each other. Secretly, both Assam and Balthasur had been having discussions about the growing influence that the Egyptian priestess had been having on the King. They had both mutually agreed that something had to be done to stem the impact. They were both feeling in danger of becoming irrelevant. Xerxes arrived face to face with the Egyptian. He stared into her eyes, testing her resolve, and the priestess didn't flinch. Her dark eyes appear to widen as she stared back at her sovereign. Golnar raised her amulet and spoke in a soft, almost hushed voice.

"My King, there is a double meaning to the events of the last hour. I believe the Gods are issuing you a warning. The war that we are heading for will not be an easy conquest. At times the Greeks will cover the sun. They will have victories."

Xerxes' face seemed to harden at the report. Golnar continued. *"There will be times when you become discouraged, like the sun being covered in darkness. But as with the sun, the moon will be vanquished."*

At the exact same time that Golnar was speaking to her King, hundreds of miles away, Cypencant was advising the Warrior Queen on the same event. Her interpretation of the Eclipse although like Golnar's, was more disturbing.

"My queen, be very careful. The moon, much smaller than the great sun, still can darken the skies. Do not underestimate the Greek capability. They can darken the sky with their persistence. Overconfidence is the lesson to learn from the heavens."

Chapter V- Demos

The wine flowed and the men around the table drank as though they had never tasted liquid before. They laughed and reveled for hours in the corner of the tavern. One by one, over the course of time, they all dropped off their chairs ending up on the floor. Their compatriots made valiant but vain attempts to come to their rescue, but they too ended up on the dirt. Since early the evening before, this group had been arguing over the politics of the time. Of course, the impending invasion of the Persian Empire was the most hotly debated topic. The plan that had been put forth before the Athenian parliament was the complete evacuation of the populace of the city. The debate was quite lively, although they all knew that it was a fate acomplie. From what was readily known, the Persians were coming to seek vengeance on Athens. They had heard that the great Persian King wanted to see their beloved city in flames. All the men worried for their families and their acquired wealth. There was much crying at this gathering.

As the early morning sun grew closer to midday, the floor was cluttered with Greeks. The snoring was deafening, although the smell outweighed the noise. Into this disgusting montage of vomit and urine walked a weather-beaten man with a yellow bandana. Every few steps he spit on the floor, often hitting a prone, unconscious body. His face was heavily wrinkled, and yet his eyes appeared as sharp as any raptor. He seemed to walk with a limp and did not seem to care that he stepped on the patrons as he made his way through the masse. As he walked, he exposed a large stick that he carried strapped to his back. He used this instrument to turn men over to identify them as they lay insensible in front of him. He did not spend much time on most of the people, as he was clearly looking for a person amid this inebriated conglomerate.

Finally, he approached the table towards the back of the bar at which the men had been arguing. As he grew closer, he did not seem to use his stick as much. He suddenly stopped and looked down at the man who lay at his feet. He identified the man lying in front of him, not by his face, but by his exposed ass. He had seen it many times, oddly in this same position. It was easily recognizable for the old sailor. He stood and slowly shook his head. It was no longer amusing for him, but he knew that his future, and the fortunes of the city and peoples he loved, depended in part on this broad ass that lay on the ground.

Thantos bent over and put his hand on his friend Themistocles. There was no movement from the famous Greek as he snored in a louder grunting fashion, not feeling the touch of his friend. As Thantos bent over, covering his nose, memories of the many of the experiences he had with this man flooded his mind. He learned to love him and what he stood for. It was these deep feelings that brought him to this bar. He had performed many extraordinary events for Themistocles. He had gone to Corinth and conned a major shipbuilder into making ships that would be the template for the Athenian navy.

He had a pirate ally kidnap the shipbuilder's daughter and then appeared to "rescue her". He followed that up by transporting three spies to the Persian Empire to evaluate the strength of their enemy. Thantos accompanied the men inland, leaving his friend, Phecontalis, to guard the ship that would bring them back to Athens. Thantos and the three spies were captured, and this old sailor was the only man to make it back to Athens. The great Persian King let Thantos tour the troops, attempting to intimidate the Greeks. His best friend, Phecontalis, was murdered while guarding the hidden ship. The loss still stuck in the sailor's throat and he silently vowed to avenge the death of his close compatriot. The man who committed the murder was the leader of one of the Persian Immortals units. These so called Ausiya. His name was Smerdomences, and that name was burned into his consciousness. When he was a captive in the Empire, Thantos noticed that the Immortal general carried his friend's scabbard. He wanted to murder the man at that moment, but it would have cost him his life and he would not have been able to return to Athens with his acquired information.

Thantos bent over but couldn't lift the heavier man without help from him. He attempted to sit the man up but again failed, as Themistocles fell back to the floor with a thud. The sailor shook his head in frustration and then attempted the lift again.

"I appeal to Zeus, for such a brilliant man you are such dead weight."

The Greek politician was now sitting up on his behind. His red eyes looked up at his friend and he farted and threw up again on the floor. Themistocles then spit on the floor and smiled at Thantos. With help from the sailor, Themistocles precariously struggled to his feet. The two men slowly made their way towards the door. Thantos kept his arm on the Greek's shoulder and said, *"So what number is this, my friend?"*

"Number?" Themistocles moaned, still half unconscious

"Fifteen, twenty?"

The sailor questioned his friend. *"Fifteen, twenty what?"*

Themistocles moaned, holding his arm up to his forehead.

"Fifteen or twenty times I've had to search through these disgusting places to lift your fat ass up off the floor."

Themistocles smiled in sarcastic fashion. In a low voice he said "And *depending on what the future holds, there will be more visits."*

Themistocles was considered a political radical by the more conservative Athenian hierarchy. Others believed him to be a strategic, yet unorthodox genius. Athens had always been a political power keg with the ten powerful families of the city vying for supremacy and controlling the political landscape. This was until Themistocles burst on the scene. He rose quickly in the new atmosphere of the Demos. He lived not in the exclusive high-end part of the city, but in the poorer end with the people he loved. Remarkably, his eidetic memory was such that he recalled all that he met. Themistocles was very precise with his recall. He could remember specifics that he had heard months earlier. He processed information at a remarkable rate. Themistocles' ability to out-debate, outthink, out-strategize and out- manipulate any adversary was astonishing. Some called him a scammer, as he was not opposed to bribery and underhanded manipulation to achieve his goals. But what he possessed was given to him by the Goddess, Athena. It was called Metis. The Metis was hard to define. It involved charisma, magnetism and foresight. But even though his personality factors always carried the day in arguments, it was his ability to strategize, anticipate and foresee the enemy's moves which made him remarkable, and in many ways, the only hope that the Greek city states had against such an overpowering enemy.

Themistocles was an enigma. He lived with the poor and, yet he loved money. He was a rational thinking man, yet he would regularly drink himself into oblivion. He seemed to trust everybody, and yet, in fact, he trusted very few people. Themistocles was bold in his decision making and in his innovative tactical approach. But the biggest paradox for this man was his devotion to the Demos. His commitment to the idea that the common man should have a say in the decision-making process of the government was his mantra. And yet as the crisis approached, the unchosen leader of the Greek resistance abandoned the democratic ideals in favor of his own far-sightedness.

Themistocles had engineered many unanticipated and astonishing events that solidified the notion of his Metis. Against all odds, he successfully argued to build a strong navy almost from scratch. An unexpected silver discovery at the mines of Laurium had come at a propitious time for Athens. But the question had become what should happen with this new-found gift. Most of the aristocrats wanted the money divided amongst the citizenry. It was enough to give many poor merchants and farmers a relative bonanza. But even though Themistocles saw the Persian nimbus cloud on the horizon, he did not argue that Athens should build ships to defend against the Persians. For twenty years, Athens had in a protracted conflict with the island of Aegina. The Aegean's had successfully blockaded the Athenian harbors, draining the coffers of the city. All Athenians had felt the financial sting of the Aegean war.

Themistocles argued that the ships should be built to fight the Aegean's. He had reasoned that to argue the need for ships against a known enemy would likely yield a higher chance for success than scaring the public over an enemy that was still outside of the horizon. This was beyond the eyesight of the populace and therefore not their immediate concern.

But this parliamentary victory was followed up by an even bigger political shock.

The government of Athens had an ostracism clause in their constitution. The ostracism rule was instituted as a way of eliminating political diversity and internal governmental conflict. A man sentenced to ostracism by a vote of 6000 citizens had to leave Athens for a period of at least 10 years. Not only did he have to leave with his family, but the bones of his relatives were dug up and had to be taken with him.

At this time in Greek politics, the only other man besides Themistocles who conveyed a substantial following was a man names Aristides. He was called Aristides "The Just", because he was among the most honest citizens in the city. Aristides and Themistocles were political rivals, with Aristides favoring more power to the nobility over the majority vote of the people. Aristides also opposed spending the city's monies for a navy which he considered more of a luxury than a necessity.

Aristides, himself had a stellar past. He was a successful general in the defeat of the Persians at Marathon. Because of his experience at Marathon, Aristides believed that the Greek hoplite army could defeat all comers. The tension between the two political rivals reached a zenith during the vote on ships. Aristides decided that the only way to rid the city of this impulsively dangerous man was to call for an ostracism vote. A vote was taken and to his surprise, Themistocles prevailed, and Aristides himself received the number of votes to be exiled. Leaving his city was an emotionally devastating situation for this hero of Athens, and his isolation brought him to the brink of despair, contemplating self-destruction.

Although in a surprise move by Themistocles, when it was clear that the Persians were on the march, all the expatriated Greeks were asked to return and fight with their brothers. In an eerie ceremony that occurred out of the eyes of the populous, the two former political enemies, Aristides and Themistocles, met in a forest clearing. The two men made eye contact and hesitantly approached each other. When they came within arm's length, Themistocles bent to his knees and put his right hand on the ground, digging and covering his hand with dirt. Aristides followed the same procedure, and the two hands met under the earth. The rite meant that the two men were putting aside their differences, uniting to defend their city. Themistocles knew that this would be the first of many compromises that would have to be made if he was going to save his city, his culture and his Demos.

And now, this man with Metis was being rescued from a drunken holiday by his friend Thantos. It was beyond imagination that the future of the Greek democracy rested on the back of this half-conscious, intoxicated man, covered in his own vomit. Gingerly, the two men stepped out of the bar, but they were surprisingly met by darkness. Thantos looked to the heavens, although Themistocles could barely lean his head back enough to see the sky. Thantos appeared stunned as he said, *"Zeus be praised. The Gods are telling us something. The moon is covering the sun."*

Themistocles belched, spit again on the ground and said, *"The moon can try, but it cannot cover the sun. No matter how hard it tries, we will not be defeated. It is my belief Thantos that our ideals are stronger than any army, stronger than any God."*

As well as he could, the great Greek politician smiled, then farted. He ended his talk with "that felt good."

****

Adon walked into the room and was almost hit by a flying chair. In her usual fashion, the Warrior Queen was in the midst of a tirade. It had been going on for a day and a half since the confrontation with the moon-woman, Cypencant. Adon was very careful as he made his way slowly into the room. He had seen this before and he knew the dangers involved in trying to contain this volcano. He did not speak, but stood by the entrance watching the storm. Already three slaves had been injured trying to intervene in this tirade. He anticipated that the Queen was soon to run out of energy. Finally, after standing for nearly an hour, Adon noticed that Artemisia began to slow down. Then the Queen put her hands on her knees and bent over. She was breathing heavily as she turned her head to her friend and bodyguard.

"I am tired of this place. We will leave tomorrow."

"Leave, my Queen?"

"I have waited long enough. We will ride to Macedonia. I want to go to Mt. Athos."

"Mt. Athos, my Queen?"

"You remember, Adon, the King had his engineers build a canal through the peninsula to save the fleet from the vicious winds of the Aegean. I will be there when the fleet comes through. I have heard, Adon, that Xerxes sent a message to the mountain not to create trouble for the fleet. I will either wait at Mount Athos or return to Sardis to speak with the King."

Adon nodded and smiled. The King of Kings wanted to show nature that he was not going to succumb to its wrath. One of the events that undermined the first Persian invasion of Greece that ended with the disaster at Marathon, was the loss of many of the Persian ships navigating the dangerous waters around the cape of Athos. Having learned from his father's failure, Xerxes sent his engineers to build a canal through the peninsula, so his navy could avoid the danger. The undertaking was colossal to say the least. Such an enterprise was unheard of, yet Xerxes believe in his divinity and the omnipotence in his mission. Adon turned his back on the Queen and cursed in a voice loud enough to be heard.

"Build a canal?"

He said in a sarcastic manner. The Queen looked at him, and Adon spun around and looked back at the woman.

"Build a canal?"

He repeated. In a harsh, intense voice, the tall Phoenician said, *"The King put many peoples in their work crews. Idiots. I have heard the stories. The engineers dug straight down, and as they achieved the necessary depth for the canal, the sides fell in on them killing five workers. Idiots. It was only the Phoenician engineers who realized the sides of the canal must be on a slant to avoid such disasters. Stupid pigs."*

The Queen laughed. She liked seeing Adon seethe with anger. It created one of the few bright laughable moments for her. Laughing was an unusual behavior for Artemisia. When she laughed it was not out of humor. It was either conquest or watching people betray their inner selves that seemed to elicit an amusing response in the Queen. She hesitated and slowly looked at her bodyguard who was standing in the middle of the room with every muscle in his body taut. Again, she smiled and turned toward the wall. As she did, she said, *"Tell the brothers to be prepared. We ride tomorrow. And Adon, make sure the Moon Woman is joining us."*

"But my Queen, the King of Thessaly might not allow this woman to leave. She is quite powerful."

Artemisia smiled again. She moved her head to the right and said, *"Kill as many of those Thespians as need be, but the woman comes with us."*

She turned and walked, again smiling to herself.

The King of Kings stretched out on the bed. He was barely breathing hard, but his body was covered with sweat. As he lay on his back, the woman stroked his chest in celebration of his well-toned body and the intimacy they had experienced. She gently scrapped her fingernails over his chest and down to his thighs. The King seemed distant as he breathed through his nose. The woman said, *"You are beautiful, Khahayarsha."*

Nobody in the Kingdom could call Xerxes, Khahayarsha, except for Hadassah. Khahayarsha was the pet name that Hadassah's people, the Jews of Persia, gave to the King of Kings. One day, while walking through Babylonia, an onlooker had called out, *"Khahayarsha."* And Xerxes had his tongue cut out. But Hadassah was different, she was immune to the great King's anger. She was able to get away with things that few other humans could.

The King turned his head slowly considering the woman's eyes. Of all the woman at his disposal, he relished her the most. He actually made love to her, not just using her as a sexual relief. Her long black hair had natural curls and reached down her back to her waist. As she lay on her stomach her beautifully shaped hips slowly bounced on the bed. Her legs were bent at the knees, with her feet flexing and relaxing themselves. More than anything, Xerxes appreciated her even temper and her gentle attention. Unlike others, Hadassah never put pressure on the King, and he seemed to relax in her arms. But even with her in these intimate moments, Xerxes never lost composure. He was a hard man who couldn't afford to show weakness, even during intimacy. An entire Empire rested on his shoulders, and the young man could feel its weight. Although he would never show it, the pressure of Xerxes' ancestors was constantly in his thoughts. They even came to him in his sleep, urging him forward. Their glory even rested in Xerxes' actions. As she continued to stroke him, Hadassah commented in a soft, whispery voice, *"My King, you are so alone in your responsibility. It must be a heavy weight. And yet you never let anyone get close to you. What is your secret, Khahayarsha?"*

Xerxes continued his stare to nowhere. He then turned his head back and looked at the ceiling.

Hadassah continued, *"I know you are religious and a devoted man."*

Finally, after a few moments, Xerxes remarked, *"Tell me about your Jewish God. I only know a few things."*

Hadassah thought for a few minutes. She then said, "God is very old. *Our religion is made up of many principles. They are simple ones. They are that God exists and he is one and unique. He is incorporeal and eternal. All our prayer must be directed to God alone and to no other. We believe that God knows the thoughts and deeds of all men and that he will reward the good and punish the wicked."*

Xerxes seemed deep in thought. He said, *"You mean those who follow truth will be rewarded and those that follow the lie will suffer?"*

Hadassah nodded in agreement.

Again, The King of Kings thought deeply. He looked seriously at Hadassah and said,

"A prayer, Hadassah, before I cross into Europe, give me a Jewish prayer."

"Khahayarsha, any prayer I say I must say in my language. You must repeat it as I say it."

Xerxes nodded again.

Slowly, Hadassah began speaking ancient Hebrew. She spoke slowly so that Xerxes could properly repeat every syllable. She did not interpret what she said. Therefore, the King was blind to what the prayer meant. *"My God, the soul which thou hast placed within me is pure. Thou hast created it; thou hast formed it; thou hast breathed it into me. Thou preserves it within me; thou wilt take it from me and restore it to me in the hereafter. I offer thanks before thee, Lord, my*

God, Master of all creatures, Lord of all souls. Blessed art thou, O Lord, who restores the souls to the dead."

After the Hebrew prayer, Xerxes rose off the bed and walked naked to the opening in the tent. It was not unusual for the King to walk without clothes. Finally, he turned to Hadassah and said, *"A great leader cannot show weakness."*

In surprise, Hadassah raised her head off the bed and walked slowly to the King. As she arrived at his side, she stroked his back.

"So things do bother you, my man of stone"! Hadassah said in a low whispery tone.

Xerxes smiled, looked down at his concubine, and began stroking her back and hips.

"Maybe, but even so," the King of all lands said. *"I would never let anyone know if they did bother me."*

Xerxes lifted the girl up and brought her back to the bed. Later Hadassah continued her inquiry, *"My lord. Why do you have such hatred for the Greeks?"*

Again, staring at the ceiling with a blank look on his face, Xerxes thought for a moment then replied, *"When I was a child, my father sent our army to quell an uprising in the western end of the Empire. This uprising was instigated by Athens, feeling some loyalty to the Greek population in the Empire. To punish the Greeks for their offense, my father sent an expeditionary force to Greece. At Marathon, the Greeks destroyed this force."* His stare immediately turned to resentment.

Xerxes suddenly rose and spit on the ground at the mention of that poisonous word. He turned his head to Hadassah and she noticed the subtle yet qualitative negative change in his expression. *"We were betrayed by that son of a pig, Datis. And then the Greeks built a temple telling the story of the Persian inferiority. I go to Greece to burn that temple"*

"So, you fight out of shame?"

Hadassah asked in a childlike tone. Xerxes considered. He had never framed his anger in this manner before.

"I suppose you are right"

"My lord, can shame be healed by death?"

The King of Kings stared for a few heart beats at Hadassah, then rose from the bed and dressed. Rather than agree or disagree with that statement, he decided to just ignore it.

****

It was almost two weeks since Sakarbaal was able to sleep comfortably. It wasn't the weather nor the comfort of the bed in which he lay. The sailor was disturbed by his thoughts. He was having trouble rectifying the moral dilemma he was facing. He was asked by his King to murder the man that has become his friend. He had never been asked to accomplish such a mission before. Sakarbaal had done many things for his King and country, but this, this was something he had not anticipated. He was almost frozen with indecision as he tossed and turned through the night. In theory he knew how to murder. He also knew when it would be propitious. What he didn't know, was if he could do it. No matter how much he examined his inner strength, Sakarbaal knew that until that moment he could not be sure where his actions would take him.

Today was the day. He knew Themistocles' schedule like the back of his hand. He knew that the Greek politician meditated in the morning down by the docks. He liked being there when the sun rose. It was his quiet time, and no one would be around. Sakarbaal had heard that the Persians were marching. He knew that his window of opportunity was shrinking. Soon the Greek would be leaving Athens to attend a conference in Corinth, as the Greek cities were gathering to prepare their defense to the invasion.

He rose from his bed. He had been keeping precise track of time, as he wanted to get to the docks before Themistocles would. Sakarbaal had already set up an escape route. A small boat waited off shore. It would take the Phoenician to a safe harbor so he could return to his home. He had to trust that the boat would be there when he anticipated it. Everything was in order. It had to be now. As Sakarbaal dressed he tried to steady the shaking in his hands. He took two knives with him. He really didn't know why he needed two, but it seemed to make him more comfortable. He knew it was irrational, but he found himself putting them both in his robes.

As per his plans, Sakarbaal arrived at the place where he knew that Themistocles would be. He had been here many times, memorizing the idiosyncrasies of the place. When he slept, he dreamt of this place. He knew where he would hide and wait, and he took a deep breath and settled himself behind one of the bails that were positioned on the dock. He knew he was virtually invisible. The seconds went by as if millennium. Every second seemed to drain him of his resolve. It was disconcertingly quiet as he sat crouched in his hiding place.

And then the moment arose. Sakarbaal heard movement and he instinctively knew that Themistocles had arrived for his daily constitutional. His arm felt frozen as he began to reach for his scabbards. But even at this late hour into his plan, the experiences and thoughts kept bombarding his mind. He had come to admire the fledgling democracy that was growing in Athens. When he first heard of the ideals of a democracy, he thought it irresponsible. Leave important decisions of state to the populace, how ridiculous. But over time, the idea grew on him until he came to admire innovation. Should common people have a say in their own destiny, or should it be controlled by the King and nobility? Such philosophical questions made his head hurt. He finally concluded that it was much clearer with a King. You didn't have to think as much.

Sakarbaal found his shaking fist tightening around the scabbard. But more surprisingly he felt wetness on his cheeks. He rose from his crouch and headed out from behind his hiding place. As expected, there sat Themistocles with his back to him. Sakarbaal approached, making sure that he was stealthy. He looked around to assure that they were alone. Themistocles sat still, not expecting anything or any danger. But when Sakarbaal reached him expectantly, the Greek turned his head and stared into his eyes. It was a prolonged stare, icy and cold. Sakarbaal did not see either fear or surprise. He saw resolve. Themistocles glanced toward the scabbard in the sailor's hand. He looked back at Sakarbaal's eyes. Burning his vision through the sailor's skull.

Suddenly the Greek politician rose and faced his aggressor. But rather than attacking, he bent his head and looked at the floor for a few seconds. Sakarbaal stood unmoving with his right arm by his face, holding his weapon. Themistocles again looked at his friend and noticed the shaking in his hands. His eyes seemed distant, but he said, *"I will not defend myself. I put my arms down."*

He looked past Sakarbaal and said, *"Either plunge that into my heart or put your weapon aside."*

Sakarbaal then noticed the shadow of another man standing behind him. He turned and saw Thantos standing with his own knife. With eyes wide, Sakarbaal again looked at Themistocles in surprise. Themistocles held up his hand, indicating to the sailor not to come forward and defend him. Thantos looked at Themistocles in protest, but the Greek said, *"No, Thantos, put down the weapon. This is Sakarbaal's play. My life is in his hand."*

He again turned his gaze on Sakarbaal.

"If this is your destiny, I open my arms for you. I am surprised but not shocked. But I will not resist. If you still believe that what we are doing here is wrong, then plunge your knife into its target."

"I have no choice, Themistocles. You know that." The Phoenician pleaded.

"I know nothing of that, Sakarbaal. This is what we fight for. From the beginning you have always had a choice, you just chose not to use it. Only a fool believes that he has no choice, and you, my friend, are not a fool."

Themistocles continued, *"Our Demos is based on every man controlling his own purpose. You can either choose the future and control your own destiny, or sink back into the past and blindly follow others. It is your choice, you must make it."*

Sakarbaal's face was now completely wet, as was his chest. His eyes were popping out of their sockets. His face was contorted. He raised his arm, and rather than burying the knife into Themistocles' chest, he began sobbing. Themistocles took a few steps to the sailor and put his arms around his friend. He whispered into Sakarbaal's ear, *"What you didn't do took more strength than what you were planning to do. You shouldn't feel guilty, you should be proud. You have not betrayed your country, you have betrayed the idea that we should all be slaves to the ruling class."*

*Th*emistocles backed away from the sailor, and Thantos rushed forward and picked up the weapon that was dropped. Again, the Greek politician held up his hand, stopping Thantos. He focused on the teary face of Sakarbaal. Again, he spoke, *"Don't get me wrong, my friend. I admire your civilization. The Persians and Phoenicians are both proud peoples that should be gratified with their undertakings in architecture, trade, exploration, engineering, art, and religion. My fight is not with the culture, it is with the King of Kings, and with his* *dedication to absolutism. We here in Athens have lived that for generations. We will not return to the black earth."*

He turned his back and walked away from his friend. After a few steps Themistocles turns back and said to Thantos, *"Let him go Thantos, let him escape into oblivion. He is not welcome here anymore."*

Sakarbaal stood, his arms by his side, his shoulders slumped. He could not go home to Phoenicia for he failed his task given to him directly by the King. He had now lost his adopted city of Greece. He felt like a man alone in the world without a country, without a place to turn. He had never felt this alone before. He was always a part of something, but no longer. As Thantos turned to follow Themistocles, he heard a moan and a soft cry. Turning to look, Thantos saw the Phoenician dropping to his knees with blood coming from his neck and mouth. The knife that he brought to kill Themistocles was now stickling noticeably out of his neck. Thantos turned to follow his friend. Neither man turned again.

Vashti was outwardly a very religious woman. As part of her entourage she kept two priestesses, a magus, and two seers. Her devotion to her religion was more show than actual piety, yet she said the right words and followed the rituals. Yes, she participated in most of the ceremonies and professed her dedication, but in truth, her dedication was to rationalization and denial. Zoroastrian preached commitment to truth and living the proper way. There was a fear of demons and evil spirits from the afterlife. But the belief was that if you followed the truth, you would not be overcome by the lie. And yet Vashti had been turned to the lie many years before. There was no truth within her, there was no compassion for others, just a hedonistic necessity to have her needs immediately met. Vashti lied about most things if it satisfied her. She created story after story leaving everyone around her in turmoil. She lived in her own fantasy dreams, justifying her own behavior by her misguided rationalization. Drama and histrionics ruled her world. If something did not exist on its own, she created it. She believed the world was what she conceptualized it to be, not what it was. She was impulsive, paranoid, and sociopathic. She baited people and enjoyed their suffering. But Vashti's specialty was setting people against each other.

All her life, Vashti was spoiled. She held her name up to everybody. Yet when she wanted to, Vashti could present a convincing act, which like a deadly arachnid would draw others into her deceit. Many times, Xerxes had turned his head in disgust at his wife's behaviors and schemes. He had warned her often, but his threats seemed to be toothless. It had become very rare for the King of Kings to spend a night with his wife. Usually when he would enter her chambers, she would act in a way to repulse him. Xerxes also knew that the rejection his wife felt when he left hurt Vashti as much as any physical blow could.

On this day Vashti strolled through the encampment. She would regularly review the troops for her own reasons. Many soldiers had spent the night with the Queen, putting themselves in potential life-threatening danger if the King found out. Little did they know that the King knew every time the Queen satisfied herself with a soldier. He really didn't seem to mind, as it kept this woman out of his hair. The only predicament he considered was if his Queen became pregnant. But it was a problem that he would ignore until it became an issue. Xerxes wondered why it hadn't already happened.

But during this walk, Vashti had a hidden agenda. She was walking to the tent that held one of the Kings concubines, Volesmo. A slave announced her and Volesmo was bowing when the Queen entered.

"Hello, my dear."

Volesmo looked up, obviously surprised by seeing her Queen. Vashti rarely even spoke with her.

"My Queen, I am honored by this visit."

"Rise, my dear, rise."

"My Queen, I hope I haven't offended you in some manner!"

"No, Volesmo, no. I am just here because I miss your company."

Volesmo was a very naïve, immature young woman. Even though the Queen had never visited her before, the concubine was gladdened by the comments. She had always hoped that she could be friends with the more powerful and more sophisticated women in the Empire.

"My dear, I have realized that I haven't spent enough time with you."

Vashti sat on a pillow, looking up at the young woman.

"Now you've known the King since you were very young."

"Yes, majesty."

"I know that my husband likes you very much. He has frequently mentioned your name."

These last two comments were true, Xerxes did like her, and she was like a childhood friend to him. Vashti continued, *"Tell me, Volesmo, do you get lonely?"*

The young woman blushed and partially covered her face. After a moment, she said, *"I do, your highness. I do"*

"So do I, Volesmo, so do I. That's why I am here. We should meet more regularly."

"I would like that your highness."

"One other thing before I leave you to your peace. I am concerned and I need your help."

"Anything, my Queen."

"I am concerned that that Jewess, Hadassah, would like to hurt my husband."

"What, my Queen? Hadassah has always been so pleasant."

"Yes, yes, I agree she puts on a good front. But I have information that she blames my husband for the blight of her people. I fear she is plotting against him. Besides, her people have a history of violence"

Volesmo was quiet, obviously considering what she thought of the Jewish woman.

"Volesmo, I need your help. I need you to be vigilant. The day might arise that you and I will need to act to protect the King's life. "

"My Queen, rest assured that I will do anything that needs to be done to protect the King"

Vashti smiled and walked over and hugged the young concubine. The seed was planted and now she had to water it and watch it grow.

****

Eudocia struggled to climb the cliff. Ever since he was a young child height made him nervous. He always recalled the time when he slipped and rolled down a steep hill as a young boy and was made fun of by all his friends. Up until this time he had avoided having to climb. But this cliff was strategic for it overlooked the Hellespont. The Hellespont was a body of flowing water that separated the two great continents. It was deep, dangerous and very difficult to cross.

The rumors had spread for long periods of time that the Persian King, Xerxes was going to attempt a crossing from Asia to Europe over the Hellespont. But this body of water was treacherous. It was over a mile wide at its smallest breach. Eudocia had heard the rumors but disregarded them as speculation and over exaggeration. How could anyone take a large army across such a distance without considerable losses in both men and animals. It was ludicrous. If true, it meant that the Persian King had lost his senses. True, making a successful crossing would save the Persians almost a year for having to go around this spot would add many extra miles to the journey, but realistically it was a foolish gesture!

It had taken Eudocia weeks to reach this place. He had to travel directly north from Attica. His journey took him through Thessaly, Macedonia and Thrace. This was not only long and arduous, but these northern territories had all Medonized, succumbing to, and allying themselves with, the Persian King. Being from Athens, the center of the resistance to Persia, Eudocia would be considered either an enemy, or more likely, as a suspicious character. The testiest moment for Eudocia came in the Thracian city of Doriscus. It was so close to his final objective of Sestus that Eudocia let down his guard. He was an unusual spy for he worried about everything and everyone. But most importantly, Eudocia was a patriot. He loved Athens and he loved the philosophical ideas that underlined the fledgling Demos.

Eudocia was surprised when he was called to Themistocles' house one evening. Even though he was a member of the parliament, elected from one of the powerful families of Athens, he never expected to be called by Themistocles himself. It was a great honor, he thought. He swore on his way to the meeting that he would present himself as a brave and courageous man ready to perform any duty in defense of his city. Eudocia had heard the rumors of the impending Persian hoards. Because of his noble position he had guessed that Themistocles would ask him to organize some type of resistance within the city.

As he approached the house of the great politician, Eudocia was surprised by his anxiety. He had met many important men in his life, but he had never felt this way. He was led into the main sitting area by another man whom he didn't know. As he sat and waited, his leg shook in anticipation. It wasn't long before Themistocles entered the room, and after a brief period of awe, Eudocia composed himself and stood to greet his hero. As Themistocles approached, he waved his hand for Eudocia to sit. Themistocles spoke, *"You probably don't remember, but we met two years ago."*

Themistocles had an uncanny memory. All he had to do was meet someone once and it became engrained in his mind. Themistocles realized that the man that stood in front of him had no recollection of their meeting. Eudocia nodded his head in affirmation even though Themistocles was correct in his assumption. The great politician continued, *"We met at a gathering to honor the great thinker, Solon. Do you remember now?"*

Eudocia smiled in recognition. Themistocles turned and took a few steps before he spoke.

"He was my hero, you know….Solon."

Themistocles looked to the sky and repeated a Solon quote from memory.

> **"This my soul commands me teach the Athenians:**
> **A bad constitution brings civic turmoil,**
> **But a good one shows well-ordering and coherence,**
> **As it puts shackles 'round about wrong-doing**
> **It smoothes out the rough; it checks greed, tempers hubris,**
> **And withers the fruits of reckless impulse.**
> **It takes crooked judgments and makes them straight,**
> **Softens arrogant deeds, halts seditious acts,**
> **And ends the bile of grievous strife. And so under it,**
> **Everything for mankind becomes whole and wise."**

Themistocles appeared distant and encompassed when his thoughts shifted to his hero, Solon. After a few moments, he refocused and looked at Eudocia, *"I'm sorry, I am taken by his reforms and brilliance."*

Again, he turned and looked toward the sky, and began another quote,

*"**Some** wicked men are rich, some good are poor.*

We will not change our virtue for their store,

Virtue is a thing that none can take away

But money changes owners all the day."

Eudocia was stunned by the man's recall of Solon's poems. Themistocles took a few seconds to recompose himself again after his second muse. He then turned to Eudocia and smiled, "I become enthralled *when I think of Solon's brilliance."*

Themistocles' eyes seemed to redeploy. He smiled at the younger man, then said, *"Eudocia, I have always admired you."*

Eudocia pointed to his chest questioning Themistocles last statement. He looked surprised.

"No, I am serious. I attended the last games outside of Delphi and I was very impressed by your athletic ability."

Eudocia bowed his head in recognition of the compliment.

We need brave, athletic men like you to defend our civilization from the Persian horde. *I know that you are a patriot."*

These who met Themistocles, were taken by his presence. It was such that one immediately felt greater just standing next to him. His Metis rubbed off on others and left them willing to do anything to satisfy him. Now Eudocia stood and bowed in recognition. He impulsively blurted out, *"What will you have me do?"*

Themistocles took a few steps away from Eudocia. He had his hand on his chin and then said,

"I need a fearless man to make his way to the Hellespont and scout the Persian advance. It is a very dangerous job. The man must make his way amidst many areas that are rich in Persian supporters. But it is crucial. We must know the Persian path."

Themistocles was now in Eudocia's face.

"Are you up to this task?"

Without really thinking, Eudocia said, *"I am!"*

Eudocia cursed his quick decision many times during his trek through northern Greece. Many times he was overcome by fear as he believed he was about to be discovered. He worked hard to control his emotions, willing himself to stop shaking. But his fright of climbing outweighed his fear of the Persian. He had now finally reached the city of Sestus. Sestus stood directly opposed to Abydos, the place where the Hellespont was at its shortest distance. It was here that the Greeks expected Xerxes to attempt to cross the mile wide tributary.

Eudocia reached the apex of the hill and had a perfect view of the area. His eyes widened in disbelief as he looked down from his perch. He instantly looked to the heavens and gasped, *"Athena, protect us!"*

****

Chapter V- Mount Athos

Themistocles and the Athenian delegation arrived in Corinth a day before most of the other cities. It was an unprecedented gathering, as many of the cities were still at war with each other. There were many hidden agendas and past blood feuds, and it was possible that the Greek alliance could implode before the Persians arrived. All indications were that the Persians had already arrived at Sardis. They would winter in that area and cross the Hellespont into Europe in the spring. Therefore, the Greeks had only a precious few months to prepare a defense.

Although all Greek cities were invited, many had already Medized or formed puppet alliances with the Persian. Then there were those cities that wanted to hedge their bets, remain neutral until the Persians arrived on their soil. Themistocles was in Corinth early to meet with the Spartans before the rest of the delegations arrived. There were many problems to be addressed.

Themistocles' second in command was a man named Eudox. Eudox was an experienced negotiator. As he arrived at Corinth he was still reeling from his perceived failure at the negotiations with the dictator, Gelon, in Syracuse. The Greek cities on Sicily were approached by Eudox to join in the defense of the homeland. Gelon boasted a very large army numbering almost 20,000 troops. He also had two hundred Triremes, which would have made the odds against the overwhelming Persian force more palatable. The dictator welcomed Eudox with open arms and pledged his support, with only one stipulation. He wanted to control both the army and the navy. This was, of course, out of the realm of possibility. The Spartans would want to head the army and Athens would want to lead the Navy. When Gelon was told he could not control the alliance, he threw a temper and banished Eudox from Syracuse. Eudox was not used to failure and it weighed heavily on his heart. In truth Gelon was worried that the Phoenician colony of Carthage would attack behind the Greek defense. He was correct in his assessment, as the Persian King had planned for the Carthaginians to attack Syracuse when he attacked Athens. This would he believed, eliminate the ability of the Greeks to withdraw to the east. He would have them trapped in the Peloponnese. For these reasons, Gelon had never seriously considered allowing his troops and ships to defend Greece. He knew his demands of leadership would be opposed by both Sparta and Athens, leaving him free to remain on his island.

At this conference in Corinth, Eudox had two goals. Both were difficult. Athens and Aegina had been at odds for over ten years. It was Eudox's task to make the peace. It would be impossible to defend Greece against the Persians and fight each other at the same time. The second conflict that he needed to resolve was between Sparta and Argos. Those two Peloponnesian cities also had a long-standing feud. It was rumored that Argos had secretly joined the Persian allies.

It wasn't long before Eudox got to work. On his first night in Corinth he met with a man from Aegina named Lason. Lason was connected in high places within the Aegean government, but was considered a very difficult negotiator. His reputation was that he hatred Athens. It was ironic that he considered Athenians elitists, as he was a member of the hard-handed royal family that ruled Aegina. Lason was a member of the aristocracy, and the infantile Athenian Demos was very threatening to the ruling Aegean families. It had been rumored many times that Athens was attempting to support an insurgence against the ruling Aegean oligarchy.

Eudox was aware of the games that governments played to further their agendas. He had presented disinformation himself in support of his beliefs. He always thought it ironic to present deliberately false information in support of truths that were held. But in the case of Aegina, it was Athens who presented more distortions. The Aeginians had successfully neutralized the Athenian Navy and had blocked imports. Eudox held no cards at this game, which meant in some way he had to bluff and promise.

The two met in a very quiet room off a famous bordello. Corinth was well known for their beautiful woman and their ability to pleasure customers. But today this room was being used for a very delicate meeting between these two traditional enemies.

The room was fashionably furnished. The captain, Thantos, had secured this space for Eudox to use. Thantos had visited this house before and knew the proprietress very well. Both men would be offered many hedonistic pleasures this night, especially if their meeting was brought to a successful conclusion. But this particular evening the two men were not here for pleasures of the flesh. Eudox believed they were here to save the world they knew.

Eudox sat waiting for his opponent who was already quite a bit late. He knew that this was part of Lason's negotiating strategy. Unbeknownst to Eudox, Thantos stood behind a curtain just in case the Aegean was somehow going to be vindictive. Thantos wondered whether the Aegean had already medized and were here to lay a foundation to destroy Athens. In that case, killing Eudox would be a feather in his cap.

Finally, another curtain opened and Lason entered the room. Never having met the man, Eudox was surprised by his appearance. Lason was a very large, a mountain of a man. Eudox's experience was that very large men were not very bright. He supposed that all the energy in their body went to supporting their bulk, leaving little left for thought. Food and drink were important to such men. Lason stood silently slowly looking around as if evaluating the surroundings. This appraisal in and of itself told Eudox much about this 'mountain' man. Finally, he spoke, *"I have heard of you, Eudox. Aren't you the man that was supposed to gain the support of that hideous dictator, Gelon?"*

"Son of a pig," Eudox thought. Not only had he heard of the failure, but he was trying to shake Eudox by mentioning it as soon as they met. Eudox also ascertained that Lason was nasty and vindictive. The purpose of such a comment was to belittle and undermine the other man's position.

He took two steps toward the Athenian and bowed in admiration. The comment about his failed negotiation stuck in Eudox' throat and he thought he noticed a slight smile on the big man's mouth. Eudox rose and bowed in respect.

"Lason, I am honored that you have agreed to meet me this evening in this lovely place."

Lason rolled his eyes as he looked around again.

"Lovely place, are we in the same building? May I sit?"

Eudox nodded as he pointed to the chair next to him. Ignoring the gesture, Lason sat opposite the Athenian. Eudox smiled and again nodded his head.

After taking some wine, Lason spoke.

"Well, Eudox, have your people suffered enough *under o*ur pressure? Our navy has enjoyed crushing the Athenians."

Eudox held his emotions in check. He was practiced at this art. He would stay out of this power struggle so as not to lose the purpose of this meeting.

"You should be proud of your people's prowess, Lason. They have spanked us like a father disciplines his child."

Lason smiled, but Eudox continued

"But as you are aware, children grow both in strength and in mind. When the parent least expects it they can be made to look and feel foolish by the punished child."

Lason bowed his head in recognition. He began to respond.

"Let us say, my friend, that the Aegean are not matched equally by the Athenian, but that we are superior in experience to them."

Eudox smiled and Lason laughed out loud. Lason continued: *"I have heard rumors that the Athenians have planned to undermine my government and try to install a system closer to their misguided concept of Demos. I think to myself, is this the sign of a true friend?"*

Eudox thought for a heartbeat, then said with a confused face,

"You know, I heard such rumors as well. He slapped Lason on the shoulder. Mine said that Athens secretly purchased ships from Corinth to give to Aegean rebels. I even tried to find such ships, but only found seawater"

Lason smiled, but Eudox continued.

"Rumors are funny things, like shadows. Another bit of gossip that spread through Athens was that Aegean sailors stripped the skin off

Athenian captains of the ships they captured. But Lason, when I heard such horrors, I said to myself, we might not be best of friends, but the Aegean are wise and civilized people, not like the Persian barbarians."

Lason again smiled. Both men drank more wine.

"Silliness,"

Lason said in a low tone, and lifted his glass to Eudox. After another glass, Lason continued, *"Besides rumors, trust is also a funny courtesan, as a lover it is very fickle. You never know which way the tide will turn. But a man's character is also capricious, one day saying and promising one thing, the next day acting as if no words have been spoken. How do we solve this riddle my friend?"*

Eudox ordered more wine and some of their fine lamb stew. After the meal was served, he said, *"Lason, you and I are not lovers. But we both share the same desire. We both find ourselves on the same slowly sinking ship. We can either swim together or drown under the waves."*

After a long while, Lason's expression changed. He looked Eudox in the eyes. The Greek could see that the landscape had shifted away from the relationship as enemies to at least, reluctant allies.

"Eudox, I will be honest with you, my people are scared. Many people believe that the Persians are undefeatable. There is a strong element in Aegina that feels we should abandon this illusion that we can defend ourselves against such a superior force. Many think your mentor, Themistocles, is too drunk to face the reality of the situation. They do not want our island to burn with Athens"

Eudox was quiet, surprised, and almost shocked at the change in directness of this man. After a second or two, Lason continued, *"My King is anxious. He does not want to lose power. What is being asked of us is to put our faith in the wisdom of this man, Themistocles. We have heard of this man. A drinker, a gambler and a briber. There are those who believe that he has already made a deal with the Persians to further his own wealth. And then you have this political foolery. A government of the people! Nonsense. The people cannot vote for their own well-being. They have to be told what to do. They always have been sheep and always will be."*

His face now became more serious, as he looked directly at the Athenian and said, *"This Themistocles, Eudox. His decision making is radical; it's hard to trust such a man. He believes that his small new navy, what do you have maybe 200 ships, can withstand an attack of 1200 ships? And the Spartans. They are superior fighters. But the Persian army will outnumber them 10-1. It is ridiculous. Do you think we should commit our future to a drunken man? Better we should give the Persians earth and water and remain neutral. In fact, when we consulted the great Oracle at Delphi, Apollo recommended that we keep our swords in their holders and bow to the storm."*

Eudox's expression did not change. He smiled and said, *"You would be foolish not to trust him."*

Lason considered Eudox's words. He leaned backwards and continued to stare at the Athenian. Lason's blue eyes seemed to stare straight through Eudox.

"Foolish hey. You're asking me to trust this drunken man over the Oracle?"

"Yes, foolish,"

Eudox quickly responded. Now it was Eudox's turn to lean forward. He stared directly into those blue eyes of Lason and said, *"Have you heard of Metis?"*

"Of course I have. It is that magical ability given to human by the Goddess Athena. Are you saying that the Goddess has intervened on the side of Greece? The last mortal that was given Metis was Odysseus. "

He seemed to be pondering this, and then he continued, *"Even if that is true, it is still a major risk."*

Eudox smiled inwardly and said, *"Lason, I will promise you two things. First, if you do not join this resistance to the tyranny, your people will be forever enslaved under the Persian yoke. Second, after the Persians are routed, the Greek army will turn against those cities that have been treasonous. Or should I say coward?"*

Lason again leaned back covered his mouth with his large hands, contemplating this unlikely prognostication.

****

Adon was tired. He and the other Phoenicians had ridden for almost two weeks straight. The small group had ridden north past Mount Olympus and through the Southern Macedonian shore. Even though Macedonia was a Persian ally, the small contingent had to fight its way through many confrontations. It confirmed the belief that even with allies, the situation was fluid. Adon's sword had tasted much blood.

Their first encounter happened just north of Mount Olympus where the group had camped out in the foothills of the range. They had set their fires and placed three of the guards higher up the slope. Artemisia was jittery this night, as she was usually uncomfortable on land. Horses made her edgy. No matter how hard she tried, she could not relax. What she did learn from the animals was that they were vigilant and very sensitive to changes in the environment. Therefore, even though she disliked the smelly creatures she tended to sleep near them. This night, the horses were more skittish than usual. Artemisia took their nature very seriously. Her fears were well founded, as halfway through the night the small band of Phoenicians were surrounded by one hundred men. It was not an ambush as the tribe walked into the camp. The Phoenician guards formed a ring around the Warrior Queen.

Artemisia rose from her bed and could feel the surge of excitement in her stomach. Her sword hand was already on the hilt, and as she stepped forward, she secretly hoped that this encounter would end in a conflict. She had been controlled for too long. The head of the tribe stepped out of the background and approached Adon. He was not a well-kempt man, probably in his fifties, with knotted hair and a dirty long beard. Adon stared him down, and it was clear that none of the Phoenicians were frightened by this conflict. The leader of the tribe took another step forward and said, *"This is our land, and you cross it without permission. You must pay tribute to safely go on."*

Adon breathed heavily through his nose. He stepped forward with his eyes focused on the tribal leader.

"We pay no tribute to walk the earth. It belongs to all."

The tribal leader began to raise his hand to signal an attack when Artemisia stepped forward.

"Halt,"

she demanded. The tribal leader smiled sarcastically.

"A woman? A woman speaks for this group?"

"What is your name?" Artemisia asked. The leader looked her up and down as if he didn't need to respond to the questions of a woman. The Warrior Queen smiled and stepped forward. She walked to the leader and stepped close enough to speak so nobody else could hear. The Warrior Queen looked directly into the leader's eyes and said in a low voice,

"We have already paid tribute, for you still stand in this world. You will die this night, as surely as you smell of piss. I would suggest that if you value your life you will withdraw."

The leader looked a little shocked at the brash words. He composed himself, but as he did, the Warrior Queen silently touched her elbow giving a signal to the rest of the Phoenicians. The chief began to laugh but before the sounds were audible, his head was rolling on the floor. Artemisia, with her catlike movement, had sent him to his ancestors with a sudden, single stroke. In a split second ten more of the tribesmen fell under Phoenician swords. Shocked by the suddenness of the assault, the tribe was stunned. In that time Artemisia dropped two more and her Phoenician guard killed seven others. The remainder of the tribe quickly turned and ran into the hills. Adon stood in the center of the group covered with tribal blood. He looked at the Warrior Queen and she turned her head and with her eyes, smiled at him.

It was now weeks later and the group had almost reached their destination. The closer they came to Mount Athos, the more the Warrior Queen became visibly excited. They were met almost 20 miles from the canal by Persian soldiers. Surprisingly, the Phoenician contingent was met by both Persian and Phoenician guards. The Persians were surprised that the Phoenician guards bowed to one knee when they saw the Warrior Queen. One of the Persian guards almost lost his life when he laughed at seeing the Phoenicians bowing to a woman.

As the group approached the canal, even Artemisia stood in shock. Before her was an engineering marvel. She was so stunned that her mouth almost fell open. No enemy had ever gotten this type of reaction. Wide-eyed she looked at the Phoenician engineer who was standing next to her and asked, *"How long?"*

"Over a mile," The engineer said with a smile.

"Remarkable,"

Adon said.

"Is it deep and wide enough so that two ships can pass together,"

Artemisia asked. Proudly the engineer said *"Of course."*

Before long she saw a man-made canal cut through the Mt. Athos peninsula that would allow the Persian navy to avoid treacherous waters. A gleam shown in the eye of the Warrior Queen. Now that this diplomacy and Oracle nonsense was over, she was about to reenter her element. The beautiful Aegean stood in front of her. She would soon defeat the Greeks and the entire ocean would belong to her.

****

The two men were oiled down. They were both large muscled individuals and clearly athletic. They circled each other brandishing their swords in one hand and their daggers in the other. Both men turned around in a spherical ballet. One would fake a blow, then back off. The crowd kept urging the combatants on. After a few minutes of this dance, a loud voice was heard over the cheers of the crowd.

"Halt!"

The great King had risen off his throne and stood with an irritated look on his face. As usual, the King of Kings was adorned in a white Egyptian loincloth. His chest was unclothed and when he was angry his muscles tended to twitch. The King's arms were decorated with leather strips that ran from his shoulder to his wrist. Around his thick neck was a tight necklace of pearls. His right arm was extended toward the circle where the men stood. His eyes were gleaming. As always, his eyelids were impeccably painted in dark shades making the King look feline.

"Halt, I said, Halt!"

The two men rose in their tracks and both stood facing the King. Xerxes slowly stepped toward the circle. His eyes looked distant as he strode forward. He was obviously not in a hurry. The King of Kings stared at the two men in the ring. He put out his left hand as his eyes stayed focused on the two men. A personal slave handed the King a sword and he walked into the circle with the two men. One could see that his personal body guard, Penish, was quite anxious as the King confidently strode into the makeshift arena. Xerxes' eyes shifted away from the two warriors and onto the gleaming object in his hand. Xerxes lowered his sword but pointed it at one of the warriors. He said, *"It is time for a real trial. I challenge you both. I grow tired of this useless dance that you both do."*

Before the King could move an inch, his shadow had jumped into the circles standing at his monarch's side.

"No, Penish. Return to your seat."

Xerxes took on a serious air and said, *"Unless you both try to kill your King, I will not hesitate to slaughter you both. Your effort will determine if you survive this day."*

He backed away and the men looked confused as to what to do. Xerxes stepped forward and with a quick slice, cut through the knee of the man on his left. The other warrior jumped back in shock then raised his sword to defend himself. Xerxes stepped to his right and engaged the man who was now in front of him. The other man was moaning and rolling over on the ground. As Xerxes stepped to engage the second warrior, he quickly turned and with an upward and quick downward motion, ended the man's life as he cut his throat. The crowd was shocked by the suddenness of the strike.

The second warrior stood wide eyed in front of the King and desperately blocked his advances with his own sword. It was clear who the aggressor was, as Xerxes kept attacking and moving forward. The urgency in the warrior's face was evident as he kept retreating under the barrage. Finally, under the continuous attack from Xerxes, the man took a misstep and fell backward. Before the man could make a sound, the King of Kings swung his weapon downward and the man's sword flew out of his hand. Xerxes then lunged and put his sword at the man's throat. There was a hush and a pregnant pause, until the King smiled, lowered his sword, and helped the man up. It was obvious that the warrior was in shock, being pulled from death's doorway. It was completely quiet as the King of Kings walked from the confrontation. Penish could now continue breathing.

Later that night, Xerxes had been washed down by the slave girls. He leaned on his right arm as he lay on his side. He had called a meeting of his generals and admirals to discuss strategy for the invasion of Greece. Xerxes and the army would winter here in Sardis and cross the Hellespont in the spring. Naval forces were assembling at Cyme and Phocaea off the Ionian coast. Again, the generals gathered. They all entered in a disheveled manner as the area was experiencing a violent storm. The winds and the rain were wreaking havoc with the tents and the animals in the army settlement. Only one of the admirals was available as the other two remained with the fleet.

Gergis and Mardonius were the first to enter the King's tent. Both prostrated themselves to the King of Kings. As they rose, they blew kisses to the monarch symbolically expressing their love and devotion. Tritantachmes soon followed with the expatriate Greek, Demaratus. The other general of the Immortals, Smerdomences, was the last to enter the tent. Besides his bowing and blowing of the kiss, Smerdomences withdrew his sword and placed it under his own neck. A smile arose on Xerxes face, acknowledging the total devotion that this man showed to him and his Empire. Sitting in the back of the room, out of sight but not hiding, was Xerxes' personal body guard and advisor, Penish, the executioner. Penish was still reeling from the fight the King put on that morning. Penish almost wanted to scold the young monarch for putting his life in danger, but he wasn't sure of the response, and he knew it wasn't his place. This was the man anointed by God. If God wished to punish him, then he would be punished.

The King finally rose from his position and spoke, *"I have asked each of you to formulate plans for the unified assault on Greece. Have we reached agreement?"*

"We have, Lord, "

Mardonius replied. He continued, *"The march through northern Greece will be spearheaded by our two Immortal-Ausiya units. Gergis and his units will defend our right flank and Demaratus' unit will advance along the left flank by the coast. "*

Xerxes stood silently and listened. Mardonius continued, *"The fleet will progress down the coast and keep the army supplied."*

"What do our spies tell us?"

Xerxes inquired. Smerdomences now responded, *"Lord, northern Greece will offer no opposition. Macedonia and Thessaly have agreed to neutrality. Out of all the Greek cities, only 30 have refused our offers of submission. By far the two most important elements of the resistance will come from the Peloponnesian Greeks from Sparta and their allies and the navy from Athens. They only have enough troops to offer us token resistance. When we break through their initial defensive positions, all lower Greece including Athens, will be at your mercy."*

"And the Greek colonies on Sicily?" Xerxes asked.

Tritantacechmes laughed and said,

"The dictator, Gelon, will offer no help to the Greek alliance. Sicily will be invaded by the Phoenician colony of Carthage. They are preparing, at this moment for their assault. The Carthaginians will coordinate their attack with our march on Greece. The Greeks will not be saved by western reinforcements. Carthage has cleverly released suggesting information confirming their invasion, so the pig, Gelon, will not release his troops to protect Athens. It is a funny story lord.

What we have heard is that Gelon never was considering sending troops and ships to the Greek alliance. But rather than just saying "no" and be considered a coward, Gelon made a request that he knew the other Greek cities would not agree to. "

Xerxes asked, *"What did he ask for?"*

Tritantacechmes laughed out loud and said, *"He wanted to control both the army and navy."*

Now it was the King's turn to laugh

"Excellent. The man might be a pig, but he is not stupid. "

Xerxes mused. Smerdomences began talking again. *"Northern Greece is mountainous. There are many passes to be defended. We have spies positioned at each of these areas. The Greek army will only be able to sufficiently defend one or two of the passes. Once defeated, the rest of the Attica will be naked in front of us. We have heard Lord, that the Greeks had sent an army to defend the Tempe pass in northern Greece. As per our instructions, our friend, King Alexander from Macedonia, warned them that the pass was undefendable. They then retreated."*

In his usual style, Xerxes was now pacing while listening. Lightning and thunder rang through the encampment. Everyone stopped for a moment at the force of the event. Then the only admiral at the meeting, Zephan, spoke, *"The fleet is prepared to support the army. Supplies will not become an issue."*

"What about the Greek navy?"

Zephan laughed.

"They have 300, maybe 350 ships at best. We outnumber them almost 3 to 1. Yes, they will make a stand, but after the first battle, the shores will belong to Persia. There will be no supply problems, lord."

Xerxes snorted loudly. His arms were folded on his chest as he walked and thought.

"Where is Artemisia?" he asked. Now it was Zephan's turn to be uncomfortable. The Warrior Queen was a very touchy subject with the Persian admiralty. In fact, all the foreign contingencies were a source of wariness for the Queen from Halicarnassus. Zephan knew that the Phoenicians were the greatest sailors in the known world. The Egyptians were competent as well, although they were more river fighters than open ocean men. But all the foreign contingencies would be led by the very inexperienced Persian admirals. It created a delicate situation. Zephan was very sensitive to the dilemma. He was especially touchy regarding this woman from Halicarnassus. All he heard over and over was Artemisia. He was sick of hearing about her exploits and her capability. She had attained almost Godlike status in the Empire. He scoffed at her specialness, although he also knew of the King's feelings about her. Most of all, during battle, he did not want to be upstaged by a woman.

"Our spies have told us that she and her Phoenician comrades have made their way to Mount Athos. They stay at the canal."

"Excellent,"

Xerxes remarked. He now faced Zephan and directly said, *"Send her composite of ships to meet her there. She will spearhead the naval attack."*

Although he bowed in acknowledgment of the order, Zephan was seething inside. A non-Persian spearheading the naval attack, and a woman no less! But Zephan held his posture. His face revealed none of his disappointment or annoyance at the edict. Xerxes continued, *"When the storm subsides, I will inspect this miraculous bridge that the engineers have assured me has been constructed to transport our army over the Hellespont in the spring. I have heard it is quite a sight to see. You are all excused, except Demaratus. I wish to speak with you."*

The other generals and the admiral all bowed and backed out of the room. Demaratus, the ex-Spartan King, remained as the others left. He had a surprised look on his face at the unexpected meeting with the King. Xerxes waited for the room to be cleared and then he said, *"This must be difficult for you."*

"What, Lord?"

"You are here with a foreign army readying to attack your homeland. Does it bother you that you will be seen as a traitor?"

Always bold, Demaratus said, *"The conqueror is never the traitor, only the vanquished."*

With a nod of his head, Xerxes acknowledged the witty reply. The King then continued, *"I have considered what will happen to you after our victory in Greece."*

Demaratus held his breath. *"Because you are a Greek and are familiar with the customs and the Gods, I believe you would be the logical choice to rule this peninsular. Do you think you are up to such a challenge, after all you were outwitted by the other Spartan King, which led you to me?"*

Xerxes rarely pulled punches with his direct underlings. Of course, he did not trust Demaratus, for he believed that he had warned his fellow Spartans of the impending invasion. Xerxes had heard from a spy that a strange stone tablet had arrived in Sparta. It was blank with no message, but it appeared to originate within the Empire. Many had questioned whether Demaratus had sent this strange message. Even so, Demaratus had shown himself to be a superior leader during the campaign to crush the rebellious Egyptian magi. In fact, in Xerxes' eyes, he outperformed his elite Persian Immortals in the quelling of the insurgency. He also needed Demaratus because he knew the terrain, but more importantly, he knew the minds of the Spartans.

"Tell me, Demaratus, what are the Spartans like as soldiers?"

A tricky question for the ex-Spartan. He had to be truthful, but at the same time not offend the Persian army.

"Lord, the Spartan soldier is like no other that you have, or will ever encounter. They are bred for battle. Death is considered glorious. A regime of Spartan Warriors can stand against an army of any enemy."

Xerxes looked intrigued, but he had heard the boastings of men before.

"Continue" he said. *"Tell me about their strategy."*

"Lord, they will not retreat. They will hold their position to the death of every soldier."

Xerxes laughed and said, *"But any good soldier will do that."*

"It is different with the Spartans lord. They will punish you in battle, not just kill you. They have no mercy, they have no fear. You will never see a Spartan turn and run. Blood is their companion."

Demaratus decided it was time to prognosticate. *"I believe, Lord, they will pick their most defensible position and meet our army there."*

"And where do you suppose that will be?"

Xerxes asked in a serious manner.

"The northern passes are not defensible. There are too many, at least four. They will not split their army to defend all four. Each pass can be turned by conquering one. I believe they will concede northern Greece and make a stand farther south. The pass I believe they will defend will be at Thermopylae."

"Why that one?" asked the King.

"It is perfect for them. The pass is narrow, bordered by the sea on one side and the mountains on the other. There is no known way to

outflank it. It is there at what is called, the 'hot gates' because of local hot springs. That I believe, is the place you will first see the Greek army."

Xerxes turned and slowly walked away. He abruptly stopped and turned to Demaratus. He had an ironic smile on his face.

"You realize that once we trample these invincible soldiers, and sink the Athenian navy, then your boasts about the Spartans will have to change."

He now took three steps back to Demaratus. His face was distorted with tension. He lifted his right arm in the air pointing it at the ex-Spartan and said, *"Athens will burn before my feet and I will let you, Demaratus, clean up the ashes."*

Demaratus bowed again. But Xerxes said, *"Who do you suppose will lead the Greek resistance?"*

"I believe, Lord, that the Greek army will be led by a Spartan King named Leonidas."

Xerxes jumped at the sound of that name.

"Leonidas! That man will die under the Persian sword. I will give you enough gold to last your lifetime if you bring me his head. If Leonidas is at Thermopylae, then that is where we will take the army."

Demaratus had heard about the anger that Xerxes had for Leonidas. It was Leonidas that murdered his teacher, Hamas, on the mission to Delphi. He knew that the King would not rest until the Spartan King was dead. Demaratus bowed and backed out of the tent.

****

Chapter VII – The 17th of the Agiad Line

The son of King Anaxandridas II and the 17th of the Agiad line had prepared for this meeting for some time. As he walked through the beautiful gardens of Corinth, he had many things to consider. Leonidas knew that he was going to lead the ground defense of Greece even though he had no misconceptions about the task in front of him. But he also had unbounded confidence in the Greek resolve. This conference to unite the allies in the defense of Greece had reached an impasse. The conflict of the representatives wasn't over who would lead the land defense, it was who would lead the nautical one. The Athenian position that the Spartans did not know the seas was a logical one. But the Spartan delegation was stubborn, standing on the position that a warrior was a warrior, whether on land or on the sea. Unfortunately, the conference was at the abyss and it was threatening to fall apart. It was already polarized over this issue and there were threats that delegates were getting frustrated and threatening to bolt. The defense of Greece was on the brink of defeat even before the Persians arrived on the continent. They all knew that their chances of success if they banded together was slim enough, Greece could not stand in disunity. Sparta could not succeed without Athens and vice versa.

As Leonidas walked past a beautifully laid out flower bed, he noticed his new friend walking toward him. Athens and Sparta had had a relationship for many years. Both cities had vied for superiority in the Greek world. But Leonidas had gained much respect for Themistocles since their meeting at Delphi. And now, it would be up to these two great leaders to break this impasse, to forge the agreement that would at least give the Greeks a fighting chance. Themistocles bowed in front of the King of Sparta, another gesture that impressed Leonidas. The Spartan spoke first, *"Welcome my friend, we both find ourselves surrounded by wasps."*

"Wasps indeed,"

Themistocles smiled. The son of King Anaxandridas spoke again. *"My Athenian friend, if we cannot find a solution to the defense of Attica, it will be simple for the Persian to split us and crush each side in turn."*

In a pensive manner Themistocles said, *"I have no opposition to you leading the land defense of Greece."*

"Thank you for your confidence."

"It is not confidence, my Spartan friend, it is realism. The Spartan army can overcome any enemy."

Leonidas bowed his head in acknowledgement of the compliment. Themistocles went on, *"But on the sea............sailors from my city are more adept."*

Leonidas tightened, swallowed and spoke, *"I cannot in good faith accept any other city to lead the navy. I will concede that Athenians are more experienced on the seas, but Spartans are more prepared for war. We are disciplined and direct."*

Themistocles frowned. He looked to the sky and began a slow pace. He knew that this was a saving face issue for Leonidas and his city. To follow any leader other than a Spartan in a conflictual environment was just an unthinkable condition. He wondered whether they could even conceive of the situation. But an answer must be found. To his surprise, Leonidas spoke again: *"I have learned many things over my years, one of which is that sometimes people are called Kings, yet the power rests in other hands. But even though that is the case, the King is still called the King'."*

Both men hesitated at the suggestion, but Leonidas continued. *"The Persians are fools. I hear that they have their own admirals directing the Phoenician and Egyptian navies. If this is true, they do not understand the nature of war. They are bullies. We should not make the same mistake. But we can call an admiral an admiral when the decisions during the battle are really made by his Athenian understudy."*

"A Spartan admiral would accept such an agreement?"

Themistocles queried

"They will accept what I tell them to accept. Part of war is subterfuge."

Themistocles looked directly into the eyes of the King. He remarked, *"I had revered the Spartan King for his resolve and his bravery. But I thought my admiration for him had reached its limit until this day. I am the fool Leonidas, please forgive my lack of intuition."*

Themistocles fell to a knee in front of his Spartan ally. After a few moments he arose, took a few steps away, then said, *"I will agree to this compromise. I will lead the Athenian contingent. I will agree to an overall Spartan commander with limited power. Decisions will be made by a meeting of the commanders with the Spartan at the head."*

Leonidas smiled at the compromise. It essentially meant that the Spartan admiral would be a figurehead and that Themistocles would be the true commander. But this would save face and insure an alliance. After a minute, Leonidas bowed his head in agreement. The two men approached each other and Themistocles bent and put his right hand on the ground in front of the Spartan King. Leonidas bent and mixed the dirt as he touched his right hand to that of the Athenian politician. This was the ancient rite of brotherhood. After they stood, Themistocles said, *"What do you see as the defensive strategy?"*

"I have given this much thought. I would like you to lead an expeditionary force to northern Greece to determine which pass is the most defensible. Remember though, our army will be small. We cannot defend multiple places. We must concentrate our strength both on land and on the water."

"I agree," responded Themistocles. He continued, *"I suggest the following declaration. We will all agree to band together to defend Greece. We will all agree that any city that goes back on this declaration will be subjected to punishment by the alliance. We will all agree to give sacrifice to the Oracle at Delphi."*

Leonidas showed no emotion, but by his stance it was clear he agreed with the points that Themistocles made. The two great men stared at each other. In each of their faces one could read the desire, dedication, and resolve that they brought to the table. And yet there was sadness in their eyes as they silently acknowledged the tremendous mountain that they needed to overcome. The men stared into each other's eyes as if to say that, they might not see each other again once this war started. And yet they both instinctively knew that success would depend on the other's skills. Themistocles finally spoke, *"This war will be the greatest conflict that the world has known."*

A small smile appeared on the King's face. He said, *"Every conflict is a great struggle. All blood drawn is honored. But you know that once we engage, we will not yield an inch of ground."*

Both the Athenian and Spartan knew that the Delphi Oracle had warned them both about the upcoming conflict. First the Spartans were warned by the Pythia:

"Your Fate, O inhabitants of the broad fields of Sparta
Is to see your great and famous city destroyed by the sons of Perseus
Either that, or everyone within the border of Lacedaemon
Must mourn the death of a King sprung from the lines of Heracles."

Leonidas had sworn not to allow his city to be destroyed by the Persians. If it came down to a choice between his life and that of Sparta, the choice would be an easy one or him.

The Athenians had two messages from the Oracle. Eudox had received both, and the first was very discouraging. The Pythia answered the Greek question in this manner:

"O Pitiful man, why do you come here? Fly to the ends of the earth, leave your houses and wheel shaped city. Everything will fall to ruin. Fire and Ares, God of war, destroy all. Many fortresses will be obliterated, not yours alone. Many temples will be devoured by fire, black blood dripping from their roofs, portending inevitable suffering. Leave this sanctuary and prepare yourselves with courage to meet misfortunes."

Against his better judgment, Eudox returned for a second prediction. This one gave a small window of hope.

"Athena, the Pallas cannot appease Zeus in spite of devoted persuasion, entreaty, and prayer. Yet I shall make a second and unyielding prophecy. When all Attica shall be taken, Zeus will permit Athena a wooden wall. It alone will not be taken and will assist you and your children."

"Do not await the approach of horsemen, nor await the arrival of foot soldiers from the continent. Turn your back and depart. A day will come when you shall face them again."

"O divine Salamis, many offspring of men and women will perish, either at the time of sowing or at the time of reaping."

What did this second message mean? There were varying interpretations. The Athenian parliament argued vehemently over the points of the prediction. Many believed that Athenians should build a wooden wall around Athens to defend against the Persians. Themistocles reasoned that the "wooden wall" did not literally mean a wall, but referred to wooden ships. He backed up this logic by pointing to the phrase,

"Do not await the approach of horsemen, nor await the arrival of foot soldiers from the continent. Turn your back and depart. A day will come when you shall face them again."

Themistocles also argued that Athens should not be defended but abandoned. He didn't believe that the Greeks would be able to vigorously defend the city. He would move the people back when the Persian grew tired of occupation. He also debated that finding an abandoned city when they arrived would take away some of the Persian glamor, thereby frustrating them either further. The other reason for this logical conclusion of abandonment was that most of the male population would be needed to man the navy, in one way or the other.

Leonidas again spoke; *"Forevermore, this garden will be called the place of hope and forthcoming"*

"No, not hope my friend. Hope is an empty word. Without resolve, planning and action, hope is a delusion of those who wish and pray, but never act",

Themistocles responded.

As they left the garden, Themistocles touched the shoulder of the Spartan and said, *"We shall be victorious."*

Leonidas stopped the Greek and said, *"I have one last warning"*

The Greek politician braced himself, as the King said, *"Be careful of the one that is called the Warrior Queen. She had me under her sword but let me live. She is destruction and hatred, worse than the Furies ever were. You might have Metis on your side, but she has death on hers. Kill her quick if you get the chance. Show no mercy to this hell creature."*

Themistocles tapped his friend on the shoulder and they both departed.

That night the Greek politician was startled awake. The house in which he stayed was covered in pitched darkness. His anxiety rose, and his heart was fibrillating. There was something amiss and he could sense it. Themistocles rose up from his bed and decided he needed to walk and try and calm himself. Outside a cool wind touched his face which seemed to relax him a little. But even so there was a strangeness about the sky. An imperceptible sound came from the firmament and Themistocles jerked his head skyward. He could barely make it out, but there seemed to be a creature circling overhead. He was spellbound as he watched this aberration. The animal seemed to be circling lower and Themistocles backed up and lost his footing. He fell on his bottom and seemed to cower, ending almost in a fetal position. He could barely speak as words stuck in his throat. He wanted to cry out, but only whimpering sounds left his mouth. The space in front of him seemed to shiver in a yellowish glow. The creature that had been circling landed in the glow and began to hop in front of the Athenian. The owl appeared angry as it screeched in agitation glaring at the politician.

"What do you want?"

Themistocles shouted, although the words were too low to be intelligible. The owl seemed to breathe a bluish mist. It continued its screeching. After a few seconds Themistocles started to regain his composure. He could not stand as his legs were useless, unable to sustain his weight. It was as if they were detached from his body. He crawled forward toward the owl, trying to suppress his terror at the aberrational sight.

"What is your nature?"

The bird appeared confused as the man approached. It began flapping its wings, but then it settled. It approached Themistocles, but as it came to within arm's length a female apparition appeared out of nowhere. It was a ghost-like face, but Themistocles noticed a particular facial feature. The woman had bright green eyes that shone through the clouds. Themistocles bent his neck touching his head to the ground. Without thought, he knew instinctively who this spirit was.

"I am your servant Athena, what can I do to appease you?"

The Goddess' face seemed to be electric. Light shone through her hair. Themistocles was not frightened, but stunned by the beauty of the image. Athena did not smile, but spoke in slow measured terms.

"You have been a loyal servant. Over the years you have offered many prayers to my glory. You have built many temples to celebrate me. In return you were offered Metis. Search deep into your sole Athenian, you will know this to be true. For all we Gods exist within

you. My reign on Olympus is ending, in part because of your Demos. I glory in your accomplishment and mourn the passing of a ten-thousand-year-old trust. It is the way of things. We create our own destruction, either through our acts or our inaction."

"I will never lose faith. Your power and glory has never left my mind. No matter how strong the democracy becomes, our faith in you will not waver. Even in egalitarianism there is place for adoration and worship."

Themistocles replied. Now the ghostly face smiled.

"You now lecture me."

There was a pause, *"I know your faith, but you have sown the seeds for your children to believe otherwise. It will take years before new voices are heard, and the belief will be reestablished. The great Oracle will perish under the weight of hedonism from the west. It will take new form, but it will not vanish. Belief remains as the vessels change"*

"How can I serve you?"

Themistocles begged.

"I will build more shrines, will make more sacrifice."

"No!"

The voice emphatically rang out.

"You have heard from Apollo. He only partially sees the future. My great city will waver under the threat of the invader. Be assured, my olive tree will survive. The task you have is a difficult one, even with Metis. You must convince the people that it is the Gods' view that they must abandon their homes. You have chosen the correct path, now you must be their savior and lead them into the unknown. It is better to search the unknown, rather than be slaved in the present."

*"No more prayer to me Themistocles, no more. From now on **pray to the wind**. It will offer you salvation."*

The face moved closer. Its eyes bulged.

"Do you understand, Pray to the Wind?"

The Greek, prostrated on the ground, acknowledging the message.

With a small eruption, the face of Athena vanished.

Themistocles was still unable to move. Feeling was only slowly returning to his legs. He tried to process what he just saw, what he just heard.

"Was it real?" he thought, or was it just the aftermath of one of his wine stupors? He had heard Athena say to abandon her, Abandon her! And abandon her city! Was she really in agreement with his strategy or was this just wishful thinking? A hopeful hallucination. And what did the Goddess mean that Apollo only partially saw the future? Themistocles felt that he should be more confident in his path and yet, without the Gods' protection, where would this path lead? His stomach churned and the Greek politician threw up on the ground. His eyes grew heavy, and sleep came quickly in this spot.

****

"I won't have it!"

She angrily banged her cup on a wooden chair.

"I won't have it,"

she repeated, but this time the cup flew across the room at the slave's head. The cup hit him between his eyes, as it was protocol that he was not allowed to duck to avoid a punishment. Now Vashti jumped up and ran to the slave. He immediately fell to his knees even though his head bled and pounded from the blow of the cup. Vashti arrived at the slave and began kicking him in the side. She ranted, yelling, *"Tell your master I won't have it! I will not attend the dinner with that whore!"*

She now grabbed his hair and jerked his head backwards. In a gasping voice the slave said, *"I was only to tell you that the state dinner begins at seven o'clock. The King of Kings will expect you there."*

Unable to rise the slave crawled out of the room, leaving a trail of blood behind him.

The table was beautifully decorated. Many flowers of varying colors made the sight extravagant. Large potted plants adorned the floor surrounding the table. It looked more like a garden than the inside of a tent. For all his harshness, Xerxes loved nature. On the way to Sardis, The King of Kings stopped the entire army for two days, for he noticed a tree on the side of the Royal Road that he considered an exceptional beauty. Xerxes had little compassion for humans, or animals for that matter. But trees he worshipped them as a gift from the great God, Ahuramazda. On this occasion, Xerxes sacrificed twenty head of cattle and ten slaves to the glorious tree. He also immediately commissioned an obelisk to be erected on the spot. It was to read:

Xerxes, the King of lands, King of peoples, King of Kings rested his army on this spot. Let the world know that his army, the strongest in the world, will go on to destroy the Greeks and add their culture to our own. We will drink them like water and walk on their bodies like the mud.

All the nobles from the army, as well as envoys from the western satrap in which they rested, sat around the large wooden table. Behind the chairs stood the advisors and the slaves. Behind the throne, but out of her cage, was Simeron, Xerxes pet lioness. She seemed content as she lay on the ground. The golden throne sat at the end of the table.

Surprisingly, to left of the King's chair sat Golnar, the Egyptian lector priestess. She seemed to be gaining power and influence by the day. An empty seat was open to her left. To the right of the King sat Hadassah an unusual arrangement, considering that to the King's left usually sat his Queen. Although Xerxes had not yet entered the tent, the tension was high as the gathered invitees anticipated that when Vashti arrived her rage at not sitting next to the King would erupt. They would not be disappointed. When Vashti entered the room, it was as if fire erupted from her face. Ignoring the gathered dignitaries, Vashti threw a memorable tirade. Food, flowers, silverware all flew through the tent. Even though the gathered people had expected the tantrum, their eyes were still as wide as the harvest moon. Even Simeron began paying attention, growling with anxiety.

But then, as if a candle was pinched out, Vashti stopped. Her arms were stiff at her sides and her face was distorted. She stared across the room to see her husband, the King of Kings, standing by the tent's entrance. Utter silence covered the room. Even Simeron stopped her growling. Xerxes stood silently with his hands on his hips. He stared at his wife, and she bent her head and began to stare at the floor. He continued to glare as Vashti walked over to the empty seat. Xerxes stood watching as his wife walked silently across the room. After she sat he pointed to the floor and slaves hurried to clean up the mess. When the task was completed, the King proceeded to his throne. He sat and lifted both of his arms into the air. In his right hand he held "the Answerer." He bent his head said, *"My ancestors are all gathered in this tent with me. Our people began as wanderers in tents and I have returned to my lineage, my pedigree. We will soon be leaving our domain to carry our seed past our boundaries. I have prayed to Ahuramazda the only true God, for our deliverance and for his protection in our quest. My ancestors have been calling to me in my dreams, urging us to seek revenge for the embarrassment that was Marathon. I swear to this gathering and to my lineages, that Athens will burn below my feet."*

Xerxes lowered "the Answerer" and the slaves began bringing out the food. As he sat, his hand instinctively moved to cover Hadassah's hand. Vashti caught the movement and bristled, but there appeared a slight smile on her lips. But then suddenly a female slave, bringing food to Hadassah, fell to her knees and began writhing in pain. From her mouth oozed a white substance. Xerxes rose in horror. He had seen this before. He stepped over to the slave girl and looked at Hadassah. Xerxes knew that Hadassah had just had an attempt on her life. He instinctively turned his head at glared again at his wife. Vashti did not make eye contact with the King, but he now understood the true heart of his wife. He glared at Vashti as he motioned for a slave to remove her from the gathering.

****

The storm lasted over two days. When it was over the land appeared soaked and muddy. The sun shone through the clouds and Xerxes mounted his horse. He was accompanied by the Executioner, his personal body guard, and by Smerdomences, his favorite commander and one of the heroes of the Ausiya. Smerdomences brought 500 of his crack troops to help with security. Xerxes' horse was an animal he raised from birth. His name was Roshanak. He had been bred for size, strength, and intelligence. Xerxes would speak to the horse as if he were an advisor.

Today was the day. Xerxes had heard stories about the marvelous structure that had been constructed for his army to cross the mile-wide Hellespont. Although this was the shortest distance in the waterway that was bridged, the water that flowed in this area was turbulent and treacherous. From the great lake, the water in this area was forced into this mile-wide pass, increasing the intensity threefold. Because of this, there were arguments among the engineers over the place to build the bridge. This shortest length was also the most dangerous. In the end, two engineers assured Asanaladace the architect, that this was an accomplishable task.

Asanaladace was the greatest engineer in the Empire. He had been given this assignment by Xerxes himself, who had unbridled confidence in his ability to work structural magic. Asanaladace wore the King's opal, an honor that very few men could ever achieve. He served Xerxes' father, Darius, as well. It was Asanaladace that was behind the building of many of the great Persian temples and monuments. He also laid the plans to build the great canal by Mount Athos. Asanaladace had studied his craft in both Phoenicia and Egypt. In this case, Asanaladace would devise the scheme how this bridge would be built. He then turned over the actual construction to a Phoenician engineer for one of the bridges, and to an Egyptian for the other. Both would use slightly different construction procedures, but the design for both was from Asanaladace.

The Egyptian that oversaw one of the bridges was named Amon. His father and grandfather were both architects. His name meant builder in ancient Egyptian. Even though he had the pedigree, Amon did not like construction, but was forced into this business by family tradition. He did not pay much attention to detail, but preferred drink and revelry. The Phoenician, on the other hand, was a very serious man. His name was Hailama and he was greatly esteemed in his home city. Even though this assignment was supposed to be an honor, Hailama did not want to take it. He considered it too risky.

The bridges themselves were remarkable accomplishments. The bridge closest to the Black Sea consisted of 360 boats lashed together, hull against hull, by huge cables. They were anchored at specific places that were chosen to avoid any difficulty with the rushing waters. Wooden planks were then tied together, connected to the gunnels, and laid on the boats with earth covering them to make the appearance of a road. The second bridge was made up of 320 boats. The Egyptians and the Phoenicians used different types of cable to tie the boats together. To show the preciseness of the building, sides were built so the animals wouldn't be spooked by the rushing water when they crossed. The bridges were secured together both under and over the water line. The Phoenicians used white flax for their cables, while the Egyptians used reinforced papyrus.

Xerxes and his entourage arrived in time to see a large section of the Egyptian bridge floating down the river. He dismounted and stood motionless, hiding his fury as he watched the sections of both bridges disintegrate. No emotion was displayed. The King of Kings stood overlooking the Hellespont, again with his hands on his hips. The other men stood in astonishment, watching the fragmenting of the "roads on the water". The storm ravaged the bridge, ignoring all the engineering expertise that built it. The workers tried in vain to save the structure, but nature won out. Finally, the King of Kings had seen enough. He spoke no words, turned, and briskly walked back to his tent. A slave followed him into his resting area. The King stopped suddenly and said, *"The lead engineers, bring them to me."*

The Egyptian, Amon, was the first to arrive. He immediately fell to the floor prostrating himself in front of the supreme monarch. Xerxes stared at him, almost in disgust.

"I am sorry, Lord, we were not prepared for such a violent storm. It arose without warning as if the Gods themselves ordered its arrival."

Xerxes did not respond to the ministrations of the engineer. Instead he sat perfectly still, allowing the man to remain on the ground. It wasn't long before Hailama, the Phoenician engineer, appeared at the entrance of the tent. When he saw the scene, he too fell to the floor. He seemed to sweat profusely as a small puddle appeared under his face. Xerxes spoke to Hailama, *"Your counterpart, the Egyptian tells me that you were not prepared."*

Hailama looked surprised at the comment. He began stuttering, not knowing how to respond to the question. Finally, he said in a very broken tone, *"Lord, our bridges were prepared, it was the Gods who did this."*

"It was the Gods?"

Betraying his underlying anger, Xerxes barked, *"Gods, whose Gods do you suspect did this??"*

The King of Kings gave a strange look. He thought, *"such a blatant, absurd denial."* But outwardly his appearance returned to its stoic facade. Finally, after a few minutes, the King rose slowly from his seat. He said, *"Rise gentlemen. Don't be scared. I shouldn't punish men for something the Gods have done."*

The men didn't move, but their trembling was obvious. He let the men sit and walked to the corner of the tent. Xerxes raised his arm indicating that he needed the help of a slave. Almost as if out of a cloud, a young woman appeared at the tent's entrance. She ran to the King but he didn't turn to greet her. She stopped quickly as she reached him and froze in her place.

"Bring me Harpalus."

The slave girl disappeared. Xerxes walked to his throne and sat. He did not speak to either of the engineers or give them leave to rise. The three sat still for over two hours until the slave girl returned out of breath. Both men had lost feeling in their legs by this time. Ten steps behind her walked a large man. Xerxes smiled and said, *"Harpalus the Macedonian"*

The man had stopped walking forward and bowed his head. Then lifted his head up and blew the King a kiss, showing his love and devotion for the Empire.

"My lord, I am here. How can I satisfy you?"

"Harpalus, these two engineers have failed me. They have built substandard structures. My entire army is now stranded here."

"But Lord..........."

Xerxes raised his arm pointing at Amon. The Egyptian immediately stopped talking and bent his head back down to the floor. The King turned back to Harpalus and said, *"My army will cross this water in the spring. I need a reliable man to rebuild the two bridges. Are you able to successfully rebuild these structures?"*

"I am, Lord'

Xerxes slowly walked to the Macedonian and drew his sword. Harpalus stood between the two prone engineers. The King of Kings walked to within six inches of Harpalus' face, and said,

"I don't like failure."

And with those words, Xerxes dropped his sword and cut through the Egyptian engineer. The man withered in pain as Xerxes fell to a knee and beheaded the man with a single fluid stroke. The King rose slowly and returned to stare in front of Harpalus.

"Macedonian, do you understand my concerns?"

Harpalus seemed to tighten and his eyes were as still and wide as the spring moon. He quivered, but nodded his head. With this affirmation, Xerxes impaled Anon with his sword. Harpalus jumped at the suddenness of the attack on the second engineer. With the two dead engineers bleeding profusely on the ground, The King of Kings turned his back and left the tent. It took five minutes for Harpalus to stop shaking, as he tried averting his eyes from the carnage that lay at his feet. The King of Kings spent the evening in the secondary royal tent. Ten slaves cleaned his primary residence as he would have no evidence left of the engineers.

After supper, Xerxes was visited by Golnar, the Egyptian Lector priestess. He sat in the corner of the tent staring out at the moon. The priestess walked over to him and put her arm on his back.

"Lord, you will need to respond to the water."

Xerxes looked at Golnar. Again, he said nothing, but his look was questioning.

"You are being tested, my Lord. The Greek Gods are trying to interfere to stop your invasion."

Xerxes stood and said, *"The Greek Gods have no say over me! I will not allow them to intervene."*

The King of Kings began to pace, clearly more agitated than he had been. He banged his fist on a wooden table emphasizing his irritation. Golnar stood watching the display with her arms folded.

"The river must be punished. It must know that Xerxes is the King of Kings, Lord over even the water."

Suddenly the King stopped. He slowly looked around, *"I heard something,"*

He said as he looked at Golnar.

"I hear nothing Majesty"

Golnar responded.

"What did you hear?" the priestess inquired. Xerxes moved around the room looking behind curtains. Surprisingly, he looked at Golnar, *"I thought I heard laughing."*

The next morning, Xerxes and his entourage walked to the river. He carried a leather whip with him. The King stopped at the water's edge and looked to Golnar. The priestess fell to her knees, looked to the clouds and said, *"You salt and bitter stream, your master lays this punishment upon you for injuring him, who never injured you. But Xerxes, the King of Kings, will cross you, with or without your permission. No man sacrifices to you, and you deserve the neglect by your acrid and muddy waters."*

After the Lector priestess made her salutations, the King of Kings walked to the waters and began lashing the waters with his whip. He took 300 strokes at the river. Xerxes performed the action with vengeance in his eyes. After it was done, Xerxes sweating profusely, retreated again to his tent

Chapter VIII – Rejection of Tempe

Her eyes almost left her head. Artemisia stood on the high ground and watched as the Phoenician Trireme passed its way through the Athos canal. It was her ship, and the Warrior Queen was again in love. Ever since she was sent to Delphi to meet the Oracle, Artemisia longed for her return to the sea. It was physical pain for her to be without her lover. The ache inside of her for the water was greater and more intense than any sexual urge could be. Sexual desires were fleeting, yet the longing for the sea was limitless. She was like a salmon, instinctively returning to her safe place, her place of infinity.

The Warrior Queen squatted and her hands went to cover her mouth. Next to her stood Adon, her personal guardian, Agatha, the slave she stole from the Oracle, and Cypencant, the Moon Woman. Also, there were the two engineers who made this engineering miracle possible, Artakhaies, the gigantic Achaemenid, and Bou-Bares. The excitement seemed to be contagious as the others all had broad smiles feeding off the exhilaration of the Queen. It wasn't long before the Warrior Queen was rushing down the side of the mountain. She demanded that her entire entourage spend the next three days exclusively on the Trireme. Artemisia isolated herself in the bow of the boat. By the third day she emerged and called all of her counselors together.

"Tomorrow we will take our four boats and return through the canal. We will head to the Hellespont and I will speak with the King of Kings. I have been studying the information we have of the Greek coast. There are some traps that we must avoid in our attack."

Later that night Adon begged a meeting with the Queen. He was concerned that the Queen's aggressive impulsivity could have negative consequences. He knew she yearned for combat. Yearned for conflict. Yearned for blood. He had seen this face and demeanor before. He recognized it and it scared him. Fear is the wrong word, as Adon didn't fear much. But he had learned that Artemisia sometimes let her aggressiveness cloud her judgment. Upon entering the Queen's quarters Adon said, *"My Queen, I have concerns about returning to the Hellespont. Would it not be more propitious to wait for the fleet to meet us?"*

Artemisia smiled at her guardian and said, *"Yes, it would, but I don't intend to proceed with the fleet down the Greek coast. I intend to lead the fleet. It is time, Adon. Our time in history has come. The Greeks are inexperienced sailors.* They do not have the skills to stop us. We will prove that. *Be happy, Adon. We will soon be among the enemy and covered in their blood."*

Stoically Adon stood ingesting the Queen's words. Artemisia noticed the hesitancy and again commented. *"Why do you fret, Adon? We are back in the ocean, our element, our birth. Nobody can sail like we sail. Nobody can fight like we fight. Nobody can lead like we lead! We must grasp the time- it is our destiny!"*

"The Greeks think it is their destiny."

"Adon, I have shown you that the Greek Gods are false deities. I killed their priestess in front of their great God, Apollo. He did nothing. They are afraid of me, Adon. The Greek Gods are illusions of their warped culture"

Adon stared at her. He spoke again, *"My* Queen, is *it not self-righteous to have such thoughts? You are the greatest warrior that I have known, but the Gods being afraid of you? I fear such thought will lead to impetuous decision making"*

"Oh, Adon. *Our journey has just begun. It will lead us to great heights. The world will know the great Queen from Halicarnassus."*

****

"It is impossible, it can't be!" He empathically stated.

"The pass is undefendable. There are at least three other passes that could flank the position. It would be disastrous."

The Spartan King walked slowly up and down the length of the room. He knew, as did every other military strategist worth his salt, that at best the Greek alliance had one maybe two defensive stands against the Persian invasion. The numbers were too skewed, even for Spartans. They had to choose the defensive location that maximized their limited resources. It was obvious that the son of King Anaxandridas II, and the 17th of the Agiad Line was tense as the muscles in his arms tightened. There was no fear in the man, but he also wasn't foolish. He prided himself in not rushing in, in planning and strategizing vs. just fighting.

This was not political for Leonidas. It didn't matter to him that the Persian tyrant was attacking the Athenian Demos. Leonidas didn't care about the fledgling democracy. He didn't care about Athens or the nationalism surrounding Greece. He didn't care about Xerxes, or for that matter, Themistocles. Leonidas was a specialist when it came to war. He was a skilled practitioner. His domain was war and death and he saw in his future the opportunity to practice his craft. But as a practitioner he wanted to maximize the chance for success. He was obsessive in his planning. The philosophy that Leonidas was brought up in, taught that death in and of itself, was a desired accomplishment. But Leonidas could not stand defeat. His own death to him meant defeat. It meant he couldn't continue to fight.

Themistocles stared at the man pacing in front of him. He knew of his singular obsession. It's not that he disliked him or his ways, he counted on them. Leonidas was the kind of man Themistocles and Greece urgently needed. Without his kind, they had no chance against the superior Persian force. Watching Leonidas pace almost put Themistocles in a trance. He finally shook his head and continued talking, *"Tempe is not defendable. That was clear to me when the locals showed us three other passes that could flank Tempe."*

Finally Leonidas said, *"It must be the hot gates, we must meet them at Thermopylae!"*

"I agree,"

Themistocles responded, and both men walked to each other and locked arms. After a minute of both men staring into each other's eyes, Themistocles continued speaking, *"It is my belief that the Persians will use its navy to shadow and supply the advancing army."*

"They must!"

Leonidas agreed. The Athenian responded, *"I will take the navy, and while you are defending the Hot Gates at Thermopylae, our navy will engage the Persian navy off the Island of Euboea at Artemesium.*
"

The men locked arms. Again, they stared into each other's eyes. Both knew that the odds against them defending either position was not encouraging. In fact, the odds of either surviving the first confrontation with the Persians was not promising. For the King of Sparta knew that the Delphic Oracle had already predicted his death.

"Your Fate, O inhabitants of the broad fields of Sparta

Is to see your great and famous city destroyed by the sons of Perseus

Either that, or everyone within the border of Lacedaemon

Must mourn the death of a King sprung from the lines of Heracles."

The way Leonidas interpreted this prediction was that either he sacrificed himself, or he must wait and watch his beloved city of Sparta burn. The son of King Anaxandridas II, and the 17th of the Agiad Line wanted to prove the forecast wrong. More than that, the King wanted to stop the Persian because of their xenophobic arrogance.

Themistocles already had the embryonic plan in his mind for the initial defense of Greece. The Hot Gates at Thermopylae was perfect for defense. The path was narrow between the mountain and the water. Yet it was raised so the Persian navy couldn't directly support the advancing militia. A small but staunch force could wreak havoc as a much larger force attempted to advance through it. As he turned to leave, the Greek politician gave one more glance at the Spartan King. Would they ever meet again on earth, or would their next meeting be in the afterworld?

****

Artemisia was agitated as she stepped off her boat. She and her other Phoenician vessels had sailed nonstop to Sardis. She wanted to make sure that Xerxes understood her concerns and recognized her importance. She also wanted to clarify her role in the multicultural navy. She silently worried that the great King would put her in a compromising position. He had done it before. Although she would never say out loud, she believed that Xerxes was a poor strategist and therefore a poor leader. In the past she had been disappointed by the King's decisions, especially on how to use her unique skills. She had wrongly assumed that she would lead the invading navy to reconquer the rebellious province of Egypt. Instead, Xerxes sent her on a negotiating mission to the Delphic Oracle. A negotiating mission! She was anything but a politician. She loathed their kind. Men who compromise for the good of no one. They often saw their compromises burn in the night. Artemisia viewed compromise as weakness, bending beliefs to avoid something. She recalled that on the way to Delphi she had heard others speak of mutual concessions. Artemisia spit on the ground at such thoughts.

She believed. *"Only death resulted in such agreements,"*

The Warrior Queen was beyond herself in rage. She was insulted that Xerxes did not invite her to the alliance meeting. All of the allies met in Susa. Artemisia was there, but no invite followed. Eventually she ignored protocol and burst into the meeting leading the Phoenician delegation. No other living person could have gotten away with such an act. Xerxes was amused by the entrance, which betrayed his enormous respect for the Queen from Halicarnassus.

Artemisia would not take a minor role in this upcoming war. If she needed to, she would lead the Phoenician contingent without the King of Kings' approval.

Upon her arrival at Xerxes' encampment, the Warrior Queen was told that the King of Kings had greatly anticipated her arrival and would like her to join him for supper. She had almost killed a guard who questioned who she was. She was restrained by Adon before doing any harm. She was eventually told that after the meal the great King would grant her a private meeting. Although she had very little patience, the Queen of Halicarnassus had to accept this arrangement. She would prepare for this meeting with her entourage awaiting, what they considered, her inevitable confrontation.

Xerxes sat on his throne and contemplated the upcoming invasion. Spring had come and the crossing of the Hellespont would begin within the next few days. The bridges had been rebuilt without incident and the time he had so greatly anticipated had finally arrived. The world weighed heavily on the young King's shoulders. The reconquering of Egypt and denying the Babylonian rebellion were both minor incidents compared to this current undertaking.

Persia had a grave history fighting the Greeks. Xerxes could still taste the bile that the word Marathon brought to his throat. Xerxes was not worried about death. He believed that if he were a pious man he would find just reward in the afterlife. It was his ancestors that scared him. He dreamt about his father and grandfather many nights. They implored him for revenge. His entire destiny was centered around this invasion. History would remember him either as a great conqueror or as a failure to return the honor of his fathers to the Empire. Xerxes regularly reflected on these extremes.

After his father Darius died suddenly, Xerxes inherited the vastest Empire ever built. He had now put together the largest army ever assembled. The odds of success were overwhelmingly in his favor. The trek to Greece would be more challenging than the actual fighting. His biggest enemies in this enterprise were not the Greek hoplites, but the terrain and the ocean. But the odds were overwhelming at Marathon and an inferior Greek force embarrassed them. They outwitted that son of a pig general, Datis. Xerxes threw his cup on the floor thinking about the debacle of Marathon. Datis had been conned by a Greek counterspy to believing that if he transferred his cavalry to Athens, the city would immediately capitulate to him. Datis left his army at Marathon and took the navy and cavalry to Athens. Of course, he was met by resistance at Athens, and the army was attacked and overwhelmed at the plains of Marathon. Without the support of the cavalry, the Persian soldier was no match for the Greek phalanx.

Xerxes wanted to see Athens burn for the deceit and insult of Marathon. He promised his ancestors and swore to the Gods to accomplish this vengeance. Again, the King of Kings became angered thinking about the history. He began banging his table but immediately gained control when a slave girl entered. He turned red faced to the slave and demanded:

"Bring me Smerdomences."

An hour later the general of the Immortals entered the tent. He blew the King kisses and immediately pressed his sword to his own neck, offering his life for the King. The general had heard about the King's tirade and assumed that his anger might be directed at him. As the general stood, Xerxes smiled and immediately approached, placing his hands on his shoulders.

"My friend, even seeing your face relaxes me."

Smerdomences smiled in relief. Xerxes continued, *"Are the armies ready to march?"*

"They are, Lord."

Good, Smerdomences, good. But I have another request.

"Lord?"

"We will be entering northern Greece in a few weeks. The northern portions of the area have already aligned with us. No resistance will be offered from Thrace, Macedonia, or Thessaly. Our

ambassadors have done a good job preparing the collapse of northern Greece. I want you to send delegations again. I have heard that the remaining Greek leaders have met in the city of Corinth to ally themselves and prepare a defense. I want every Greek city that has pledged allegiance this unholy alliance, to be contacted and offered a chance to rejoin an association with the Empire. They must understand the suicide they commit by opposing us."

He stepped forward and in an urgent manner demanded, "A*ll cities must be offered the chance to join us or remain neutral. All cities except Athens and Sparta. I want them isolated. Do you understand?"*

"I do, Lord, it will be done!"

"One more thing, Smerdomences. You and your Immortals will be the first to cross. The army will follow, but at a slower pace. You will lead the Immortals and other contingents to prepare the way and serve as an advanced force. You will keep me in constant contact. Take a division of cavalry to work as messengers. Also take many divisions of slaves to help clear the path."

Smerdomences bowed as if saddened by the task.

"You have a concern?"

Xerxes enquired.

"Lord, I will do as you ask, but I must admit that I am saddened to have to leave your side."

The King walked toward his trusted friend.

"I trust no one else. You will be the tip of the spear that will puncture the Greek heart."

Smerdomences paused, bowed his head again, and then continued talking, *"Lord, when I came into the tent, I noticed that Artemisia was waiting quite impatiently to speak with you"*

The King smiled and his smile grew as he approached the general.

"Everyone is impatient, Smerdomences. She will wait until I call for her."

"I understand Lord."

Now the general smiled. Xerxes slapped him on the back and said, *"Before she enters have the slaves bring me Golnar."*

"Lord."

Smerdomences backed out of the tent. It took almost an hour till the lector priestess entered the tent. Although she bowed, it was not the movement of somebody devoted to the monarch. It did not go unnoticed by the King.

"You called for me, Lord?"

Xerxes turned to Golnar and said, *"In a few minutes, Golnar, a woman will burst into this tent. She will be agitated and angry. I want you to watch her and you will tell me your thoughts later this evening."*

"I will stand in the corner, Lord"

Xerxes began to turn when a commotion occurred right outside the entrance. Two guards fell and in strode the Warrior Queen, her face red with rage. She immediately noticed the other person in the tent and raised her arm pointing at Golnar.

"Be still woman, or you will taste your own blood this day. The King and I will have words."

She turned to Xerxes and with a directed tone said, *"You enjoy having me wait."*

The King smiled at her irritation.

"Artemisia, it is inspiring to see you again."

"And why was I asked to leave my weapons outside of this tent? If I so wanted, I do not need a sword to strangle a man"

She was dressed in black. Her hair was braided and her green eyes were large as limes. She stared at the King, not flinching. She took two steps closer to Xerxes. The King stood his ground and his expression remained as stoic as ever. Two narcissistic heavyweights, neither willing to give an inch to the other. Finally, the Queen took a step backwards and bowed her head. Xerxes smiled to himself. He knew that she had no choice. She had to bow even though he knew that it went against every cell in her body. One of the reasons Xerxes admired this woman was that there was not an encounter he ever saw her back down from. He knew that her step backwards and her bow had nothing to do with submission. It had to do with protocol. In an unexpected move, Xerxes returned Artemisia's bow. She now smiled in recognition. Artemisia did not change her stare, yet she pointed at Golnar and said, *"Who is this woman and why does she deserve to be in my presence?"*

Xerxes waited *and then* said, *"She is here because I wish it."*

The Warrior Queen did not press the issue. Instead she said, *"The army is ready to march. Your navy is standing by."*

Xerxes turned and walked away from the Queen. After a few moments of silence, he said, *"Out of all the generals and admirals that are taking part in this invasion, you are the most important to our success."*

The statement took Artemisia by surprise. She didn't expect such a validation. That it was important to her was also a shock. The comment seemed to take the wind out of her sails. Her anger seemed to float away and her face softened. The King continued, *"The Greeks sent an army to a pass in northern Greece called Tempe. We have heard from the King of Macedonia that they abandoned that position. Unfortunately, there are other passes that we could have used to surround and destroy their army. It would have quickly ended their resistance. But it would have lessened my satisfaction in victory."*

The King turned to face Artemisia directly.

"They have now decided to make their stand at a pass called Thermopylae. The navy will support the army as it makes it way down the Greek coast. It is likely that the Greek navy will make its stand off the Thermopylae coast."

Xerxes walked to Artemisia. He got within an arm's length of the Queen. He then said, *"Persia needs a commander that will lead the naval attack off the coast of Thermopylae. Are you that commander?"*

As before, the Queen locked eyes with the monarch. *"What do you believe, Lord?"*

Xerxes smiled.

"You will lead a force of Phoenicians. I want you to be the first to encounter the Greek navy. The navy will wait 11 days before following the army. You and your Phoenicians will not. You will leave when the army does and return through the canal at Mount Athos. You will proceed down the coast of Thessaly till you reach the Mount they call Pelion. You will then scout the Magnesian coast and prepare for the naval battle when the fleet arrives."

Although no outside change was obvious, Artemisia smiled to herself. The Queen began backing away, but she didn't leave the tent. Instead she walked slowly to Golnar standing in the corner. The priestess took a step backwards at the approach of the Warrior Queen. Artemisia walked up to Golnar. She bent over and whispered into the priestess' ear. *"Stay away from me. Next time you spy on me I will have your head and no King or God will be able to protect you."*

The Warrior Queen now turned back to her King. Her voice was even and tempered as she spoke, *"You say I am the most important part of the invasion, yet you let me wait as a dog waiting for a bone."*

She turned half way toward Golnar and pointed.

"You send a spy to evaluate me"

Back to Xerxes she said, *"You don't need a spy, my King. What do you want to know? A*re you worried *that the pressure of the invasion will buckle my legs? Is that why you did not send me to Egypt with the army?"*

Xerxes stood stoically with his arms folded on his muscular chest. Artemisia waited a few heartbeats then said, *"And when the battle begins, who will the Persian officers take their command from? Will they listen to my direction?"*

Again, silence from the monarch. The Queen of Halicarnassus turned to Golnar and pointed at her. She said nothing. With that warning she left the room. Xerxes looked at Golnar when the Queen left. Her face was white, and she said, *"Dangerous, very dangerous."*

'Yes dangerous, but for who Golnar, for who?"

****

Eudocia could not believe the spectacle. He had been at his perch for many days. Luckily, he had found an old goat herding shack that offered him protection from the elements. It was less than a mile from this. Eudocia was an excellent marksman and the area offered plenty of hunting opportunities. He even killed a lion one day who had been sizing him up for supper. Eudocia's bow was too quick for the animal. He ate well for a few days. He even fashioned a jacket and a headdress out of the skin and mane. Fresh water was also plentiful, so his major difficulty was loneliness. All this was about to end. He knew that even though this place was primitive and dirty he had come to enjoy the adventure of having to completely fend for himself. He made up songs and stories to keep himself occupied during the long arduous times. He figured he hadn't spoken to a real person in many, many weeks. He kept seeing Themistocles in his mind, quoting Solon and putting his faith in him. At times it was as if he stood by his side.

Eudocia knew that once the army had crossed the Hellespont he would have to leave and return to find Themistocles. A mass of humanity that size would move very slowly, and he wasn't concerned about reaching the Greek politician in time to give his report. He had watched the crossing of many small parties. He figured they were either spies or advanced reconnoiter groups. He even thought about confronting one of them, but decided against it. He couldn't risk his life and not bring the information back to Athens. What Eudocia hadn't considered was that the Persians might be looking for him. It was only logical that they would assume that the Greeks had spies watching them. The thought rang through his mind like a lightning bolt one day.

One day, when returning to his hut he noticed two horses tied up outside. A rush of fear flew through his chest. After a few seconds he calmed and realized he had his bow. He slowly advanced toward the hut, making sure that whoever was in it couldn't see his approach. He was startled when a man appeared from behind a tree bringing water to the hut. The man did not see him and Eudocia readied an arrow. His aim was true and the man slumped over after one hit. He had aimed for the man's upper chest to discourage him from making a warning sign to his compatriot. Now Eudocia again approached the hut. He figured the other man was inside. His strategy was simple, casually walk through the door and attack. His mind was racing too fast for any more sophisticated tactic. When he walked through the door, he saw nothing, no other person, until he felt something heavy bang against his neck knocking him to the floor.

Within a second the second Persian was on him, brandishing a knife. Luckily, Eudocia was able to grab the man's wrist and stop the trajectory of the weapon. He lay on the ground with the man on top of him, straining to overcome his strength and plunge the blade in his chest. He then remembered that one of the events that he had won in the Olympic games at Delphi was wrestling. He hooked the man's leg and with his free arm transferred the man's energy that he was putting on the knife to flip him over onto his back. The Persian was spitting and biting as Eudocia jumped on top, now gaining the advantage. The man still held the knife but now his eyes showed fear. Eudocia had seen that sight many times and he knew that he had to react before the man gained composure. With his free hand he swung and broke the man's jaw. Yelling in pain, the Persian dropped the knife and Eudocia grabbed it and swung. His first assault with the weapon cut open the man's forehead. The battle was over, Eudocia plunged his second swing through the man's throat.

For the next half hour, Eudocia sat in the corner of the hut staring at the corpse on the ground. He had never killed another man in close hand to hand combat, and he mused on how swiftly he acted. Then a realization overtook him. He now had two horses with which to return to his beloved city. It would make life much easier.

Using the horses, he dragged the two bodies about two miles from his hut. He left them on a rudimentary path that he figured might be used by lions or other scavengers. He had stripped the corpses of anything of useful worth. Eudocia would not be surprised again. He found a patch of fertile ground where he tied the horses up. He would now be watchful.

As he lay on his perch overlooking the bridges that were constructed over the Hellespont, Eudocia couldn't help but admire these Persians. What they did to construct these structures was truly extraordinary. Because of all the hustle and movement of people, Eudocia supposed that the crossing was beginning this morning. He was then shocked. Out in the distance he noticed a man being brought to the water by slaves. He sat on a gold throne. Eudocia was transfixed at the sight. He supposed this was Xerxes, the King of Kings. In his wildest dreams he had never anticipated that he would see this man who was considered a "man-god" throughout half of the known world. Eudocia needed to see this man up close. He came up with a dangerous plan. Eudocia ran back to his hut and put on the Persian garments that he had taken from the two scouts.

Eudocia swallowed hard and made his way down the slope. When he reached the bottom by the water there seemed to be guards everywhere. But surprisingly, he walked with authority and nobody questioned him. He actually made it to the bridge. At this close distance the engineering accomplishment was even more impressive. There were quite a few men mulling along the length of the structure, so Eudocia gained his nerve and stepped onto the overpass. Gaining momentum, he confidently strode toward the other bank. He wasn't sure how far he would venture, but he just kept moving with a confident stride. He was able to get more than halfway across when he was stopped by guards who had set up a barrier. He bowed and backed off standing by one side. Then he noticed the reason for the barrier. He saw that Xerxes was being carried onto the bridge. Unconsciously his mouth dropped open at the sight.

The throne that he was carried on was placed down about a quarter of a mile onto the walkway. Eudox found himself only about a quarter of a mile away from the great King. If only he had his bow. The King of Kings got off the throne and slowly walked on the planks, staring at the water. Eudocia was taken by what a marvelous physique this man had. He was oiled down and every muscle seemed taunt. The King carried a golden goblet that he emptied into the water. As he did, he appeared to make a prayer and an offering to the Gods of the water. Next to the King stood a woman who Eudocia assumed was some form of priestess. She did not look Persian to the Greek. She was from a different land than the Persian King. The priestess threw a few objects into the water. Eudocia couldn't make out what they were. As she did, the King kept his stare fixated on the water. He then raised an amulet and touched the water many times. At least 15 cattle were brought to the side of the bridge and their throats were cut. Their handlers held them as the blood flowed into the water.

Eudocia was fixated. He could not remove his stare from this man. The King was so confident in his walk and his demeanor. He was so close to this man who ruled the largest Empire in the known world. If he had his bow, he was close enough to loose an arrow.

A loud noise by an animal shook Eudocia from his mesmerized stare. He realized that he did not want to push his luck, so he slowly made his way back off the bridge. He went back to his perch to watch the procession. First the King and his entourage crossed the waters. Marching in superb order after him were what Eudocia identified as crack troops. After two of the highest decorated men, Eudocia estimated that there were 30 divisional commanders, each supporting about 60,000 men. The marching appeared endless. Over the next few days Eudocia saw a cavalry that numbered about 80,000 men with horses. He even saw riders with lasso's. Chariot after chariot followed the cavalry. He watched in amazement as undisciplined troops from the Dark Continent passed in their traditional outfits. He noticed Assyrian, Cappadocian and Lydian banners. It was a spectacular sight, and the Greek spy concluded that his long wait in isolation was well worth the performance. What's more, he saw at least 1000 ships passing by the bridges, some cargo carriers and some war ships. After all the troops came a never-ending number of slaves and carts. He thought, *"Where the King goes, everybody goes."*

When Eudocia saw the herds of cattle, oxen, and camels, he decided it was time to leave. He kept repeating numbers in his head so he could remember all that he saw. He went back to his hut, kept his Persian garments on, loaded the horses and left the hut.

Chapter IX – The Revenge of History

King Leonidas had argued extensively with the Spartan elders that their city must respond to the advance of the Persians. There were many elements of the Spartan hierarchy that favored keeping all Spartans in the Peloponnese to spend time building a "wooden wall" across the Corinthian Isthmus. They had argued that the Delphic Oracle had suggested they should build this wall, it being the only defense against the oncoming Persians. The secondary argument of the elders was that the religious ceremony honoring Hercules was about to begin and having the army leave the city at this time would be an insult to the Gods.

For days the argument continued. The nobles were empowered by the Magi and the Priests who were tenacious in their intransigence. But as obstinate as they were, Leonidas was more resolute. He would not budge. On the fourth day of this argument, King Leonidas, son of Anaxandridas, was visited by a friend. His name was Aristodemos.

Aristodemos was not of nobility. He had passed the age of 30 and was now a full citizen of Sparta. Aristodemos had been one of the most successful students of the Agoge, the Spartan training program for young boys. The Agoge was a training system in which every Spartan boy was required to participate. The young boys were subjected to continuous training in fighting, survival, singing, and dancing. Resourcefulness and discipline were emphasized. These boys were given little food and were encouraged to learn survival under extreme circumstance. There was a famous tale about a young Spartan boy who was so hungry that he went out and captured a fox. He hid the animal under his shirt but was stopped by an elder returning to his barracks. While the boy was being questioned about why he was returning at that late hour to the barracks, the fox began chewing on his stomach. The boy did not cry out or complain. The young man eventually died, choosing his discipline over physical pain, choosing his training over his life.

Aristodemos told the King that he had negotiated with the priests. To end the disagreement, they would give him a religious exception. He would be allowed to take 300 soldiers and march to Thermopylae. Part of the arrangement would be that he could only take older men who had already had children. Aristodemos was promised that after the religious celebration the Spartans would reinforce Leonidas with an army division. Aristodemos had learned, from experience, that future promises often did not materialize. The King was contemplative at this news. Compromise was not in his nature. With his hand on his chin, Leonidas walked around the area. Sweat began appearing on his forehead as the King focused closer on the agreement. He turned to his friend and with a low assertive voice said,

"They have broken promises before. I must assume there will be no reinforcements."

Aristodemos followed the King, and when Leonidas stopped muttering to himself, he said, *"I hope I haven't assumed too much majesty, but I have already asked for volunteers and have received many more than 300 responses. All the men have pledged their allegiance to you and this mission, including myself. We would all be proud, my King, to stand with you against the Persians."*

Leonidas felt proud and smiled at his friend. Aristodemos said, *"This will not be easy, my friend. I am honored by your courage, my King."*

"No Aristodemos, it is I who is honored. We will leave in two days. Prepare the men."

****

It was a side visit and would delay the army's advance, but Xerxes was insistent at the stopover. Before the crossing of the Hellespont, The King of Kings woke up one morning and called for The Executioner. His voice sounded as if an emergency existed. The warrior arrived post haste and clearly wasn't ready to wake when he was summoned. He bowed so quickly upon entering the King's tent that it almost appeared as though he tripped. While on his knees, Penish pulled out his sword, laying it on the ground in front of him.

"Lord, is there an emergency?"

"Yes, Penish, an emergency. We will leave in a half hour. Prepare my horse. I have been called by the Gods."

"Where are we going, Lord?"

"Penish, we are going to the River Scamander. On the plain of Scamander is the Phrygian city we will visit."

Xerxes was a strong horseman. He and his entourage rode almost nonstop. They finally arrived on a hill where one could see ruins. The remains of a walled city lay before them. Xerxes suddenly stopped his horse and stared at the ruins. The executioner rode by his side and asked, *"What is this? Where are we?"*

Xerxes was quiet, ignoring the question. He rode slowly toward the ruins. The King of Kings slowly dismounted, as did Penish. After a moment of silent contemplation, Xerxes was back on his mount. The two men rode up the hill to the ancient walls. The grass was high and vines had taken over the bricks that remained. Xerxes stopped again suddenly. He pointed to the surroundings. His stare was straight ahead and he raised his arm pointing out over the land and the ocean that lay beyond.

He now looked at his royal bodyguard.

"800 years ago, Penish, 800 years ago! In this spot stood the greatest warrior that ever lived. Can you imagine it, Penish? In this place stood Achilles, the half-man, half-god. He and his King,

Agamemnon, came to this place to destroy this city."

He continued, *"This is a strategic point, very important Penish, very important. It protected the northern land that the King of Argos brought the Greeks to this place and destroyed the city of Troy. On this spot Penish, it happened here. The Greeks killed the Trojan King, Priam, and took the entire population into slavery. The woman were raped and brought back to Greece. The entire population Penish, the city was leveled."*

He looked at his friend. Xerxes appeared pensive. Penish had never seen emotion in the King before. Xerxes took a few steps to the wall. He continued, *"The army, Penish. Many men.*

The King of Kings looked into the eyes of the Executioner.

"Do you realize that in 100 years we will all be dead. Every man in the army, every slave, every animal. But all we accomplish in this

invasion will be remembered. Do you know why we march to Greece, Penish?"

The bodyguard thought for a moment. *"We march to Greece to avenge Marathon."*

Xerxes smiled.

"Partially true, my friend. Partially true. Marathon will be avenged. Athens will burn, I have sworn on my heritage to that. But we also march for greater reasons. More ancient vengeance Penish. We march for Priam and the thousands of dead and enslaved Trojans."

The King now became even more serious. *"The Greeks consider us monsters. We are not enlightened. They think of themselves as superior to the Persian and Median races. They are arrogant. They plunder, enslave our people, kidnap entire cities. But we are considered the infidel. The Greeks are the civilized race. We build great cities, we use math, search the stars for answers, yet we are the barbarians in their eyes."*

Pensive now, Xerxes took a few steps away from Penish.

"No, Penish, we are here for a greater vengeance more than the deceit at Marathon, more than their instigation in the Ionian revolt, more than the lack of respect they showed to our emissaries, killing them when we only wanted them to join our alliance. More than for my father Darius and his ancestors. We also march for Priam and for Troy. We are here to show who is the superior race. It begins now, Penish, it begins now. We will show the Greeks where the strength in the earth lies. It does not lie in Athens, it lies in Sousa"

Xerxes fell to one knee. Penish could see tears drop to the ground from his cheeks. The King of Kings rose and walked to his horse. Out of the saddlebags he brought a bottle of the finest of Egyptian wine. He took out his magic amulet, "the Answerer," holding it to the sky.

"I am Xerxes, King of peoples, King of lands, King of Kings. I come to this holy ground to promise to you, Priam, that your glory will be revealed. Your souls will rejoice again. You will be restored to your rightful place in history."

Xerxes lifted the wine bottle to the sky and smashed it on the ground. He rose from his knee and walked back to his horse. As he walked, Penish heard the King say,

"I now return to revenge history."

The two men began to ride back to the army.

****

In the distance Artemisia could see the gray shape of Mt. Pelion. The ten Phoenician ships she led had been sailing the coast close to Thessaly. South of the mountain was the rocky coast of the Magnesia peninsula. It was a dangerous place and the Warrior Queen knew of its treacherous currents. This rocky coast was famous for storms and there was little space for ships to harbor. There were 30 miles of unforgiving coast, a daunting place. The Queen knew that a storm could rise without warning, and that would easily destroy her entire entourage of vessels.

Artemisia's task was to evaluate the strength of the enemy and preview the coast. At the bottom of the Magnesia coast lay the city of Artemesium. Forty miles west and slightly south of this city was the pass at Thermopylae. She knew that the first contact with the Greek ground troops would probably be at the "hot gates" of Thermopylae. Because of that, the Persian fleet would need to support the troops by the city of Artemesium. Logically then, the Greek fleet would also be at this place. Therefore, it only made sense to the Warrior Queen that two battles would be fought in this area, probably at the same time.

The Phoenician sailors were the greatest in the world. They were very coordinated fighters, and had a very complex system of communication while on the seas. They were closely synchronized in both their reconnaissance and in battle. It made them the most formidable navy in the world.

Artemisia took a step to the front of the boat. The Warrior Queen stood at the railing, appearing to stand up straighter than usual, breathing through her nose. She waved her arm over her head and all ten of the ships seemed to stop in their tracks. She twisted her head slightly then turned it to the other side. The Phoenician captain walked up behind Artemisia and silently stood. It could have been ten minutes as she stood perfectly still looking out over the horizon. There was something amiss.

"It's coming," she said as she pointed at the eastern horizon. The captain stared but saw nothing but shadows being cast by the setting sun in the east. Finally, the Queen said to him, *"Let the other ships know. We head out to sea. I can feel it in the tides."*

"It is almost sunset my Queen."

"I know friend, I know. We will head out into the seas and sail by night."

Artemisia looked at the surprised boat captain. She enjoyed the feeling of his shock. She waited for a few minutes and then she turned to the captain and said, *"We will head to the sea. If the Greek ships are stationed by the island of Shiathos, as our intelligence indicates, then they will not be watching for us coming in directly east. We will surprise them if they are there. We will sweep in with the sun at our backs and catch them looking north along the coast. If we can catch them it will set a model for the upcoming conflict. We will bloody them first. It will send fear through the Greeks."*

Chapter X – The Troezen Inscription

Engagement

The Acropolis sat on a large hill in the center of the city of Athens. It is the highest point in the city. It was built in this location so every Athenian could always view their center. Dedicated to their patron Goddess, Athena Parthenos, it was the focal point of their culture and civilization. Just gazing at the Acropolis helped the citizens find guidance and understanding to life's most daunting questions. The hill was so high that the entire Greek open-air parliament could sit on its slope and hold their debates. And such was the case this day, as the male population of the city sat with their backs to their beloved Acropolis and faced their city below. In the background the three mountains that surrounded the city could be seen, Parnes, Mymettus, and Pentele. It was this gathering that would decide the fate of both the city and the population. Themistocles had a daunting task. The aristocrats, representing the affluence and the conservative view did not want to abandon the city, for it meant leaving behind their wealth.

They were interpreting the "wooden wall" that the great Oracle at Delphi mentioned meant a wall to surround the Acropolis. But these men were also against the idea of meeting the Persians at sea. Their experience had been with successful land forces. So, to have every male citizen partake in the navy was a ludicrous idea for many of them.

Then there was a group of professional seers who believed in their own interpretation of the message of the Oracles. They wanted to abandon the city to flee and not fight the Persians, either on land or at sea. They wanted to offer no resistance to the invader, but to just leave and resettle the entire population in the western Greek settlements.

Themistocles understood both positions. They were both founded in fear. One wanting to hold tighter, the other wanting to let go. Of course, the seers didn't have much to lose with their position, whereas the aristocrats did. What he also understood was that these decisions would probably be made from fright. Fear was an interesting reaction. It could freeze some and cause others to act irrationally. But Themistocles also knew that it was contagious. It could spread like a wild fire in a dry forest. But its presence also made people more able to be manipulated, and if used correctly, could bind people together to accomplish things they never thought they could.

The aristocrats sent one of their most influential members to argue their case. The man's name was Bardyia and he was a successful farmer. He was known for his shrewd business deals. He was an interesting choice to present the nobles' position, as the general population did not have positive thoughts about the man. He was aloof and distant. And in the end, the choice was a poor one, as Bardyia's speech was dry and focused on the economics of leaving Athens and settling in another part of the world. For such a tense moment, when history was held in the balance, the speech was void of insight or passionate fervor. The commoners either didn't understand or care about the specific issues of which he spoke. But the speech wasn't a waste, for it would serve as one of the reasons that the populace would turn to their hero.

The seers were different. They tried to play on the utter horror of the Persian invasion. In the end they were all pessimistic when the city, the culture and the new Demos needed foresight and direction.

Themistocles had a specific plan. He knew that the details were irrelevant, that the people wanted to hear from someone who understood the larger picture, someone who could see into the future to give them hope for renewal. He argued that to temporarily leave Athens bound them to their beloved city. After all, the city structures were mere bricks and mortar. Athens was its people. The life of the city came from the people not from the buildings and causeways. As he spoke of commitment to history, to the Gods and to each other, one could almost feel the power of the masses growing. This thing, this passion was alive, and it came not from tyrannical rule but from free men willing to place their futures in each other's hands.

Themistocles then shifted to prophecy. The Oracle, on first reading, could seem defeatist. But the underlying message was that of hope and ultimate victory.

"O Divine Salamis"

The Greek politician screamed. He repeated it three times.

"What does this teach us, my fellow Athenians. What is Apollo trying to say?"

He let the words hang as the crowd murmured. Finally he spoke what was now clear to everyone.

"The Wooden Walls are our ships, our navy. It is not the wall surrounding our beloved Acropolis. We have the means, my fellows. Our victory will come at Salamis."

Themistocles raised his arms and the crowd exploded in agreement, waving their arms in the air. The master manipulator let the enthusiasm burn through the hearts of every man present. He finally raised his arms again and begged everyone to sit. It took a minute or so, but eventually all the people sat in silence. The conductor of this symphony now paced slowly across his stage. It was not over yet. Themistocles had more. He knew the debate was already over, but he wanted the final blow. Finally he spoke. *"The Goddess' snake has left the Acropolis. Is the snake fleeing? Does this foretell destruction? Are the evil spirits, the Keres that fought in the Trojan war, back to seek revenge? No, I say!! Athena remains with us. She will ride the waves with us as we drown the tyrant!"*

His voice began to crescendo. *"History is now, my fellows, and we will write it with Greek valor. This is not the end of our culture NO! This is the beginning of our revival. The birth of the Demos!"*

The people of Athens again exploded in support. They were being asked to be brave and put aside their own wants and needs for the good of the civilization. They understood it and they accepted the challenge.

After the crowd calmed, the orator, Aischines, read the doctrine that would be known as the Troezen Inscription.

*"**It was Resolved by the Council and People of Athens***

Themistocles, son of Neokles of Phrearroi, proposed:

To deliver the City in trust to the Goddess of Athena and all the other Gods…. And that the Athenians themselves and the foreigners who dwell in Athens shall deposit their children and wives in Troezen. The treasurers and priestesses on the Acropolis will remain guarding the things of the Gods. The other Athenians all, and the foreigners of military age will embark on the 200 ships which have been made ready to defend against the barbarian.

All the Athenians will be of one mind in the defense against the barbarian."

After the end of the session, the Greek politician prepared to leave his city and lead the fleet. As he walked to the docks, Themistocles looked back with tears in his eyes. He knew that if the defense in central Greece failed, the road to Athens would be unprotected. His friend, Leonidas, would defend on the land at Thermopylae, and he and the fledgling Navy would attempt to stop the Persian fleet at Artemisium. If Leonidas was defeated, the Greeks did not have the land troops to launch a second stand. All the Athenian men were to be manning the boats in the navy. If Themistocles was also defeated at Artemisium, then for all intents and purpose, the war would be over.

The Spartans were building a wall along the Corinthian peninsula to prepare to defend their city against the oncoming Persian army. But Athens had no such defense. The Persians, if they broke through, would be able to walk into the mostly deserted city with little resistance.

Themistocles stopped and looked back at the Acropolis shining in the early evening sun. He stood for a few moments watching the priests attempting to build a wall around the temple. They would not leave the city with the rest of the populace. They believed that the "wooden wall" that the Oracle referred to, meant a wall around Athena's temple. He felt for these men and woman, for if the Goddess didn't intervene, their lives would surely be forfeit. And from what he had heard about the Persian tyrant, their deaths would not be easy.

As he stood looking at the Acropolis, he felt a hand on his shoulder. His friend, Thantos the sailor, was standing next to him.

"I heard about your triumph in the Assembly."

Themistocles looked at him with a sad expression.

"Triumph, Thantos? No triumph. I have sentenced my beloved city to destruction. Xerxes will burn it down. Black ground will be all that is left."

"Yes my friend, but you saved the people. Is it not a worthy sacrifice?"

The politician turned away. He then turned his face back to his friend.

"I don't like to lose, Thantos, you know that."

Again the sailor patted him on the back. Thantos said in a low soothing voice, *"Many men will die, no matter how the next year occurs. Magic, my friend, we will need magic. Athens needs your magic, my friend. You need to read the future. We need the Metis. Whatever the Gods have given you, we all need you to find it."*

The Greek turned to him with tears in his eyes. His lips began to quiver.

"What if I have no magic, my friend? What if the Gods have abandoned me?"

The captain turned to his friend and the two men hugged. The Greek politician spoke, *"The upcoming weeks will not have many hugs, but many tears."*

After a minute, Thantos replied, *"I believe in you. The people of Athens believe in you. I am sure the Gods also believe in you"*

Themistocles looked at him and with a seriousness rarely seen said, *"The Persians are a test. They are a test of our resolve. Is our new government so important that we are giving up our Athens, our earth? Many nights, my friend, I ask myself whether I have misread history, whether I am sacrificing our beloved city for a dream."*

Thantos seemed to understand the importance of the moment. He seemed to realize that even in this self-questioning, his friend was still in control of fate. He responded to Themistocles by saying, *"I am not a smart man. I have been a lucky man. I could walk into the west and live a happy life. But I don't walk. And why don't I walk?*

Themistocles turned to him and with a smile said, *"Good question, why don't you walk? Why don't you run? It would be the smart thing."*

Thantos turned to him, *"I have never run away in my life. Leaving Athens is not running away. We have put our resources together to meet the threat. We will bleed my friend, but we will live and rebuild. I have NEVER run. Today I follow my faith. I follow you. We will walk into the future together."*

"If we have a future."

Themistocles grimaced, *"Are you ready? Our ships wait."*

Themistocles turned to his friend and smiled.

"We head to Artemisium. May the Gods come with us."

****

He was stationed outside of the tent. The guard was quietly told to leave and have supper. It was unusual for the great King to snoop around, but in this situation, he didn't want witnesses. Witnesses would have to be put to death. So Xerxes stood silently and listened. He had a smile on his face for he knew what was coming. Outside of listening range, but in visual contact was the Executioner. He was the only one allowed within 25 yards.

It wasn't long before sounds were coming from the tent. Over only a five-minute period, the sounds grew louder and more primal. Slowly and gently the King pulled back the tent opening and silently entered.

What he found he was not expecting to find. In the bed were two soldiers servicing his wife. Xerxes expected one, not two. He smiled to himself and gained some respect for his wife. Penish was now not far behind, standing at the tent opening watching the King and the show that was happening not ten feet from him. The bodyguard rolled his eyes while he watched.

Xerxes began slowly walking toward the bed, yet, the three involved in their amorous dance had not noticed his arrival. Penish noticed that the King was reaching for his long knife.

As he approached, one of the men finally noticed the movement out of the corner of his eye. The soldier froze, noticing the King of Kings. Xerxes continued to approach, finally lunging and stabbing the man who was on top of his wife. The man's body began to spasm and the blood flowed over both men and bed, and covered the King's wife's, Vashti.

Vashti began screaming and had some difficulty pushing the man off her. She sat up in her bed covered by her lover's blood. As she screamed, Penish stepped into the tent and flung his knife, hitting the other soldier in the neck. Vashti watched as her second lover fell off the bed spurting blood. As his wife continued to scream, Xerxes stood silently, watching the scene. He stared at his wife but remained silent. Then, without a word, the great King turned and exited the space. Penish followed. As they left, the screams of Vashti followed the two as they walked away. A slight smile was on the King's face, and he spit on the ground.

****

The three captains met every morning. They were accomplished men. Asonides was from Aegina. He was a very hard and disciplined man. He ran his ship with methodical exactness. No issue was too minor for his attention. His sailors called him "the Tree". He stood steadfast and never wavered in the face of any storm. This morning he was met by Praxinos, the captain of a Troezen ship. The two men didn't dislike each other, although they were not friends. They each tolerated the other's presence. As they stood and discussed minor things about each of their cities, the third captain arrived. His name was Phormos of Athens.

Phormos did not have the history of being a great military tactician, but he was a survivor. The other two captains resented him because of his arrogant attitude or what they perceived as a cavalier attitude.

These three unusually connected men all had a singular mission. They were the advanced warning system for the Greek navy in three ships stationed off the island of Shiathos. Their job was to warn the Greek navy of any approaching Persians. On this day, the three ships of these captains were all beached. It was much safer to beach the Triremes than leave them at sea. The ships were defenseless to inclement weather and rough seas unless they were on the beach. In fighting a naval battle, finding the places to beach the ships was paramount to success. Without such a haven, the ships were extremely vulnerable.

The three men sat around the fire and were having a laugh when Phormos jumped to his feet. The other two captains reacted, immediately following suit.

"What, what?" Asonides demanded

Phormos pointed to the horizon. What the men saw was ten small black dots. With every second they seemed to be closing in on their position. Without speaking, the three men abandoned their gathering and raced towards their ships. The orders were dispatched and the men scrambled to their positions.

By the time the boats were launched, the ships that were bearing down on them were now distinguishable. The three captains seemed to take different approaches to the ten oncoming ships. Praxinos, the Troezen, appeared frozen. His ship was not moving in any direction. Praxinos couldn't decide whether to fight or flee, so in response his ship seemed to list. The Aegean ship captain, Asonides, was confident and direct. On his ship there was no indecision. On its own, without any support from the other ships, Asonides ordered his ship to attack the incoming Persians. Phormos the Athenian captain quickly decided that attacking ten ships was not in his favor. His ship headed north to outrun the attackers and escape this attack.

Praxinos, after his long hesitation, finally decided that he needed to follow Phormos and attempt to outrun the enemy. The Persian ships, or more specifically, the Phoenician ships, immediately split when the different Greek strategies were identified. The lead ship veered to its right to cut Praxinos off from following Phormos. Four of the Phoenician ships began giving chase to Phormos. The remaining five ships pushed forward ready to engage the Aegean vessel.

Within what seemed like minutes, the lead Phoenician ship was engaged with Asonides. The five Persian vessels attacked in an arrow formation. But Asonides immediately noticed that the lead Phoenician vessel separated itself from the other four. The remaining vessels seemed to stop as if they had lost their oars. The lead boat bore down directly on Asonides' vessel. It appeared the vessel was planning to ram the Aegean head on. In the few seconds from noticing this strategy, Asonides had to decide how to deal with this aggressive tactic. In that time the Phoenician veered quickly to the left, bouncing off the front of his vessel and sheering off the oars on the right side of the Aegean vessel. Without hesitation, Asonides ordered his marines to board the Phoenician boat. The Phoenicians were as quick as the Greeks. The Phoenician marines quickly boarded the Greek ship. The fighting was initially intense, with the defending Greeks appearing to gain an early advantage. The screams of death filled the air as blood stained the floor of the boats. It did appear that the Greeks had stopped the Phoenician advance on their deck, holding a line and trying to push the enemy back.

But then, a black object seemed to fly over the confrontation, landing behind the Greek position. In one motion, two of the Greek defenders fell and the momentum changed quickly. With the break in their defense, the Phoenician split the Greek defense into two weaker positions. Asonides rushed to the split and engaged the Phoenician who had turned this battle. His eyes wide, Asonides raised his sword and rushed forward. As he began to swing, he noticed that he was facing a woman. Steel clashed and the Queen from Halicarnassus rolled to the right, slashing the Aegean in the leg. In the time it took for Asonides to reach for the wound, the Queen swung again, knocking the sword out of his hand. The Aegean appeared shocked and the Queen doubled him over with the butt of her sword. She dragged the man up to the front of the boat and gave a blood curtailing yell. Time seemed to stand still, as all the fighting pairs turned their attention to the noise. As the crews from both ships watched, The Warrior Queen impaled Asonides with her sword. She held his head as his body began to slump and fall to the deck. She pushed it down as if it were a bag of potatoes.

"On your knees. This battle is over."

Almost in unison the Aegean marines dropped their weapons as if they tired of the fight. The Phoenicians quickly herded many of the marines and Greek oarsmen to the center of the ship. They were all to lay on their stomachs. Artemisia strode through the mass of now naked, quivering men. She walked over to one of the deckhands and stepped on his neck. Her Phoenician bodyguard, Adon, stood stoically behind her. He was now a strange looking man, covered in blood, as if painted. He was silent when she turned her head and looked him in the eyes. Their continued silence lasted for a second and then she said, *"The best looking, Adon, bring him to me."*

The Phoenician strode through the mass of naked bodies. He lifted heads and pushed them back down. Finally, he stopped over a man, placed his sword on his neck and signaled for the other Phoenicians to lift him off the ground. The man was dragged toward the front of the boat. He was thrown down in front of the Warrior Queen. She looked down at the man who was obviously terrified and stared at the other Phoenicians, touching her ear three times. Adon lifted the man off the ground and held him up so Artemisia could look at him.

Very gently, the Warrior Queen ran her fingers over the man's face. She smiled as she reached down and held his testicles. A small smile came across her face. She pointed to one of the Phoenicians who said in broken Greek,

"What is your name, Greek"

The man was terrified. In a fumbling response he said, *"Leon, my lord, Leon is my name."*

A small smile appeared on her face as she repeated, *"Leon. I like that name."*

The man, still scared, began involuntarily urinating as Artemisia held his penis and testicles. She looked down at the urine as it splattered on the deck. But after he finished relieving himself, the Warrior Queen began squeezing the man's private parts. Leon's eyes seemed to bulge out of their sockets as the Queen pressed. Finally, she looked over the mass of naked Greeks and said, *"The world has turned. The Persian God will soon rule the land, all the land."*

Again the Queen turned to her Phoenicians standing guard over these now slaves.

"Put them on their knees for they will pray to the Persian God. They will pray to the King of all lands, the King of all peoples, the King of all Kings."

The Phoenicians dragged all the men and forced them to their knees. Artemisia stood on the highest point of the ship. She lifted Leon up and demanded that all the Greek slaves pray to the King. They all began chanting Xerxes' name. Artemisia again raised Leon, she turned to the water and said, *"I sacrifice this Greek to the glory of Xerxes. The most handsome of the enemy must die and be sacrificed."*

She made a slow cut into Leon's throat. She held him over the side of the boat, allowing his blood to flow into the sea. She kept him there, allowing his life to pour from his body into the waters. After he lost consciousness from loss of blood, she nonchalantly pushed him over the side.

The fighting on the Troezen ship, after it was caught, was not as decisive as on the Aegean's ship. After their initial hesitation, the Troezen fought the Phoenicians with great vigor. Their captain, Praxinos, was more comfortable with the sword than in the boat. Four Phoenician ships had surrounded the Troezen vessel and attacked from all directions. But even though the odds were overwhelming, the Troezen would not surrender and not bow to the Phoenician demands. One by one they fell under the sword until the deck of the ship was slippery with their blood. Within the first half hour Praxinos was cut in half by two Phoenician marines. He had attacked four men who were moving up the boat's bow. His voice was heard above all others as he screamed his death cry. He was speared by the second man he met. Yet even falling to his knees, Praxinos the Troezen captain, continued waving his sword and shouting his protest. Most of the men on the ship were oarsmen possessing no weapons. They fought with their hands, feet and teeth. The Phoenicians cut through the mass of men with their swords and knives. The Phoenician marines almost looked wild as the blood lust overcame them. Some of the Troezen oarsmen fell to their knees, but were summarily executed as the slaughter continued. Even though the Phoenician marines initially concentrated on the Troezen with weapons, at some point, killing became the only goal.

The Phoenician marines eventually backed the Troezen fighters into a place with no retreat. Two of the Troezen dove over the side of the boat. Out of all the Troezen fighters, one stood out from the others. His name was Pytheas, son of Ischenoos. While others fell along side of him, Pytheas maintained his balance and his attitude. Pytheas was not only an excellent swordsman, but a skilled and forceful fighter. Unlike many of the other Troezen, Pytheas had cut down a number of Phoenician marines as they charged him. During one encounter, he ducked a sword swung at his head while he took out the legs of another marine.

It came to the point that Pytheas was the last Aegean marine standing. Surrounded by ten Phoenicians, Pytheas stood in a crouched defensive position. Many of the Phoenicians began laughing and slowly cutting him with random swings. He would defend one strike and another behind him would cut through his skin. At one point he turned, surprising a Phoenician marine and impaled him through his stomach. It angered the other Phoenicians and they stopped playing with him and began advancing. Pytheas finally dropped to his knees, not because he was pleading for his life, but he was not able to stand on his blood-soaked legs. A Phoenician marine came up behind Pytheas and raised his sword. It was time for Pytheas to die. As the marine hesitated with his arm in the air a voice rang out, *"Stop. Let the man live."*

Coming over the side of the ship, in all her wild glory, was the Warrior Queen from Halicarnassus. Her presence immediately changed the demeanor of the men standing around Pytheas. In unison, they bowed and lowered their weapons. She slowly walked to the center of the ship where Pytheas sat on his bleeding feet and legs. She walked straight to the Troezen.

"On the Aegean ship the men were sheep. I killed the most beautiful of them and the rest will be enslaved, forced to clean droppings and excrement. They deserve to be sheared. "

She hesitated then continued, *"These men on this ship are not sheep. They are our enemies, but they fought like lions. Worthy opponents."*

She pointed her sword at Pytheas. *"My brothers, this battle is over. This man deserves to live and be honored for his bravery. Bring the doctor, heal his wounds."*

The remaining Greek ship was the Athenian vessel captained by Phormos. Because of his fast reaction at the sight of the Phoenicians, the Athenian vessel was outrunning the Phoenician boats that were in pursuit. But this advantage did not last long. His men were tiring and the other Phoenician vessels seemed to be slowly reducing the distance. Phormos knew that he could not fight the Phoenician ships with any hope of victory. They outnumbered him four to one. The captain of the Athenian vessel then turned his attention away from his pursuers and focused on where they were going. He had decided that he needed to beach his vessel and take his men overland back to Athens. He saw no honor in dying for no reason. After a time, with the Phoenicians continuing to shorten the distance, Phormos found the perfect beach. His second in command, a man named Pythagus, was a farmer by trade. He was surprised when the man protested his decision, for his impression of Pythagus was not that of a hard warrior. Pythagus did not become stubborn in his protest, therefore, he figured his objection was probably more a show than a serious opposition.

Phormos did beach his vessel, and most of his men were enthusiastic about not having to fight and probably losing their lives. Remarkably, Phormos, leading his men in retreat, avoided thieves, hostile tribes, and Persian patrols to guide his people back to the Greek lines. He lost only 15 men to disease, accidents and lions.

Chapter XI – The Striped Goose

King Leonidas marched on a gloomy day from his home in Sparta. He was promised that the Spartan government would send reinforcements to bolster his troops, but he knew better. The reason that only a small contingent was being sent to Thermopylae was blamed on the religious Karnesian Festival. There had been a spirited debate within the Spartan government over this mission, as there were many who didn't want to send any men in defense of central Greece, but to hold their troops on the Peloponnese. Thermopylae was in central Greece, quite a way from Sparta. Was it prudent to send a larger army so far, leaving their city and the entire Peloponnese poorly defended? The majority view was that Thermopylae should be abandoned in favor of building a wooden wall across the Isthmus of Corinth. It was the Delphic Oracle that warned of this occurrence:

Far seeing Zeus grants to thrice born Athena a wooden wall

The only place not to be sacked, it will help you and your children

Do not wait for the great host coming from the continent

Cavalry and foot soldiers; turn your back and withdraw from the foe

Halfway through the discussion in the Spartan assembly, the Apella, Leonidas knew that he had lost the argument. The council of elders, the Gerousia, were mostly against the Thermopylae campaign. Although he couldn't argue the personal point, Leonidas had given his word to the Athenian, Themistocles, that the Spartans would join a united Greek defense, not one that focused only on saving or defending the Peloponnese. The son of King Anaxandridas II and the 17th of the Agiad line, would not abandon his Athenian friend and an assurance that he made. His word was holy to him and meant more than the fear that the Apella and the Gerousia would reprimand him. With this in mind though, Leonidas was worried that even though Thermopylae was considered almost an impregnable position, sending such a small force could be disastrous.

The Spartan King knew that during his march to the Thermopylae pass he would pick up troops from some of the allied cities. Many of the troops would come from the Peloponnesian cities, but he had no idea what type or amount of support would be offered. In the end, Leonidas picked up almost 3000 more hoplites. They came from Laconia, Tiega, Mantinea, and other cities. At his side, every step of the way, was his friend and confidant, Aristodemos. Many times Aristodemos would site one of Leionidas' favorite poets, Tyrataios, for inspiration:

"It does all the people of the state good whenever a man stands firm in the front ranks, holding his ground and steadfastly refusing to even think of shameful flight. He must risk his life with a stout heart and shouting encouragement to those around him.

He who loses his life falling in the front ranks, brings glory to his father, his fellows and his city."

The King's other advisor was a man named Dienekes. He was the equivalent of a sergeant in the Spartan army. Dienekes was a hard man. He lived for conflict and would aggressively confront any questions. Although there was no fear in the Spartan heart, few would stand up to Dienekes. Even when confronted by a group of warriors, Dienekes was a dangerous opponent. In his young life he had been in many skirmishes, mostly against neighboring tribes.

Even though Dienekes was young, he was a celebrity in his city of Sparta. He was called the man who was undefeatable. Although there was some over exaggeration of his exploits on the battlefield, Dienekes generally lived up to his reputation. He seemed to love blood. His sword was swift and his conscious was small.

Every night when the army stopped to camp, Leonidas met with his Androecia council. This assembly was considered the meeting of the brave. Besides Aristodemos and Dienekes, the two brothers, Maron and Alpheus made up this inner circle for the King. When the brothers told their mother they were marching to Thermopylae, she blessed them by saying:

"Do me proud, boys. Either return with your shields in your hands or have your dead body carried on them."

There was no kissing, no fear of loss. The Spartans lived an austere life. They had a contempt for pleasure. They were respectful but denied compassion as a true emotion. They saw emotion as weakness. Death wasn't feared, it was almost worshiped, revered. Death on the battlefield was an admirable ending to one's life.

On this night, Leonidas' Androecia council had much to ponder. The army was almost at the Thermopylae pass. They had already met with several spies who provided them with valuable reconnaissance. The main force of the Persian army was at least a week away from the pass. Leonidas was told that there were three columns marching toward the pass. One column hugged the shore and a second marched inland, closer to the mountains. The main column, which contained the King of Kings and the famous Immortal-Ausiya units, marched down the center. One of the spies gave numbers of marching Persian soldiers that was beyond belief. It wasn't until the huge numbers were confirmed by another man that Leonidas believed the magnitude of the force that would be facing him. At the confirming news, there was no sense of surprise or defeat within Leonidas' Androecia council. There was no panic among these officers, and surprisingly their mood bordered on excitement.

Leonidas was impressed that the King of the Persians would lead the march into Greece. He would watch closely how the Persian King handled himself during battles.

One of the most important pieces of information that Leonidas heard from the locals was that there was a small, little-known pass that ran across the mountains that overlooked the Thermopylae pass. A Trachinian was brought before the Spartan King and told him about a pass that he called the Anopaia road. Thermopylae was bordered on the north by the Malian Gulf and the Anopaia mountains on the south. If there was a mountainous pass, then the Persians could outflank the Greeks and attack them from behind. The council concluded that a large portion of the Greek troops should be sent to defend this back road. It was crucial to the defensive position. They had decided that the 1000 Phokians who marched with them, would not go to the pass, but would be sent to defend the Anopaia road. There was really no argument about this strategy, as the Androecia council knew that it would be suicide to defend against a larger enemy with its back undefended. If this happened and the Persians attacked the Greeks from both sides, then the strategic advantage of Thermopylae would quickly become a death trap.

The Greek force arrived well before the Persians at the Thermopylae road. The pass was almost three miles long, and about halfway in, Leonidas found a partially built wall that must have been used during earlier times as a defensive position. He immediately noticed that it would be to their advantage to rebuild the wall as best they could.

****

The Goddess was obviously agitated. She paced with heavy steps. Throughout her immortality, Athena had confronted her father, Zeus, many times. She won many of these arguments, never backing down, and testing her strength against the all-powerful Zeus. He was the 'father' of all Gods and all men. All the many Greek deities referred to him as 'my father'. But Zeus was a moody and stubborn master. When his mind was made up regarding a request, no force could make him relent. His daughter, Athena was born from Zeus himself, not from his wife, but the story was that she emerged from his head. The green-eyed Goddess was nearly as powerful as her omnipotent father and they both knew it. The father had only tentative control over his rebellious and head strong daughter.

The Gods had no use for time and had no way to measure it. It was essentially unimportant. It's only use lay in the way mortals measured it. On Olympus there were no days, no nights. Any changes occurred because of immortal conflict, manipulation or influence. Unlike her father, who considered mortals in no way different than the flies or plants, Athena had become involved with human interaction. She had a soft place in her existence for these broken mortals. Their mistakes and their weaknesses meant that they needed her. Human judgments and lack of internal strength was laughable to most of the immortal beings, but Athena took their lives and destinies more seriously. Forlorn, Athena knew she was ultimately mistaken. These humans who needed and relied on her for guidance were now turning their heads. Yes, they still prayed and sacrificed, but their spirit had left their belief, as their faith waned their desire for egalitarianism and self-reliance grew.

The strength of the Gods depended on faith. Humans had to believe and hold this conviction above all other principals. The more they placed their trust in this Demos, the more the godly power slowly bled from their souls. And yet, the Goddess was ambivalent at this growth, at this political evolution. She was desperately envious of the Demos, but proud of her children's growth.

Athena's father was weakening. She and the other Gods could see it, and, more importantly, could sense it. Of course, "the father" denied any change, but Athena knew that their term, which not long ago they thought was infinite, was coming to an end. Maybe an end was a bad word, it was more like an evolution.

During this time, the green-eyed Goddess had approached her father with a request.

"Father, I require your guidance."

Zeus sternly turned to face her.

"My guidance? My guidance! The great green-eyed Goddess asking for guidance?"

"Father, don't mock me"

"No!"

Zeus responded, and the sky blackened and thunder could be heard.

"Do not ask me to intervene with the puny mortals."

He pointed at his daughter and lightening crackled overhead.

"Do what you must, I will not help those useless creatures, but I will not impede you."

And with that the Father vanished into the clouds.

Athena was quietly satisfied by her father's response.

"After all these years, he finally knows when not to challenge me," she boasted to herself. But with his departure, Athena knew the

direction she must travel. The heavenly territory in which she would enter was not one that she frequented. In all the millennium of her mastery over events, Athena rarely asked the other deities for assistance. She would this time. Following her father's direction, Athena went to the clouds. Her tasks were clearly laid out in front of her and she hoped her stature was still great enough to command obedience.

But what familiar would be suitable for this journey that she sought? As she drifted aimlessly a thought finally struck her mind. Years ago, she had contact with an extraordinary bird. It had a beautiful white head with two black bars making it an elegant looking creature. But the goose, which Athena had named the striped headed goose, was an obstinate creature. Although the green-eyed Goddess admired the animal's strength and persistence, it was an awkward and a funny sounding bird, making an unpleasant honking while it flew. Athena preferred more graceful animals, with hawks being her favorite. But this goose was something special and was suited for this journey. She knew it was capable of flying over even the highest of this world's peaks. It also made immensely long journeys, some over 5000 miles. It was perfect, for Athena had to leave Olympus and travel east to one of the highest peak on earth. She found it ironic that the place to which she travelled would be in the great Empire that she was attempting to hinder with her interference.

Without a second thought the Goddess transformed into a striped headed goose for her journey to a place that she knew of as Parbat. When she arrived at this wondrous range, the goose found a shallow lake in which to rest. After regaining strength, she flapped vigorously to make the climb to the cloud covered height of the Parbat.

The clouds were cold. The Goddess retransformed into her usual appearance. She had not felt cold for a thousand years. Temperature rarely affected her, but today she could feel the chill. As she wandered through the vapors, she sensed the existence of another immortal. She instinctively knew that this other deity had no knowledge of her presence. She approached him from the rear.

"Anemoi, it has been long time since we have spoken."

The God of the wind did not have a solid body like the green-eyed Goddess. His facial features were clear but his body melded with the clouds.

"Athena! A joy to see you again. I had forgotten the beauty that you bring to me. I know why you come. You are a sensitive soul even with your stark appearance and hard ways. You seek assistance with my brother, Notus, to help impede the men that are called Persians."

The Goddess stood motionless. The God of the Wind, Anemoi, continued: *"My brothers, Notus and Ares, are both taking a great interest in these earthly happenings. Ares' children, these Spartans, are mixed into this affair. His two specialties, fear and terror, have so far proved useless to his children. The Persians are powerful people, stubborn in their ways. They see their quest as divine, and there is some truth in this feeling."*

"You lecture me Anemoi. You do not think that I have the sense to understand these simplicities."

"I am sorry, my Queen. Notus and Ares can be found together. A small human place, in the animal place. Its name is Kifuga. It is there where you will find Notus, the God of Storm, and his companion Ares- the God of Fear and Terror."

The transformation occurred again and the stripped goose began the multi- thousand-mile journey to Kifuga. It was a strange place, this Kifuga. It was amid an astonishing jungle streaming with great wildlife. Notus and Ares played in this area. They created great storms that reached out over the large oceans terrorizing the local populace. Lightening and dangerous winds were a frequent occurrence, with the two Gods stopping only to rest. The goose arrived during one of these storms. She turned into the wind and rose to find the Gods.

Like the juveniles she considered them, Notus and Ares were having great fun in their torture. Athena appeared and with a wave of her hand the skies cleared. There was none of the pleasantry as with Anemoi. The green-eyed Goddess glowed and great balls of light flew from her jade colored face. Reading the message, Notus and Ares stopped their antics and bowed in reverence. Athena hovered by them and then demanded.

"You will both return to Mount Athos. You can play your games, but you must become active in this upcoming conflict."

Her mind now expanded and the air itself shook. The wave overcame the two Gods and they vanished almost instantly. Athena smiled. The dye had been cast. It would be the help that would turn the tide in favor of her beloved children.

****

Chapter XII – Demaratus

The Greek politician vomited and staggered across the room. His head pounded until even his hair seemed to hurt. His friend Thantos brought him some cold water to put on his face.

"How long have I been out?"

"A couple of days. You realize that your recovery from these wine excursions grow longer with each event. There will come a time when you will not return from the darkness where you go."

The Greek politician stared at him with vacant eyes. Finally, his gaze straightened and he said, *"I know, my friend. I have also found that my memory is affected by the wine. I don't remember who I have been drinking with or where I was."*

"I am curious," the sailor remarked. *"Why do you engage in this behavior? There is much work to be done. We leave today to face the*

Persian menace. Must you not have your wits about you for this undertaking?"

Themistocles turned to the sailor and a hint of a smile appeared on his face. He patted the man's shoulder as he spoke. *"You believe it is because of the enormity of the task that I drink, do you?"* he laughed.

"I guess it is time that I told you a secret."

Themistocles' face grew more solemn.

"Thantos, my friend, I see much. Other men have some foresight into the future and plan their lives by the little they see. Some men act as if there is no tomorrow and stumble through the days as if they too had consumed too much beverage. Some men are bold in their behavior, rushing into situations before engaging their thought."

He paused and let out a breath.

"I am not like any man that you have known."

Now it was the captain's turn to smile. With a smirk, Thantos replied, *"Your ass looks the same as mine. And I have seen it more times than I care to remember."*

Themistocles smiled and patted him again.

"There are times I see with clarity. The future lays out for me. Don't misunderstand me, I am no prophet. I know the course, can see its wisdom, and will force others to abide by my vision. I drink my friend, because I can see, not because I can't."

The captain thought.

"Do you ever mistrust what you believe?"

"I do not!"

Themistocles answered in a strong persuading manner.

"I do not!" he reemphasized. The captain now turned to him *"If I didn't know you I would think you an arrogant fool."*

Themistocles began walking with Thantos astride. He stopped suddenly and said to the sailor,

"Many of us think this Persian King Xerxes is a fool. But I assure you he is not. But what he is, is overconfident and inexperienced. He has a vast army and navy and feels invincible. By sheer numbers he will win many battles. But I tell you Thantos, in the end the Demos will survive and we will again control our destiny."

"Confident, you are,"

Thantos mused. Themistocles smiled, but Thantos continued, *"Or stupid."* Themistocles began to laugh *"You don't follow me because you think I'm stupid."* He patted the sailor again on the shoulder.

By this time the two men had reached the docks. The fleet was assembled and ready to sail north and meet the enemy.

Thantos asked, *"Where do you want my ship positioned? Should I say, my general."*

"We will go to a place called the Strait of Artemisium. It is near the town of Aphetae and south of the Magnesia coast. It has excellent beaches and harbors to rest our vessels. For the Persians, the Magnesian coast has no such hospitalities. We must reach this area before the Persian fleet to secure these beaches. If we do, they will not be able to harbor their ships and be forced to stay on the sea. Much more dangerous, as you know."

"Artemisium holds other strategic importance. The strait is narrow, it takes away some of the numerical advantage of the Persians. Their ships will be limited in their scope, with only a certain amount able to advance at a time. Also, their withdrawal lanes will be impeded."

"Artemisium is also across from Thermopylae. Our stand will not allow the Persian vessels to support and resupply their army, which advances to the path. If we fall, Thermopylae and the Spartan defenders will fall. If that happens, then the road to Athens will be unchallenged."

The men both stopped suddenly. Before them lay the navy. Themistocles looked at the vessels. They were lovely in his eyes, holding more beauty then any woman could. He looked at his friend with tears in his eyes.

"Do not worry, my friend. The wine is finished. It will not obstruct me anymore."

He pointed outward.

"Are they not beautiful?"

"That they are. That they are,"

Thantos agreed.

"But answer my question, where do you want me positioned?"

Themistocles put his arm around the shoulder of his friend.

"Since I've known you, you have been a smuggler, a diplomat, a spy, and one of my protectors."

He looked into the old sailor's eyes.

"I don't want you in the battles. You are worth more to Greece carrying out special tasks. I will continue to contact you. You must be ready. I need someone I can count on to carry on behind the scenes."

Themistocles became serious, looking deep into the captain's soul.

"Thantos, if Thermopylae falls, I need you to go to Delphi and rescue Lasiandra. It will be an open road to Delphi for Xerxes. He

loves money and Delphi has much gold. My guess is that he will attack Delphi. It will be up to you to rescue her. Do you understand?"

****

The Persian advanced forces arrived near Thermopylae two days before the King of Kings. They were given strict orders. Spies were sent to reconnoiter, and they returned with some remarkable stories. There were many fires from which they concluded that the defending force was in fact much greater than they had first thought. Two Greek scouts were captured and tortured, revealing that the number of defenders was far less than the fires would suggest. The spies got as close as they could to the Thermopylae pass. What they saw were soldiers leisurely combing their hair and exercising. The Persian scouts reasoned that the Greeks obviously knew of the impending attack, yet these Spartan were more concerned with their appearance. Were they bluffing?

The two scouts argued which of them would be the man to report this unusual occurrence to the great King. It was not positive for one's future to report strange things to the Xerxes. Ardalan was a young man but had a reputation for bravery. He had ventured deep into Greek territory before the Persian King crossed the Hellespont. Ardalan had met Xerxes twice, both times being called in front of the King for his courage and daring. As he rode north to report to his sovereign, he hoped that the King would remember these incidents when he made his report.

Not long after he arrived, Ardalan was immediately summoned to the King's tent. He entered and began blowing kisses to the King, announcing his love and devotion. He then immediately fell to his knees, prostrating himself. The King of Lands stoically stared at the smallish scout. Ardalan began to realize that he was more fearful here then he had been in any other situation. But he steadied himself and tried to look as proud as he could when the King gave him the sign to rise. He bowed his head, *"My lord, my life belongs to you."*

Slowly standing, the great King stared sternly at the scout. He took two steps and then a smile emerged on his face.

"The little man!"

He remarked with enthusiasm. Xerxes turned to a guard standing near him and pointed at Ardalan. *"This man is one of the bravest in the Empire."*

With those words, Ardalan felt like the great palace at Susa was removed from his shoulders. The King then rushed forward and hugged the little man. After a minute he put Ardalan down and said, *"I can depend on you to tell me the truth. What have you found?"*

"My lord, I was able to see the Spartan soldiers."

"How close did you get?"

"I came within 20 horse lengths Lord"

"Tell me what you saw."

"I saw the strangest thing lord. The Spartan soldiers were exercising and combing their hair."

The great King's eyes widened, and he said, *"Combing their hair Ardalan? Are you sure?"*

"Positive lord."

Xerxes turned his head and murmured to himself, *"Combing their hair?"*

After a minute of staring at the wall Xerxes turned and faced Ardalan.

"Anyone else I wouldn't believe. It is too unusual. But you my friend, I believe this to be true"

Ardalan bowed and smiled to himself as he backed out of the tent. When he ingested and thought over this news, Xerxes immediately sent for the ex-Spartan king, Demaratus.

Demaratus entered the King's tent and bowed down with one knee on the floor. Xerxes spoke.

"Demaratus, I have heard funny stories coming from my spies. They tell of the Spartans doing gymnastics and combing their hair while they wait for us. They must truly be mad. I would like to hear your thoughts on the matter."

The ex-Spartan King and the son of Ariston thought for a moment and then asked, *"Lord, I don't know how to respond. Do you ask me to tell you the truth or something that will make you feel good?"*

Xerxes immediately bristled with some irritation,

"Speak the truth, Spartan, I have no use for lies or gestures."

"O King! Since you command me to speak the truth, I will not say what will one day prove me a liar. Difficulties have always been present in our land, while courage is an ally whom we have gained through wisdom and strict laws. Her aid enables us to solve problems and escape being conquered. All Greeks are brave, but what I am about to say does not concern all, but only the Spartans."

"First then, no matter what, the Spartans will never accept your terms. This would reduce Greece to slavery. They are sure to join battle with you even if all of the rest of the Greeks surrendered to you. As for Spartan numbers, do not ask how many or few they are, hoping for them to surrender. For if a thousand of them should take the field, they will meet you in battle, and so will any other number, whether it is less than this, or more."

Xerxes jumped off his throne and said *"What wild words, Demaratus! A thousand men join battle with such an army as mine! Come then, will you -- who were once, as you say, their King -- fight alone right now against ten men? I think not. And yet, if your fellow citizens really are as you say, then according to your laws as their King, you should be twice as tough and take on twenty all by yourself!"*

"If size and kind of men as those I have seen at my court, or as yourself, Demaratus, then your bragging is weak. Use common sense: how could a thousand men, or ten thousand, or even fifty thousand -- particularly if they are all free and not under one lord -- how could such a force stand against a united army like mine? Even if the Greeks have larger numbers than our highest estimate, we still would outnumber them 100 to 1."

"If they had a single master as our troops have, their obedience to him might make them courageous beyond their own desire, or they might be pushed onward by the whip against an enemy which far outnumbered them. But left to their own free choice, they will surely act differently. For my part, I believe that if the Greeks had to contend with the Persians only, and the numbers were equal on both sides, the Greeks would still find it hard to stand their ground. We too have men among us as tough as those you described -- not many perhaps, but enough. For instance, some of my bodyguards would willingly engage singly with three Greeks. But this you did not know and so you talked foolishly."

Demaratus did not flinch, but continued, *"But since you wanted the truth, I am telling you what the Spartans will do. I am not speaking out of any love that I have for Sparta -- you know better than anyone how I feel about those who robbed me of my rank, of my ancestral honors, and made me a homeless exile.... Look, I am no match for ten men or even two, and given the choice, I would rather not fight at all.*

But if necessary, I would rather go against those who boast that they are a match for any three Greeks."

"The same goes for the Spartans. One-against-one, they are as good as anyone in the world. But when they fight in a body, they are the best of all. For though they are free men, they are not entirely free. They accept Law as their master. And they respect this master more than your subjects respect you. Whatever he commands, they do. And his command never changes: it forbids them to flee in battle, whatever the number of their foes. He requires them to stand firm -- to conquer or die. O King, if I seem to speak foolishly, I am content from this time forward to remain silent. I only spoke now because you commanded me to. I do hope that everything turns out according to your wishes."

Demaratus continued:

"They are preparing for the fight. It is their custom, when they are about to risk their lives to adorn their heads with care. Be assured, however, that if you can subdue the men who are here and the Lacedaemonians who remain in Sparta, there is no other nation in all the world which will venture to lift a hand in their defense. Now, you must deal with the strongest Kingdom and town in Greece, and with the bravest men."

Demaratus bowed again and withdrew. As he left, the ex-Spartan King heard the King laughing. He thought, *"I wonder if he will be laughing a few days from now."*

****

Chapter XIII – Ptea

The Greek Triremes arrived at the Artemisium beaches two days before the Persian boats arrived. The Persians sailed south along the Greek coast. Unfortunately for them, because they arrived late, there were no secure beaches for them to moor. The Pelion peninsula offered no safe havens for the Persian vessels. At least part of the Greek strategy was planned successfully. Themistocles had reasoned that if the Greek navy could arrive and occupy the beaches between Artemision and Histiacca, then the Persian fleet would remain vulnerable, having to stay by Cape Sepias on the water rather than beach their vessels. Every advantage needed to be utilized in this coming engagement. Every edge needed to be used.

As Themistocles stared from his advanced ship, his mind kept drifting to his friend, Leonidas, standing not far from his position in the pass at Thermopylae. Both positions were interdependent, as if one fell the other became vulnerable. The position at Artemision and the defense of the Thermopylae pass were both strategically chosen. Themistocles hoped that the Persians could not advance with their great numbers through the Thermopylae pass. It was too narrow. The Spartans could encounter equal numbers of Persians, rather than facing an entire army. Leonidas could not be outflanked with the water on one side and the mountains on the other. It was as if a great ocean was emptying into a small tributary. The river could only accept a certain amount of the water. This was the defensive beauty of Thermopylae.

The Artemision strait was just as strategic. The beaches were perfect for the Greek navy, leaving the Persians exposed in the Aegean. As with Thermopylae, the Persians could not advance in numbers because of the narrowness of the water way. Themistocles knew that this was the place, and this was the time.

The Greek politician had beached his boat and was now contemplating future events. His friend, Thantos, sat by the fire next to him. Themistocles had been quiet for over an hour. He seemed to just stare into the flames as if in a trance. Finally, after what seemed like an eternity the Greek politician began speaking, *"Well, my friend, what are your thoughts?"*

"My thoughts, Themistocles. You are the quiet one."

The Greek smiled at the comeback.

"You are right, my friend. I have been self-engaged. Since we left Athens, I have spent every last-minute praying to the Gods and the wind."

"The wind, my friend? You have the Metis. You have created the Demos, why do you need the Gods?"

"Oh, my friend, do you really think me foolish? This Metis if it exists, was a gift from the Gods. And the Demos, do you think that without their approval we could have proceeded this far? Do you know the story of the King Croesus and Solon?"

The sailor shook his head and Themistocles continued, *"After giving us the laws, Solon left Athens and wandered. He came upon King Croesus. Because he knew the law giver's reputation, the King asked Solos who was the happiest man that he knew. Croesus was expecting Solon to say he was because of his wealth. But Solon mentioned a young boy who died for his country. So, Croesus asked, who was the second happiest, believing that he would be named. But again, Solon mentioned another. He spoke about a man who died protecting his family."*

Thantos looked confused so Themistocles said, *"Yes, it is confusing my friend. But you see Solon believes like I do, that a man's life is judged by his greatest achievements. Not the wealth or property he gains. You see that Solon believed that the Gods were jealous of man because for all our weaknesses and imperfections, we still breathe and can feel the touch of others. But because happiness is so ephemeral it can only be found after death, and that death is exalted if it is in defense of what you believe. Solon said:*

As from the cloudbank comes the storm of snow or hail, and thunder follows from the lightning flash, exalted men portend the city's death: the folk in innocence fall slave to tyranny. Raise them too high, and it is not easy afterwards to hold them. Now is the time to read the signs.

"I think I understand," said Thantos, although in truth, he really didn't.

"We are here to defend what we believe. If we are true in defense of our beliefs, and die in the process, we will find happiness after we die."

*"I am impressed, "*said Themistocles, *"And I thought you were just a dumb sailor."*

The two men laughed out loud. Themistocles turned to Thantos and said, *"The Spartans comb their hair when they face death, and we Athenians laugh," The* two friends laughed again. Before they could stop a sailor approached them.

"Lord, a man here says that you know him and wants to see you"

The Greek politician stood and confronted the man, *"Which ship are you on, my friend?"*

The man blushed and said, *"I too, am a Greek sailor. My name is Callus, son of Jinsen. I was a farmer raising olives in a small town just west of the beautiful Athens."*

Themistocles put his arms on the man's shoulders and said, *"Callus, son of Jinsen, you are welcomed by my fire. But I must insist upon something. I am not your lord. Please do not address me with that title."*

Callus bowed his head in recognition of the request. Then Themistocles introduced his friend Thantos and said, *"Have the man"*

Themistocles began to say, but before he could continue, behind the three men, a tall thin man had appeared. He had his sword out and was walking hastily toward the group. Callus caught the man approaching out of the corner of his eye and quickly moved to intercept. But after taking a step, Thantos yelled, *"Stop, Callus!"*

And Thantos pushed him aside and began walking quickly toward this new man. As he got closer, a big smile appeared on his face.

"Ptea!"

He yelled, and the two men hugged as if they were brothers. Themistocles approached them, also with a smile on his face. He said, *"Ptea, I've heard this name. A pirate, right?"*

"Not a pirate," Ptea said, *"A brave and courageous adventurer."*

Ptea and Thantos stopped their hug. And after a laugh, the pirate said: *"I am sorry, my friend. I heard about Phecontalis. The Persian pigs."*

Thantos bowed his head at hearing his best friends' name mentioned. Phecontalis was Thantos' second in command on all of his trading and black-market adventures. The two men had become very wealthy, trading wine, commodities, and precious stones. Then, on an auspicious day, the two sailors were approached by a Greek politician named Themistocles, asking the two to join the effort to save Athens. Phecontalis was against the idea of joining an effort just for country without financial reward. Thantos and Phecontalis secretly went to the city of Corinth to purchase four Triremes that would become the templates for the new Athenian navy.

Part of the reason that Thantos and Phecontalis were able to be so successful had to do with the secret help of the most successful pirate in the Aegean, Ptea. Ptea was an oddity amongst pirates. He was ruthless and had very few scruples, but for Thantos and Phecontalis he had different rules. He treated them as brothers.

"My friend," Thantos said. *"Why do you join us at these beaches? You are far from your usual waters."*

Ptea backed away and his facial expression changed.

"I have been stalking the Persians. They have many ships, almost 1200 I count. They sail down the coast and are two days from this place. They are poor sailors, disorganized in their movement. But they

have many Phoenician ships, very dangerous, my friend. Also, Egyptians, better than the Persians, but still amateurs. Other than the Phoenician, they can be easily outmaneuvered."

Thantos stood nodding his head. Ptea went on, *"I also saw something I thought was just a rumor, a legend. There was a Phoenician contingent that was led by a woman. I can't be sure, but I think it was the Warrior Queen from Halicarnassus. Thantos, from what I've heard, this woman and her sailing skills are mythical. Out of all the Persians, Egyptians, and all the other nationalities that sail under the Persian flag, this woman worries me. She is like a cobra amongst the sheep. She and her brothers can turn the tide in a battle. However, if you are going to defend this position, be aware of where this woman and her brothers are during the heat of the battle."*

Themistocles looked very grave as the pirate spoke. After a silent moment Thantos slapped his friend, Ptea, in the arm.

"Thank you for the information, my friend."

As Ptea turned to leave, he stopped to look at Thantos one more time. He stared at his friend and said, *"One more thing, my friend. A storm is on the way. I can smell its advance. It could be dangerous. Tie down your ships. The Persian armada will suffer loses."*

He stopped for a moment then looked directly at his friend.

"We will meet again, Thantos, we will meet again. Have no fear, this is not the end"

****

Aapep was captain of the Egyptian Trireme named Bes. He leaned over the railing and watched the dark cloud coming from the east. It gave him a very sour feeling in his stomach since he could not identify any beach to moor his vessel. Aapep did not like the feeling of being so helpless. Only a very few Triremes in the Persian navy were able to beach to ride out the storm. The Magnesian coast offered little shelter in such a situation. Most of the navy would have to ride out this storm on the Aegean. The danger was not only the seas and the wind, but the rocks that guarded the coast. Most were unseen, living just below the water lines, waiting to devour unsuspecting ships like revenging angels. These formations could rip through the hull of a ship without any remorse. The storm would push many vessels into this tragic end. Aapep knew the dangers that would ascend on the helpless vessels, and the storm was ominously moving closer by every minute that passed.

Aapep decided on an aggressive strategy to deal with the upcoming calamity. He decided he was going to leave the fleet and head into the storm. His reasoning was either courageous or foolish. Aapep figured that the ships would be thrown against their will either into each other or against the rocks. If he could get into the deeper Aegean, at least those two dangers would be minimized. But there was another danger in this strategy. The waves could be more violent, and if they ended up in the water there would be no rescue. This was a life and death decision, not only for him, but for his gallant crew.

As he hurriedly gave the order to move out into the open ocean and away from the fleet, his second in command, Amun, rushed to him in protest. His eyes were wide with fear, *"My captain, we are heading to the monster? It must be a mistake!"*

"Amun, we have a difficult choice. If we stay with the fleet, we will end up on the rocks. We have no choice but to challenge the monster on his own turf."

He looked directly at his second. He had known Amun for many years. They had sailed the Nile together hundreds of times. But the Nile was a sleeping beauty compared to the raging of the monster Aegean. He could see the dread in his friend's face and he had no logic to calm it. Amun might be right, staying where they are could be a wiser decision. But the captain had to follow his instincts. Every cell in his body told him that staying where they are was a death trap. The thought even rose in his mind to sink the ship before the storm and have his men swim for the shore. But that, of course, would never happen. He was too proud a man to give such a cowardly order. Finally, after a few moments of silence, Aapep smiled at his friend and said, *"We are heading into hell. I will need you to maintain yourself. It is our time to be brave."*

As the Bes turned away from the fleet, the dread in the crew's eyes was palpable. If they didn't love him, Aapep though these men would revolt out of this fear. As they guided the vessel into the open ocean Aapep continued to remind the crew that they needed to turn into the waves, for if a wave hit their side, the ship would capsize. The sky continued to grow dark, and with each shade of gray that covered the sky, the waves reacted with the intensity of angry children. They hadn't yet reached the storm itself and crew members were already vomiting from the rise and fall of the boat. With every inch that the ship moved, Aapep had an increasing sense of death. The salty ocean spray soaked his face and body, but the ship continued to move to perdition.

Aapep correctly evaluated the upcoming tempest. The intensity of the blow was beyond anything that most of the Persian ships had either seen or experienced. What nobody expected was the length of the storm. It was to batter the ships for three days. It was relentless in its pounding of the crews. The waves rose high enough to jump the sides of many of the vessels. The panic among even the most experienced sailors was tangible on every Trireme of the Persian navy. Hard grizzly men were reduced to both tears and prayers. It was a remarkable fact that many sailors and the marines on their ships could not swim. The waves flung many of the vessels onto the waiting rocks to be broken like child's toys. Other ships were capsized as rogue waves pounded them from the sides. The raging of the wind and thunder could not drown the blood curdling cries and screams of the drowning men. The winners in this encounter were the rocks, and the sharks.

When the carnage was over, 250 ships from the Persian navy had been flung against the shores of Magnesium. Not only was a fifth of the entire fleet destroyed, but most of the remaining crews hadn't slept for over three days. Another 200 ships were heavily damaged and would need to be serviced before they would be ready for battle. This storm had set the Persian strategy back at least a week. It was more devastating than any Greek attack could have been.

As the admirals of the Persian navy took count, they noticed that another ship did not return after this storm. The Egyptian vessel, the Bes, had disappeared. Nobody had seen it sink and its remains were gone forever.

During this horrible storm, Themistocles watched the carnage from the beach. Surprisingly he took no joy in watching and listening to the destruction. Although enemies, most of the thousands that died were simple people or slaves serving their Empire. Themistocles knew that the stories would come in about the sections of the ships and the human remains that were washed onto the shores. He told his advisors he wanted to hear no such tales, that the only interest he had was the number of ships lost by the King of Kings.

As Themistocles watched the carnage, miles north, another figure also watched. Standing half naked, the great King Xerxes stood on a mountain and screamed at the storm. For one of the first times in his life he felt abandoned by his God. Could it be true? Could the Gods of the Greeks be more powerful than his own? He could not even consider such a conclusion for more than a few seconds. But Xerxes did not stand alone on this precipice. He ordered everyone of his magi and priests to stand with him. None of them had predicted this catastrophe, and the King seethed at them as much as at the storm. If any of them fell from the weight of the wind, Xerxes grabbed him and threw him over the cliff to be devoured by the sea.

Many times, Xerxes was begged by his advisors to withdraw to the camp, but every time he pushed the man away, saying, *"I must stand with my people!"*

So, it went on for three days. The King of Lands slept on the mountain crying for his people. His only blessing was that the storm masked his tears. Food and drink were brought to him and the magi, but only bare necessities were consumed. He wondered whether his whipping of the water back in the Hellespont was now coming back to haunt him.

The story of the great King finally reached Themistocles. The rumor was, *"Xerxes the King of Kings, had stood for three days, never sleeping and never eating until the storm abided."*

Themistocles knew the power of exaggeration. He himself had used it many times to convince people and win arguments. But there would be some truth in this rumor, and the Greek's respect for this foreign invader rose to a higher level, but it never morphed into fear.

"This is a proud and daring man. He will not be an easy enemy."

And with his respect, Themistocles gained a new sense of urgency for the future of the Demos, and for Greece.

But when the three days of storm passed, green eyes looked down on the Aegean and smiled. But she also knew it was not enough.

****

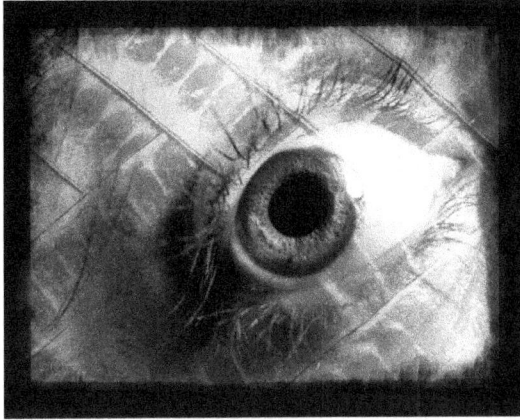

Chapter XIV – The Pearl Diver

The Greeks sat out the great storm safely protected on the Artemisium beaches. Themistocles and Thantos both knew that the Persians had been injured by storm, although they weren't sure how many ships were either lost or damaged. They, on the other hand, had lost no vessels, with the entire fleet beached in safety. Even all the scout ships escaped destruction.

Two days after calm returned to the Aegean, Themistocles was meeting with the Spartan admiral who was the figurehead leader of the Greek defense.

During the Greek congress at Corinth, many of the Greek states almost rebelled at the thought of an Athenian commanding the navy defense. There was general concern that Athens was becoming too powerful in the Hellenic world. Even though the Athenian contingent was the largest in the alliance, and they were the most experienced sailors, the other states stood firm in their objection. Eventually a compromise was reached. Initially it was made between Leonidas, the son of King Anaxandridas and the 17th of the Agiad Line, and the Greek politician, Themistocles. But it was proposed to the delegations by the Aeginians contingent. Leonidas did not want the rest of the alliance to believe a secret arrangement had been made without their input. The concession was that a Spartan, Eurybiadas, son of Eurycleides, would be the figurehead leader, and the Athenian general, Themistocles, would be his advisor.

Eurybiadas was an unusual Spartan. Most of the generals in the Spartan army were daring and aggressive. Eurybiadas was neither. He was a defensive general, preferring to fight by delaying battles rather than confront the enemy directly. It was these qualities that led to his being chosen as the compromise choice. Leonidas believed that Eurybiadas could not impose his will over the Athenian politician and therefore was a perfect choice for the job.

The two generals met on a regular basis. On this night, even though they had heard that the Persian fleet was pounded, there was quite a bit of tension in the air. The immenseness of the Persian navy, and the task in front of them, had become real to these men. Eurybiadas was leaning on a pillow and drinking wine. He looked at Themistocles and commented, *"I have a good feeling that the Persian navy might have been injured by the storm."*

Themistocles stared at him with an unbelieving look. Eurybiadas was stating the obvious as if it were a revelation. He swallowed hard to make sure he didn't say anything insulting to this man he would have to get along with over the coming weeks. He continued to stare at the Spartan, and Eurybiadas, misinterpreting the look said, *"No, no I am optimistic."*

Themistocles was less positive. He looked at the Spartan and said, *"We have won nothing yet! The Gods have intervened. It is now our turn."*

As the Athenian finished his comment a sailor entered their tent. The man was an Athenian and directly addressed Themistocles. *"General, a man awaits. He claims that he has knowledge of the Persian navy."*

"Knowledge?" Themistocles inquired.

"General, I don't know what information he has. Should I interrogate him before he can answer?"

With a pensive response, Themistocles asked, *"Where does this man hail from?"*

"He is a Greek, general."

"Is he? Search him for weapons, then send him in."

Five minutes later, a small man was ushered into the center of the tent. Surprisingly, he bowed in front of the two generals. They both stared at him in disbelief of his actions. Although diminutive in stature, the man seemed very serious. He had very short hair and was clean shaven. This little man had an unusual build. His chest was out of proportion to his legs. His legs were so thin that it was hard to believe they could support his large chest. He also had very long arms, looking more like a monkey than a human. Finally, the man spoke. *"General, my name is Skyllias of Skione. My profession is a pearl diver. I was hired by the Persian King to help salvage the ships that were destroyed by the storm."*

"Tell me, Skyllias of Skione, why would you work for the Persians, then come and talk to us?"

"I am not a soldier, General, but I am a Greek. I have no way of helping defend my country or our navy. The Persians paid me well. I saved money for them and made much for myself and my family. But I reasoned that if I could learn of their movements, I could help my country."

"So, you are a patriot?" the Spartan general questioned. But afterward, the Greek politician turned to the small man and said, *"Skyllias? I have heard this name before. There are many rumors about this man."*

Themistocles continued, *"I have heard that you are able to swim under water almost 10 miles without breathing. Are you a man or a fish?"*

The pearl diver smiled, *"I think I am a fish and who am I to argue with rumor."*

Now it was Themistocles' turn to smile. He blurted out, *"A merman, the upper body of a man and the lower body of a fish. Tell me merman, is Poseidon your father?"*

Skyllias bowed his head to the Athenian.

"General. I have information. The Persian fleet suffered much damage during the storm. Parts of ships have been found as far away as 150 miles. I have heard estimates that upwards of 250 ships were destroyed or damaged."

Eurybiadas jumped up hearing the numbers.

"250!" he yelled. But as excited as the Spartan was, Themistocles was again contemplative. The pearl diver continued his report, *"There is an important bit of information that you should know."*

Now Themistocles stood, *"Tell us, merman"*

"General, the Persian have sent a squadron of ships down the coast of Euboea. They plan to sail around the island and block your retreat. From what I have heard, the Persian admiral wants to destroy the Greek navy in one pitched battle. I believe they will wait to attack your frontal position until after the squadron is in place."

Hearing this news, Eurybiadas was clearly shaken. It was this reaction that took Themistocles back, not the news that the Persians were attempting to surround their position. He immediately lost faith in his Spartan counterpart. Such a reaction told the Athenian more than any history could. He immediately stepped between the Spartan and the pearl diver, shooing him out of the tent. When they were alone, Themistocles looked at the Spartan, *"Fear spreads like the wind. An army cannot fight if their leaders fear the enemy."*

He walked closer and came face to face with Eurybiadas.

"Control your reactions, Spartan."

Eurybiadas acted as if he had not heard any of the words spoken after the news of the Persian plan. He again appeared stunned.

"Our position has been compromised. We will need to withdraw before we are surrounded and *lose the whole fleet. There is no choice."*

Themistocles slowly walked to the Spartan, *"You are misguided, my friend."*

He pointed in the direction of the straits that separated the Greek ships from the Persians.

"This is our place. It is perfect for us. The strait is narrow. If we leave, we will be abandoning your brothers who are defending the Thermopylae pass. Their only hope is that we can engage the Persian navy and not allow them to reinforce their army."

Eurybiadas stared almost in horror at the Athenian politician. His eyes looked as if they were going to fly out of his skull. One could notice sweat forming on his brow. Themistocles closed in until he was face to face with his arms on his shoulders.

"Take hold of yourself, my friend. I know you are a brave man. Your brothers are guarding a pass with millions of men bearing down on them."

He gently shook the Spartan, *"We will not abandon Leonidas!"*

Finally, Eurybiadas seemed to regain control. He nodded in affirmation. *"It will take the Persians some days to reorganize themselves. They must wait for the squadron to get into place. We will have time to prepare."*

The two men decided to walk to the docks. The sight of the ships seemed to calm them both. The two men became quiet as they stared out to the fleet. After a while, Thantos joined the two. He came from behind the two men and put his hands on both of their shoulders

"My friends, I have news."

Both men turned to listen.

"You might not know this, but the Persians sent a squadron of ships down the Euboean coast to surround our position."

Both generals looked at the captain. Eurybiadas began to speak, but Thantos interrupted

"A second storm is close, coming in fast from the Aegean. I met with Ptea this morning. He believes the entire squadron was cast upon the rocks of the coast. There will be no ships circumventing the island. Our escape route is secured."

Themistocles looked at the Spartan and smiled. He leaned close to him and whispered, *"Pray to the wind."*

The second storm arrived as predicted. It was different from the first tempest, as this one contained lightning and thunder. Nevertheless, the weather still battered the Persian ships, still stuck in in the Aegean. Again, as with the first blow, many of the Persian vessels were either sunk or damaged. So, before any battle had begun over 400 of the Persian vessels were destroyed. Others had been damaged. Nature had taken its toll. Although the odds had been lowered to 700 against 300, the Persians were still superior.

****

It had been four days with no Persian advancement. Yes, they had sent some scouts to test the Greek defense, but they were easily vanquished without any Greek injuries. The son of King Anaxandridas II, and the 17th of the Agiad Line, showed no concern. The Spartan phalanx was a formidable weapon. Lining up next to each other with their shields touching, they fashioned their defense into a wall of metal. The hoplites directly behind the first line used their shields to cover the heads of all the defenders.

The army also had lone pikes and sasissas. The sasissas were long spear like weapons that the hoplites used to spike at the enemy as they advanced. This was an intimidating defense that took a huge toll on an advancing unit. The potential was even more dramatic on the Thermopylae road, as the Persians could not progress in a spread formation, but had to taper their structural advance because of the narrowness of the terrain. There was therefore no way to outflank or surround the defenders. The Greeks would have to be pushed back and overwhelmed. A daunting task for any army.

Still smarting from the loss of a significant part of his navy, The King of Kings had lost some confidence. He had heard of the difficulty his troops would be facing when attacking the pass at Thermopylae. His advisors had warned him that even with the enormous advantage in numbers, the cost of vanquishing the Spartans would be significant. Eventually the King threw out all his prognosticators and isolated himself in meditation. He had been supplied by his Magi with a special potion that would stimulate his thoughts. Being chaperoned by almost three thousand soldiers and his bodyguards, Xerxes left the encampment and traveled into the surrounding woods. They traveled to a low outcrop of rocks among the lush forest. After a short scouting mission, Xerxes found a small cave. Penish was called to the monarch and told how to partition his protective troops. The bodyguard protested, wanting to stay with the King at the cave. Xerxes would have none of it, demanding his isolation which would allow his consciousness to wander away from the reality. The conclusion of the argument was decided before it began, as the King never lost a disagreement.

That night the great King settled into a small crevice at the back of the grotto. The potion accomplished its task, and Xerxes imagining himself standing near his adopted mother, Ho of Sebennytos. She looked concerned as she stared at her son. The King dreamt that he could feel the heat emanating from her eyes. He felt himself shrink in response.

"What has happened to you, my son?"

"I am scared, mother"

"Scared!"

She roared.

"My people are dying and for what purpose?"

"It is your destiny"

"I do not want to go down in history as the man who destroyed the great Persian Empire."

Xerxes came out of his trance long enough to vomit where he sat. But he quickly fell back into the vacancy of the hallucinogens.

"My son, you cannot change what is already written."

"Where is my father?"

"He will not come to speak with you until you rise above your weakness."

"We have lost over four hundred ships, mother."

"Everything has a cost, my son. Did you think you can be in such a fight and not bleed?"

"You will bleed, my son……………you will bleed………………you will bleed"

The voice began fading with the warnings

On the fourth day, the Persian sent an envoy to negotiate with the Spartan defenders. Xerxes had sent his most trusted general to negotiate. Smerdomences rode with two guards down the Thermopylae path to the outskirts of the Spartan position. He sat high in the saddle and carried a red flag. The flag was meant to signal that they wanted to parlay. On his fine mare, the Persian general stood five feet in front of his guards. A single Spartan came out to meet him. In broken Greek the Persian general said, *"I am here to speak with your leader. I come under a peace flag."*

The Spartan snorted and spit on the ground.

"You come here for conquest and blood, not for peace"

Smerdomences grabbed his sword hilt, but at the last minute controlled himself. He repeated his request, *"I will speak with your leader."*

The Spartan stared back at the Persian with hatred in his eyes, but eventually bowed and walked backwards to the defensive position. It took fifteen minutes until a Spartan dressed in ceremonial guard advanced to meet the Persian general. The Persian left his horse and slowly walked toward the Peloponnesian.

"My name is Smerdomences. I am here representing the King of Lands, King of Peoples, and King of Kings. My lord, Xerxes, wishes to tell you how much he respects the great peoples of the city of Sparta. He has come to admire your bravery and your culture. He wishes to invite you to be an ally as opposed to an adversary."

"Compliments are like the breeze, Persian. They hold no power. Their purpose is to seduce. How do you wish to seduce me, Persian?"

"You misunderstand me, Spartan. My King does not wish to insult you but to offer you a peace."

"A peace! The Persian peace is subservience. We bow to no sovereign other than our own."

The Persian general swallowed hard at the implied rejection. In a terse fashion, Smerdomences asked.

"Tell me Spartan, what is your name, that you speak so foolishly?"

"I am the son of King Anaxandridas II, and the 17th of the Agiad Line. My name is Leonidas."

"Leonidas? Leonidas. I have heard this name before. Are you the man who fought and murdered the Persian Hamas at Delphi?"

Leonidas did not move but stared the Persian down. After what must have been two minutes, the Persian said, *"Leonidas. My King will be happy to hear that you are here in defense of this position. He will be happy to hear that your blood will stain the ground."*

Leonidas smiled at the Persian. *"Tell you great King to get off his golden throne and come down to avenge his friend. I will meet him, face to face, if he has the nerve"*

Smerdomences snorted at the comment, but then acted as if he were going to get down off his horse.

"Yes," Leonidas said, *"Yes, do you wish to step forward and challenge me, Persian?"*

Smerdomences stopped and the King of Sparta *laughed.* He then said, *"Tell your King of Kings that the Spartans that stand here welcome death. Neither his Gods or his army worry us. Tell Xerxes that we await his army. We have been waiting for four days and wonder whether the Persians have come for vacation or conflict."*

As he spoke Leonidas began to laugh quietly.

"Laugh if you will, Spartan, but in front of your limited defense stands over a million men that will walk over your decompensating bodies. Our archers will blacken the sky with their arrows."

From behind the King a voice said, in a jokingly fashion,

"Excellent! Then we will fight in the dark."

Leonidas turned and saw his friend, Dienekes, banging his spear on the ground as he laughed at the Persian. The Persian general turned his horse. He said to himself. *"Then you will die in the dark."*

Xerxes, after hearing that Leonidas was at Thermopylae, jumped from his throne in rage. He pointed at his general,

"Leonidas, the butcher of Hamas is here! I want him. Any soldier that brings me the head of Leonidas will become richer than his wildest dreams. Even if the Spartans agreed to peace I want Leonidas dead. Prepare the army, we attack tomorrow!"

****

Chapter XV – Kyksos

The Spartan Admiral entered Themistocles' tent in a rush. He could barely breathe in his excitement.

"The Gods have been with us again. Fifteen Persian ships became confused in the fog and sailed directly into our position. They were captured without putting up a fight. We have drawn first blood. It is a good sign."

"I agree."

Themistocles responded, as he looked towards the heavens. Eurybiadas became serious and said, *"We have an opportunity my friend. The Persian squadron that was sent to surround us was destroyed by the Gods. They are giving us a signal. It is time to withdraw."*

Themistocles looked at him with disbelief.

"Just the opposite, my friend. The Persians have given us an opportunity. Their hesitation has revealed their lack of coordination and their poor strategizing. This evening we will attack."

"Attack, this Evening?"

Eurybiadas yelled in questioning protest.

"We attack in the evening? We are not able to fight in the dark."

Themistocles smiled. *"We will attack with only two hours of light left. They will not expect such a move. They will respond, but they will be even more disorganized than usual. Attacking at that time will limit the battle time in case we become overwhelmed. We must lure the Persian out to fight on our terms. They are hesitant, we must anger them. Their bulk will work in our favor. We will attack one of their southernmost squadrons. By the time their other squadrons respond, darkness will end the encounter."*

"On the second day, after we sting them, they will be more aggressive. We will move our ships toward the Persian vessels and wait for them to come out. When they do, we will form a semi-circle, a Kyksos, with our backs to the shore. This will further confuse the Persians. As they position to surround us we will break position and each attack one ship. We will row through the Persians and then turn around and row back through the Persian fleet. We will aim our ships for their oars, sheering them off."

"When you are outnumbered, you must be bold! From what I figure, we will be outnumbered 3 to 1. We probably will not destroy them, but we must reduce the odds for the next battle. Remember, this a battle to control their minds as well. Their navy is as inexperienced as ours. I want to destroy their will, crush their confidence before it has time to build. We must beat the men, not just the ships."

The Spartan admiral looked with surprise at Themistocles. The Athenian continued, *"I want the Persians to be conjecturing about our strategy, not us guessing about theirs. If we can keep them on the defensive and bloody them, they will begin questioning everything they do. We will confuse them, offer them things then take it away. We will strike when they expect withdrawal and withdraw when they expect attack. They will think of us as witches!"*

****

Xerxes was in the midst of one of his famous temper outbursts. He had lost almost half of his navy. The storms had taken 400 ships off the Magnesium coast. The squadron of 200 that was sent to surround the Greek position and block any retreat was destroyed by weather. His admirals appeared hesitant and in disarray. Fifteen ships had sailed into the Greek position. His army had been waiting for the Persian navy to surround the Greeks before attacking at

Thermopylae, which now was not going to happen. The grand strategy to destroy the Greek resistance in a concerted ground and navy attack was in clear jeopardy. This scenario brought back many shadowy memories for this young King. During his first venture as King of Kings in quelling the rebellious magi in Egypt, Xerxes was dissatisfied in the effectiveness of the Persian troops. Only the troops led by the ex-Spartan, Demaratus, performed admirably. The defeat at Marathon, in which the Greek army out strategized and embarrassed the Persian force was one of the key elements leading to this invasion. Was it happening again? Had the God, Abu Mazda, abandoned them in this venture? Had the Greek pantheon of Gods proved to be superior to his single deity?

The young King was sensing the wrenching feeling of uncertainty. In the past, when this feeling overcame him, he could turn to his teacher, Hamas, who always had the right words to reignite the fire in his soul. But Hamas was gone, murdered by the Spartan monarch Leonidas, a man who boldly stood only yards from his current position, laughing at him in mock defiance, combing their hair and exercising as they faced certain death. But for all his anger and hatred for this King of Sparta, there was a small part of him that revered his bravery. To kill Hamas in a sword fight had probably taken the skill of the immortal Achilles. And now he faced him, Xerxes, King of Lands, King of Peoples, King of Kings. Sharply, Xerxes demanded all the servants in his tent to leave. He walked to the middle of the opening and knelt. Looking up to the heavens, Xerxes prayed.

"Abu Mazda, I have always prayed to your might. I have tried my whole life to follow the truth and avoid the lie. You have led me to this point and I trust your judgment. Give me the strength to continue on this quest to satisfy my ancestor's vengeance and right the world again."

Xerxes raised his head and yelled for a slave, *"Send me Golnar."*

Xerxes continued praying until the lector Egyptian priestess arrived. She found him on his knees in the center of the royal tent. She stood silently, waiting for the King to end his supplication. Finally, Xerxes looked up and spoke, *"Tomorrow we launch our attack at the Spartan position on the Thermopylae road. I will order my weak admirals to advance against the Greek navy at Artemision. I need to contact my father to gain his support. My mother, Ho, was a prophet of the Gods. In a sacred ceremony in the caves outside of Susa I met my grandfather and spoke with my father. My mother was also a lector priestess, but a very powerful celebrant. Ho came to me in a trance and told me my father had decided not to talk to me. But I need to speak with him. Are you able to accomplish this task?"*

Golnar bowed in affirmation, *"Prepare yourself and your potions, for this night I must consult the spirits."*

The lector priestess demanded that the King bring frankincense and other herbs to the session. She also wanted him to bring his sacred rod, "the answerer," which was given to him by his step-mother, Ho.

Golnar also warned the King of Kings that the journey he was considering is an arduous one and can be both physically and mentally draining. She also warned that there was some risk that the person will not recover his soul after it leaves his body. It is a time when Tiamat, the internal devil that lives within all of us, can steal the soul and take over the body of the wanderer.

"This danger needs to be considered before embarking on such a journey. Even those that return safely are changed by the experience. I must warn you my King, that you should not take these dangers lightly. Journey to the spirits is more dangerous than any enemy, than any animal, and what's worse, your questions might go unanswered. Your mother thought that the journey was too dangerous for you to make this attempt."

Unflinchingly, the King of Kings agreed to all the terms of this séance. His doubts overcame his fears of the procedure. That evening, Xerxes, King of all Lands, met Golnar in the woods outside of their encampment. He was naked except for a small cloth covering his waist. His slaves had oiled him down to make his journey easier. Golnar brought many potions that the King had to ingest at different times. A very large and bright fire burned in front of the Xerxes as he sat, legs folded in front of him. He drank the first potion and the lector priestess put a reddish paste on his forehead. It seemed to burn deeply into his skin, but the King showed no response.

"Close your eyes, my King,"

Golnar said in a firm tone. Xerxes obeyed. The two sat still for five minutes. The young King's head began to feel light and he felt waves of warmth penetrating his mid-section. Golnar had said that the seat of all bodily energy lay inside a person, just above their stomach. Xerxes became dizzy and felt himself starting to lose the ability to sit upright. He struggled to maintain his posture. Golnar had him drink another mixture, this one sour and smelling of dead fish. As he opened his eyes, the world had changed. Colors were altered and the King had lost all orientation. The trees that were so prominent in the forest before him had all vanished, replaced by the desert. But Xerxes mind had no desire to reason why. He began to float, rising above the fire below. The King seemed to hover, but it was not warmth that he felt from the flames, it was chill. Xerxes saw Golnar below, saying some words, but they were unintelligible. And then as if shot, the King of Kings felt a heavy beat in his chest and all consciousness vanished.

When Xerxes awoke, he was in an ethereal place. Images were unclear, but he could see people far away in white robes. It felt as though he was floating in water, the slow undulating of the waves carrying his body towards the figures in front of him. They had no faces just translucent shapes. As he drew closer one of the figures held up his hand to stop his advance. Somehow the King knew he was close to death, and moving further would push him to the point of no return. This was the place that one finds oneself after one abandon's one's body.

"My son."

The voice was gravely.

"You have lost faith. You must remember who you are. You are the leader of the greatest peoples on earth. The Persian soul and spirit are stronger than all others. You will bleed but you will overcome. Remember Marathon, remember Marathon!"

The hazy figure just kept repeating the same phrase. Xerxes' eyes flew open and he jumped. Golnar was by his side but he was clearly confused and dazed by the experience. The King slept for hours after his journey. He developed a fever, but it only lasted a very short time. Upon waking, Xerxes looked like a different man. His doubts were erased. He demanded both his generals and admirals to gather at his tent. The meeting itself was short lived and one sided. Xerxes chided the group quite dramatically. He wanted Greek blood.

****

It was late afternoon and the sun was looking heavy in the western sky. The Greek triremes left their beaches and quickly gained formation. The crews were well rested and the boats quickly moved north along the coast. Themistocles had won the strategic battle against his Spartan equivalent and the Greeks would make the first move and attack the unsuspecting Persian position. The Persian position was spread over miles on the Magnesian coast. Their plan was to attack the first squadron that they encountered.

The confrontation happened just north of the town of Aphetae. The Greek triremes had three uneven levels of rowers. The first level of oarsmen were called thranites. The second level were the zygites, and the third level was called the thalamites. When these three levels worked in unison they were an awe-inspiring propulsion element. The Greek triremes were oaken ships that were fashioned after the master ship builders from Corinth. They were 121 feet long and carried 170 oarsmen. Although they had large square sails, and when attacking they opened to the wind. They had to achieve a speed of 10 knots to inflict the type of damage that they needed. Their goal was to ram the smaller Persian vessels rendering them useless. They did not have the strong marine contingent that the Persian fleet carried. Therefore, they did not attempt to engage in hand to hand fighting.

Themistocles stood on the prow of the Athena, the lead ship in the Athenian contingent. His vessel sprinted toward fifty Persian ships that lay anchored off the coast. Each Greek trireme targeted one Persian ship and the streaked toward their pray. It was easy to see that the Persian admirals and boat captains did not anticipate this attack. The Greeks had obviously caught them by surprise because they were spread out over the sea in an unsystematic fashion. As the ships met, the cracking of wood on wood was a frightening sound as the Greek vessels furiously attacked the stunned Persian navy. Each attack ended with the explosive sound of bowed wood cracking. Before they realized what was happening, the Persian navy had lost 20 ships. The Athenians had rowed through the first row of Persian triremes and continued to secondary targets. They had taken out the oars of Persian ships and swung back to break the back of the disabled ship. As the sun began to sink behind the mountains, the screams of Persian sailors were heard in a chilling chorus of death throws. Most of the Persian sailors could not swim, so when the bows were shattered the carnage for the sharks began in earnest. Many of the men died before they drowned, as the sea reddened in the chum of the frenzy. The more they struggled, the more chum they created, the more of a target they became for the slaughter.

A mile up the coast, a hundred Persian triremes organized into attack formation and headed south to meet the Greek surprise attack. As they approached Cape Sepias the site of battle, the Persian admirals were shocked at the wreckages that floated to meet them. Their hearts sank as the evidence of the Persian massacre became more evident with bodies of Persian soldiers and oarsmen floating by in dismembered parts. Crew members and Persian marines began throwing up overboard at the putrid sight. What they eventually found were thirty sunken Persian triremes, six damaged vessels, and one Persian ship that deserted to the Greeks.

Angered, the Persian admiral, Zephan, urged his ships to increase their speed, but the Greeks had already withdrawn and outran the Persian counter attack.

That evening Zephan, the Persian admiral of the southern fleet, stood before the King of Kings with his head bowed. In front of him Xerxes paced back and forth. It was clear that the King was spending energy maintaining his composure in the face of this unexpected setback.

"Explain, Zephan."

"Lord, I take full responsibility for this tragedy. We were not expecting such an attack."

"Obviously Zephan, obviously,"

The King screamed as he slapped the general across the face. Zephan moved backwards holding his reddened cheek.

Xerxes drew his sword and pointed it at the admiral.

"Persians do not bow to Greeks. So far, my generals and admirals are acting like scared children, not brave warriors. I am confused where the spirit has gone. Have you lost faith in yourselves, or are you just stupid? Besides, I don't want you to expect, I want you to know!"

Zephan did not answer the direct question but bowed his head in shame. Xerxes shook his head in repugnance. Out of the left side of his eye, Zephan noticed some movement. Silently, like a stealthy serpent patiently stalking it's pray, Artemisia, the Warrior Queen from Halicarnassus had entered the tent. Zephan immediately reacted, looking directly at the young King, *"Why is that woman here?"*

He protested in obvious irritation. Stoically, Artemisia walked toward the admiral. She reached him and bent into his face.

"Do you have a problem with me?"

Zephan just stared into her dark eyes. Droplets of sweat appeared on his forehead. The King of Kings smiled to himself watching this confrontation between two of his leaders. Artemisia pointed to Xerxes and with a brash voice said, *"The reason we lost those ships and their crews is because we have been scratching our asses when we should be attacking."*

Zephan defended himself to his sovereign. *"Lord, we were waiting for the trap to be sprung. Once the squadron had been in place behind the Greek position, we would have been in position to destroy their entire navy in one battle. That was the plan"*

"Would have, would have! What is important is what did happen, not what would have happened. So rather than destroy their navy we look like frightened fools."

The Queen spat and looked at the King, *"Either the navy goes with me to attack these people, or I will go myself!"*

With that, she stomped out of the room. Xerxes stared at the admiral. He finally said, *"I couldn't decide, Zephan, whether to take your life today or wait to see how you responded."*

The King then walked slowly to the admiral.

"Tomorrow, our army will attack at the pass at Thermopylae. I expect that the navy will move in force against the Greek position."

The admiral bowed and left the tent, thanking all the deities he could think of that he still had his head.

****

"There is movement!" the cry went out.

"They are coming! They are coming!"

Alpheus yelled out pointing up the path. His voice betrayed his excitement.

"Thank, Ares, the God of war has heard my pleas," Leonidas yelled, looking up at the sky. He jumped up and ran up to Alpheus. After staring for a moment, he patted his fellow Spartan on the shoulder. He stood on a rock raising him above the others.

"Our time has come. Prepare yourself."

The Greek allies all rushed and began putting on their armor and setting themselves in their prearranged pattern. Leonidas' gaze was fixated, gazing up the pass. After a moment he jumped on his horse and headed to the Persian position. The others were stunned by the reactions, but he stopped and put his hand up indicating he did not want to be followed. He feverishly prodded his animal as he rode headlong into the enemy position. As he approached the Persians, they scrambled to meet the advance. Arrows flew from different angles, none of which came close to the advancing Spartan. Suddenly the Spartan pulled back on the reins and the horse stopped dead in his tracks. He scanned and found who he assumed was the leader of the Persian advanced force. He drew his sword and pointed at the Mede general. *"I am the son of King Anaxandridas II, and the 17th of the Agiad Line. My name is Leonidas.*

Your men will die this day."

The horse rose on his back feet and the Spartan began laughing. The Mede general stared in astonishment at what he was seeing. After a few moments, he regained his senses and pointed at the Spartan. In his loudest voice he yelled, *"Bring me this man's head.*

In unison, a hundred Median soldiers began rushing the horse. Hundreds of others picked up their weapons to follow. Leonidas did not move, almost challenging these rushing soldiers. Spears were thrown, bouncing off the shield of the Spartan. The horse circled in a panic at the approaching hoard. Suddenly, as the running soldiers came into range, Leonidas turned the horse and slowly began riding back to the Greek position. Again, arrows flew past his back and head without success. He continued to turn and slow or speed up his retreat, as if bating the Meads as they ran after him. Suddenly, as the horse turned a corner and a black wall of shields appeared. The King smacked his mount and the horse replied with a full out run. Riding directly into the assembled shields the horse continued to increase its speed until it appeared to fly over the assembled Greek hoplites. The

Mede soldiers turned the corner in pursuit and immediately became aware of the hoplite wall of steel. Some stopped in confusion, yet many of them continued their advance. The Greek soldiers advanced with their long spears, cutting through the disorganized Median attack. The Persians were haphazardly advancing while the Greeks cut them down with precision.

Realizing the situation, the Median general yelled again, urging the soldiers to retreat to their positions so the attack could be coordinated. Within minutes he brought his entire army of 20,000, backing up the chaotic advance. As they moved closer, the Greek position had again re-formed. Each Spartan shield fit into the side of the ones next to them, so the advancing army could not make out any individual. Some Persian soldiers began throwing up as they recognized the carnage of their brothers who had chased the Spartan King. Many men from the first Mede advance lay bleeding with limbs cut sharply off their bodies. Some were crying and praying for their salvation. Their comrades kept moving forward ignoring their pleas. Because of the narrowness of the path, the Persians had to step over and on, their fallen comrades.

The Persians stopped within twenty yards and the Median general ordered the archers to the front of the column. His name was Kurush, which meant 'little father' in the ancient tongue. Kurush's grandfather had risen to power with Xerxes' grandfather Cyrus. Kurush had been called the day before in front of the King of Kings. While he was in his bow, Xerxes spoke, *"Kurush, I have known your family for as long as I can remember. Your grandfather served Cyrus well."*

"Lord," Kurush said from his kneel.

"I am bestowing on you and your family a great honor. Your troops will lead the invasion of lower Greece and capture the Greek position in this pass."

"A great honor Lord."

"I have only one request," The King said as he rose from his throne.

"I want the head of the Spartan pig Leonidas, brought to me."

"It will be done, Lord."

Kurush remembered the discussion with the great King as he ordered his archers to the front of the column. He had already lost more men in this skirmish than he was willing to admit. He preferred to destroy the Greeks with arrows rather than swords. Unleashing volley after volley of arrows toward the Greek position, Kurush quickly became disheartened. The arrows had no effect, bouncing off the metal barrier of the Greek shields. Realizing that this strategy was having little or no effect, he quickly glanced to both sides to see if the enemy could be outflanked. The pass was much too narrow, and he immediately concluded he would have to meet them directly. But Kurush also noticed something from the fallen soldiers that he saw, the Greek weapons were superior to the Persian. The Persian shields offered only minimal protection from the long Greek spears. He had a sinking feeling at this epiphany. His arrows were generally useless, he couldn't outflank, and his weapons were of a lesser quality. For a second he considered withdrawal, but instinctively he knew that he would forfeit his life and be branded a coward by Xerxes.

As Kurush watched his arrows bouncing off the Greek shields, he noticed that the Greek position was slowly moving forward toward the Median archers. Pulling the archers off the forward lines, the Median general swallowed hard and ordered a full-frontal attack by the soldiers.

The Median shields were wicker and were not able to effectively defend the soldiers against the longer Greek spears. Since the path was so narrow that they could not outflank the Greek position they were attempting to crush the position by vastly superior numbers. Line after line they came, and line after line the Greek hoplites cut them down with gory efficacy. After two hours, the advancing Medes had to climb over the dead bodies of their comrades. A few Medes began to run and Kurush had them beheaded on the spot. He could not afford anything but total compliance. If they were going to die, they would die in service to the King, not in retreat from the Greeks.

The stench was overwhelming. Urine, feces, and blood mixed and created an eerie olfactory presence. Kurush noticed that the Greeks were rotating across the front lines, bringing in rested troops on a regular basis. Yet he was amazed that even with the change, he couldn't break through the barrier. At one point he ordered some troops to drop their shields and rush the Greek position and attempt to hurdle the Hoplites to break stalemate. Two soldiers were impaled on spears as they made this suicidal attempt, being caught in the air after their jumps. They screamed in horror as the spears exited their backs. Other soldiers actually cleared the Greek position, bouncing off the shields used to protect the hoplite heads, only to be slaughtered by the troops backing up the front lines.

The King of Kings had been positioned on a small mount to watch the Median attack. Twice he had jumped out of his seat yelling and pointing,

"No, no."

He was clearly discouraged and angered by the Median lack of success. His face was reddened and his hair was becoming disheveled.

The sun began setting in the sky when Kurush ordered the withdrawal of the Median advance. He had to order hundreds of soldiers to advance to the front lines to clear the path from the dead Medes. There were too many to bury, and the soldiers were ordered to dump the bodies of the killed and wounded over the sides of the cliff, pushing them into the bay. As they performed their ghoulish task the Greeks watched, making no attempt to advance on them. It took hours for the Median soldiers to clear the pass. Many cried as they pushed their half alive comrades over the ledge to be crushed on the rocks below.

The great King watched this morbid occurrence as well, and he also cried. Although he appeared heartless at times to others, Xerxes loved his people, and watching them be butchered and not able to affect the outcome, made him wild with anger and pain. After the retreat, Xerxes called Smerdomences into his presence.

"My friend, you know about the tragic occurrences of today."

"I do Lord."

"What is your assessment?"

"I went up close to the fighting, Lord, and stood by Kurush during part of the day. I was sickened by the slaughter. This position must be turned, and doing it from a frontal attack will cost many more lives."

"What is your recommendation, Smerdomences?"

"Lord, I have already sent men into the hills. I have never seen a mountain pass that did not have an alternative path. We just must find someone who knows it."

Xerxes thought for a moment

"Offer a large reward for any local with knowledge of another pass in which we can surround these Spartan pigs."

"Will be done, Lord."

****

Chapter XVI – Lycomedes

"Raise you glasses to Lycomedes. He has the honor of being the first Greek to take a Persian ship intact."

The applause rang out as the captains clapped their sides and their glasses.

"Today we attacked the Triremes from Cilicia and destroyed them. In all, we captured 30 Persian vessels."

Themistocles stood.

"My fellow independents, we have had triumph in our defense. But be cautious my friends, for in a war success is fleeting, as the next battle could mean destruction. We must be attentive and not overzealous. Tomorrow I suspect the entire Persian fleet will be launched against us, not just an inexperienced Cilician contingent. Remember our strategy. We will engage them in the strait by Artemisium. That will limit the amount of ships the Persian can mass in attack. They will need to bunch up to prevent any large-scale maneuvering."

Heads nodded in confirmation of the strategy.

"The Persians are angry. We have punished them, and angry men make many mistakes. They will not wait for us, they will seek us out. They will come to us so we must choose the position to best defend. We will mass off the shores of Pevki Bay. In the bay the land that projects out will help us defend flanks. Remember, my friends, the Persians are a proud people, and they are desperate for victory. We have only blackened their face. Do not be of any illusion that they will easily succumb to us. We have only faced minor contingents."

Themistocles stopped to allow the information to be digested. He continued, *"We will form a Kyksos, a semi-circle with our backs to the shore. You will wait for the horn and then break ranks and attack. Some of the Persians will have to cross our position to try and out flank us. We will not allow them to gain position, but we will attack them before they have settled. One last word. No heavy drinking of wine this evening for we need our wits."*

Themistocles raised his glass, *"To Greece!"*

"To Greece," the captains answered.

"To Greece," Themistocles said louder. The captains now stood and in unison yelled,

"To Greece! To Greece."

After the crowd dispersed, Themistocles decided to walk the beach. He had just cautioned his captains about 'keeping their heads' by staying sober. With every step on the moonlit sand, the urge to drown his fears in wine grew stronger. Themistocles had hidden bottles in different places to assure that he could reach them. He stopped, looked around and saw that he was alone on the darkened sand. Themistocles slowly walked over to a group of rocks that were located under a bush. As he kept a watchful eye to make sure he wasn't being seen, the Greek politician dislocated a rock and found what he was looking for. He took the bottle over to another rock position where he could sit and not be noticed. As he drank, the great man's mind began to relax. He began considering the plight of the Greek alliance, and tears slowly appeared on his cheeks. He really wasn't sure what was bothering him until he realized the significance of the moment that was quickly arriving. History was converging on this place and he stood in the center of the hurricane. Themistocles knew that great men had superior qualities. And yet here he stood. "What the hell is this Metis?" he thought. It is just one of my illusions he wondered as he spit on the ground. Other men saw gray areas in the world, but not Themistocles. He saw blacks and whites. Things were clear for him, and yet he himself did not trust people who had no doubts. He continued drinking as he mused. Finally, his hands went to his forehead and he quietly began to cry. After a couple of minutes, the Greek politician regained his composure and emptied the wine into the sand. Themistocles stood and looked to the heavens.

"History is indeed converging, and here I stand. And because I am stupid, I will not break under its pressure".

****

Leonidas tensed. The sun had only been up a few hours and again there was movement on the Thermopylae road. His scout had returned from the west gate to report that the Persians were forming to march on their position.

"It is different" the scout said.

"Different?" Leonidas asked, *"Yes, my King. These are different troops gathering. These troops are dressed differently than yesterdays. They are more formal and have colored banners."*

"Colored banners?" Leonidas commented.

"The Persians are sending their elite troops against us today. It will be an even more glorious victory for us."

It was about a mile from the west gate to the middle gate and Phokian wall where the Greeks were positioned. Leonidas ordered his hoplites to prepare for they were going to march a half mile toward the Persians and he wanted to arrive at the position before they had. They formed their usual wall of shields and waited for the upcoming attack. When the Persians arrived at their position they hesitated as if appearing surprised to find the Greeks standing opposite them. The Persians marched forward and engaged the Greek hoplites. Within a short time, it became obvious that these elite Persians Immortals were not going to have any more success with the Greeks than the Medes had the day before. They had changed their troops, but not their strategy, nor more importantly, their weaponry. And yet they were very valiant men, and even with extreme losses continued to press their position. And then came a surprise. After an hour of slaughter, the Greeks broke and quickly began retreating in what seemed like a chaotic route. Taking advantage, the Persian Immortals began shouting and chasing the Greeks back towards the middle gate. After about 100 yards, in another surprising move, the Spartan hoplites stopped their retreat and formulated into their phalanx position. The Immortals kept advancing and the Greeks unceremoniously began slaughtering them. After some substantial losses the Persians reformulated their position and again began attacking in order.

As with the previous day, the Persians continued experiencing large losses. Even the almighty Immortals were getting cut through by the Spartan defenders. And then, two hours later, again the Greeks broke position and began running away from the Persians. Again, the Immortals chased in a more disordered fashion. As with the previous time after about fifty yards, the Greeks reformulated into their phalanx and began slaughtering their pursuers. The fight carried on for the remainder of the day until the Persians withdrew for good as the sun began setting. Again, as before, Persian soldiers were ordered to clear the path by pushing their dead and wounded over the cliff. Many men had died and not an inch of land was taken by force.

Xerxes could not believe his eyes. He estimated that he had lost five thousand of his elite troops in the battle. He sat stunned in his tent. This small group of fighters was holding off his entire army. He sat with his hands on his head when a slave entered indicating that Smerdomences was begging to enter. The King raised his head and stood when his friend came in.

"Who is this man?"

The King of Kings inquired. Smerdomences was accompanied by a short man who appeared to be a sheep herder.

"His name, Majesty is Ephialtes, son of Eurydemos."

"And why do you bring him before me at this time?"

"He has an answer for us, my Lord. Speak, Ephialtes, speak."

The man appeared shy, as he spoke in a very low voice, *"Great King, your general has informed me that you seek a way over the mountains to attack the Greek position from behind. It is called the*

Anopaia road. I have traveled it many times, and it will lead to the east gate, behind the Greek position."

Xerxes was expressionless and said, *"And why do you betray your people?"*

The Trachinian bowed his head.

"Lord, I have no love for either the Spartan or the Athenian. They consider themselves superior to other Greeks. I will not cry when you burn their city."

Xerxes stared, trying to read another underlying motive. The Trachinian continued, *"Besides Lord, I am a poor man, and I want my wife and children to be happy."*

Now Xerxes smiled and ordered a slave to take Ephialtes and feed him a large meal. When the man left Xerxes turned to Smerdomences and slapped his shoulder.

"Good work, my friend. Prepare your troops. You will march this night over the pass and surprise the Spartans in the morning."

"Finally," The King of Lands thought, *"God has finally smiled down on us. The Greek Gods have f*inally proven no match"

The great King dropped to his knees and began to cry.

****

Chapter XV11 – 17th of the Agiad Line

The Greek Triremes headed to Pevki Bay. It was an hour before sunrise, and although it was dangerous to leave the beaches before the sun was up, Themistocles believed that the chance was worth taking. It was imperative to any hope of success that they attain and secure their position before the Persians arrived. The superiority in numbers for the Persians was such that unless the Greeks could establish a positive defensive position, they would have no chance in the upcoming battle. The other chance that the Greek strategy depended on was that the Persians would enter the bay to attack their position. Of this, Themistocles was more confident. He believed that the losses that the Persians had sustained in the previous two days baited them into a reactive mode. They wanted blood and would have to attack the Greeks wherever they lay. The bay was such that like the pass of

Thermopylae, the Persians could not bring its entire navy into it. The Persians would have to advance in smaller groups to confront the Greeks. Even with the defensive position secured, the odds of not only defeating, but surviving a Persian onslaught, were not good.

Upon arrival, the Greek politician's heart lightened when he found the position vacant. If nothing else, they would have some time to set up their defense in anticipation of the Persian attack. They did not have to wait long, nor were they disappointed. Barely a half hour after their arrival, the Persian fleet was spotted readying to enter the bay. Again, Themistocles smiled to himself. He immediately knew that the Persians would not have to be baited, they would come to them completely on their own. Pointing to the Persian navy on the horizon, and talking to nobody in particular, Themistocles said, *"Look there, look there! Here they come. Being led into the trap because of their pride. They are not thinking my friends, they will move to us with their eyes closed. They believe they are omnipotent. They walk in without thought."*

It was an extraordinary sight to watch over 600 Triremes massing to enter the small straight. Themistocles knew, just from observation, that less than half of the Persian vessels could engage in the initial attack. But what would be their strategy? Would they surround the Greek position and wait them out or would they be aggressive and advance on them? It wasn't long for Themistocles to have his answer. They would attack.

There was some satisfaction in this understanding as Themistocles correctly anticipated the Persian strategy. But along with this came a chill of reality. What would happen this day could arguably become the greatest sea battle that man had ever known. Although normally self-confident, Themistocles could not help but quiver at the anticipation of the destruction and death that was imminent. For a moment he wondered whether protecting their culture and the infantile Demos was worth such a sacrifice. If they had agreed to the Persian demands thousands of lives could have been saved. Many Greek and Persian lives would be sacrificed over principle. Themistocles looked to the left and he saw Thantos, the captain of the ship on which he stood. Even though the Greek politician had ordered him out of the fray, there he was. The captain met his eyes and both men recognized the expectation of the slaughter. Themistocles pointed west and said, *"From what we've heard, Leonidas has successfully defended two attacks from the Persian army. Many of the barbarians have died. But these are not stupid savages. They will adjust. How can such a small force defend against such an overwhelming onslaught?"*

Thantos did not speak but stared into the politician's eyes. Themistocles continued, *"And what of our beautiful city? Arrangements are now under way to evacuate the entire populace. Will we ever be able to return to our homeland, or will we all be destroyed this day?"*

"Why do you torture yourself?" the sailor replied.

"The future is not yet written, it is up to us to author it."

"I'm impressed," Themistocles replied. *"I thought I was the philosopher."*

Both men smiled. Time was shrinking in the face of the upcoming apocalypse. Now was not the time for second thinking or philosophizing. Decisions had been made and the dye had been cast. There was no turning back. It was time for combat and all thoughts had to be concentrated on the engagement. Themistocles knew that timing was crucial to the first stage of this encounter. The Persians had begun entering the bay and the Greeks were already in their Kyksos semi-circle with their backs to the shore.

As the sun started to climb in the sky, the Persian offensive strategy began taking shape. Their first line had formed and their secondary ships were beginning to row into place. Themistocles noticed that the Egyptian contingent was formed on the right of the Greek position. At the center of the offensive line were the Persian vessels. On the left of the Greeks were other elements of the Persian navy. While viewing this position Themistocles noticed a series of ships in the position with black sails.

"Artemisia!" Themistocles thought *"The Warrior Queen is on our left."*

He pointed in that direction and Thantos acknowledged the message. And then, as an eerie stillness hung over the bay, the silence was broken by a loud horn. Immediately, the Greek ships broke formation and attacked the Persians. Each ship had targeted a specific vessel. But at the sound of the horn, the black sailed Halicarnassus ships broke their formation and began attacking the Greek left. Artemisia's lead ship was the first to engage a Greek vessel. It was an easy catch for her as she seemed to arrive before the Greeks could dodge the assault. She was one of the first to board the Greek vessel as her marines began fighting on the deck. Three Greek marines quickly fell under her blade. Within a half hour the entire Greek crew was subdued. They were quickly bound and the Warrior Queen returned to her craft and targeted another Greek ship. Within an hour and a half, Artemisia's ship had captured three Greek vessels. Her contingency then withdrew and removed the three Greek ships to the rear of the Persian position.

The Egyptian contingent to the right of the Greek position also fared well in the initial engagement. Their marines were much more skilled than the Corinthians they faced. Unlike the Warrior Queen, the Egyptian marines were caught in the blood lust of the moment and disposed of all the living men on every ship they captured.

Manasus was one of the captains of the Persian navy. His ship, the Eelengar, spearheaded the Persian advance toward the Athenian vessels. Manasus was not a sailor, in fact this journey was his first off land adventure. He had been given the captainship of this vessel because he was distantly related to the great King. As he watched the advance of the Athenian vessels towards his position, his heart raced and the fear of the moment and his own death overcame him. Manasus was so scared, he was having trouble breathing. Should he just wait for the Greek vessels and then engage, or should he venture forward and be aggressive? The only option off the table for Manasus was retreat, for the Persian vessels were lined three to four deep, blocking any retreat through the channel. He had not considered that when he was offered one of the lead positions. At that time, he was proud of the honor, but the realization hit him of the death sentence that came with the honor. Manasus tried to regain composure, but his arms and legs felt uncontrollable. As the other Persian vessels advanced past the Eelengar, Manasus instinctively raised his hands for the ship to advance. The vessel jolted forward and the Persian marines on the vessels prepared for the attack.

Manasus turned his head to the right as a loud noise gained his attention. What he saw brought a gasp to his throat, as the Persian vessel to his right was hit broadside by a Greek vessel. His eyes were fixated at the sight of the Persian vessel's side crumbled by the hit. Men flew over the side of the ship as screams and the sound of wood cracking filled the air. Manasus watched as spears and arrows from the Greek ship punctured the Persian oarsmen and sailors. It seemed like an eternity, but Manasus finally was able to pull his gaze away from the attack to his right and refocus on the plight of his own ship. Almost simultaneously, an arrow passed by the side of his head. But his consciousness quickly turned to another Greek vessel closing very quickly down on the port side of the Eelengar. Manasus heard himself screaming for the boat to swerve, but as he yelled, he already knew that it was too late for the escape maneuver. He anticipated, then immediately heard the oars of his vessel being cut off by the Greek vessel.

Manasus could now see the Greek sailors and marines up close. He found himself focusing on a young man that must have been ten years younger than himself. He met the young man's eyes and Manasus thought he also recognized the fear that he also felt. But at that moment of recognition, Manasus was thrown back away from the spot on which he stood. Manasus found himself lying on the deck and he noticed a large staff protruding out of the right side of his chest. As he felt himself losing consciousness, Manasus noticed his Persian troops abandoning the Eelengar.

What Manasus didn't know before his death was that the Phoenicians and Egyptians were successfully punishing the Greeks. But just as the left and right of the Greek position was faltering, the center of the Persians was taking a beating from the Greek attack. The Athenian lead ships were clearly more skilled than the Persian and easily outmaneuvered them. The Athenian vessels rammed ship after ship, but unlike the Egyptians, the Athenians did not board their enemy; their goal was to destroy their oars leaving them useless in an engagement. The Greeks broke through the first line then quickly rotated and attacked other ships from the rear.

Themistocles was correct in his appraisal. It was a bloody day. Half of the Athenian vessels were either damaged or sunk. Luckily, most of the damaged vessels could easily be repaired. But as the sun set, the Greeks limped back to the beach. They were wounded and bleeding. One of the heroes of the day for the Greeks was a man named Cleinias. He was given a prize for valor by his fellows. Cleinias was a wealthy merchant from northern Greece. He built and paid for a Trireme by himself. He also paid the crew out of his own pocket. Considering the damage, there was little to cheer about, but Cleinias and his crew fought harder than any Greek ship. There was a saving grace for the day, for by a quick, unofficial count, the Persian navy had lost over 200 ships. But as the Greeks made camp for the evening there were no celebrations or merriments. Themistocles and the Spartan general, Eurybiadas, were isolated from the others, attempting to figure out what the next move should, or could be.

The Greek politician and the Spartan general sat by an open fire, mostly in silence. They appeared stunned by the day's outcome. Themistocles was stunned by the loss of life on both sides of the equation. He was having difficulty separating his emotions from the military strategy. But as he thought, his mind generally focused on the damage that the outnumbered infantile Greek navy did to the Persians alliance. One incident stood out in his mind. Themistocles came within a ship's length of the infamous Warrior Queen from Halicarnassus. She had boarded a Greek vessel and was lost in the blood lust of the moment, or so he thought. As if on a cue, Artemisia turned away from the attack and stared back at Themistocles. It took him by surprise, and yet he didn't flinch, he continued the glare. And then the Warrior Queen smiled, turned her head and beheaded a Greek sailor. Themistocles could not get the image out of his thoughts. His lowered his head, and thought of Leonidas.

****

Smerdomences and his men had marched and climbed most of the night. There were times when he doubted that there really was a path that led behind the Thermopylae pass. It was unusual for the army to advance in darkness, so this mission was unnerving to many of the troops. During a short rest, one of the Immortals advanced scouts reported that there was a Greek contingent guarding the road. It made Smerdomences optimistic that this pass led to the east gate, for if it didn't, why did the Greeks have to defend it. Smerdomences had the scout brought to him.

"Tell me what you saw."

The scout put his hand to his chest and his sword to his throat, indicating that his life was unimportant and at the general's leave.

"My general, I would estimate hundreds of Greek soldiers are on a small hill defending the path. I have seen their colors before, they are not Spartans, they are Phokians. They are also not very watchful. They all sleep except for two guards who are dozing. They will easily be overcome. They do not seem to be expecting us"

"Excellent," Smerdomences said.

"Excellent. Alert the men. We will march in two columns. Half of our army will attack the Phokian position. The second column will secure the road. Send scouts to let the King of Kings know that we are about to break through. I also want scouts to proceed ahead and let us know the terrain."

The scout and the soldiers left to prepare the attack.

The scout was accurate in his assessment. The Phokians were poor soldiers and unprepared for any attack. The Persian Ausiya surprised their position, and without any engagement the Phokians withdrew in disarray. Smerdomences stood in disbelief watching them flee to the woods. He couldn't understand how the Greeks could have such discrepant soldiers. The Spartans who spit blood and the Phokians who ran like deer. Not all the Phokians were cowards. A few had snuck past the Persian position and headed down the path to warn their Spartan allies of the impending attack.

When the Phokians arrived at the east gate, the Spartan guards quickly ushered them to Leonidas. It was still hours before daylight, but the Spartan king was already dressed for battle. When the Phokians were brought in, Leonidas instinctively knew why they were there.

"Tell me of the battle," Leonidas said to the two Phokians who stood in front of him.

"My name is Xyston, lord. I am from the city of Antikyra. I am not proud of what I am going to tell you."

Leonidas just stared at him with a contemptuous look on his face.

"Lord, my fellows did not put up much of a resistance. I anticipate that the Persians will be arriving a couple of hours before the sun reaches its zenith in the sky. I am sorry for this, lord. I will donate my life because of my shame."

"There is no need, Xyston, at least there is one Phokian with integrity."

The Phokian left the area, and Leonidas commented, *"Not a Peloponnesian. "*

Leonidas walked toward the men that were still half awake. When they saw the King of Sparta they all jumped to attention.

"My friends, our position has been betrayed and we will soon be hopelessly surround by the Persians. I now release you all from this defense."

He pointed to the Thespians, the Thebans and the Lokrians. In total they numbered almost 1400 hoplites.

"This position is no longer defensible. It is not in the Spartan way to retreat. You other men have all fought bravely and will again defend Greece in a future battle. We Spartans will stay and continue to punish the barbarians, assuring your retreat. Be brave my fellows. Remember how we stood in defense of our country. My fellows prepare, for tonight we dine with the Gods."

Over a thousand men bent to one knee in recognition of the bravery they were witnessing. Leonidas bowed and the Spartans stood pointing their swords at their King. The brothers, Maron and Alpheus, stood and yelled,

"To our King. To our life. To our city."

The Spartans in unison began chanting, "To our King, to our life, to our city." Even before the Spartan chanting stopped, the other contingents began retreating toward the east gate.

In hearing the news that Smerdomences and his Immortals would soon surround the Greek position, Xerxes almost jumped from his throne. He looked at his other generals and said, *"Prepare! For in a few hours we will take this pass. Prepare the troops"*

But as they began withdrawing, Xerxes yelled, *"I want Leonidas' head. Bring me his head."*

Smerdomences and his men were in position before midday. On the other side of the middle gate the Persian regulars were preparing to march on the Spartan position. To their surprise, around a bend came three hundred running Spartans. They would not stand and wait for death but would attack the Persian position. They took many of the soldiers unprepared for such an audacious move. In their front rode their King, Leonidas. With their shields locked in their phalanx, they ran directly at the Persians yelling, *"Sparta forever!"*

The three hundred engaged the enemy killing many of the first they encountered. But the waves of Persian kept coming. The Spartans fought off every advance. Leonidas, still on his mount, charged at the Persian position. He swung his sword, killing two soldiers near his steed. He turned his horse and rode back to the Spartan position. But on his way, an arrow pieced his shoulder. Leonidas showed no effect but looked back and growled at the enemy. When he reached his men, Dienekes smacked the horse on the rump and it ran down the path. One of his men reached Leonidas and put his hand on his back to help with the arrow.

"Stop," the King yelled. *"Leave it, it will give me strength."*

He faced the man with a smile.

"It is not time to beat the cauldrons yet. The King still walks."

To the left of Leonidas stood Maron and Alpheus to his right. Dienekes was at the front of the battle, cutting through Persians. A Persian archer ran forward and prepared to release. At the moment of release his knees were cut off by Dienekes' sword. But the arrow ran true and struck Leonidas in the left chest. He initially fell to one knee but rose again with a scream. More and more Persian soldiers arrived on the scene but the Spartans stood firm. The Persians realized that they could gain an advantage by chopping at the Spartan spears. They were ordered to ignore the men and attack the shields. Two Persians died for every broken spear, but the strategy was beginning to work. Smerdomences and the Immortals arrived on the scene and attacked the Greek right. Although their circle was shrinking, the Greek hoplites held firm. Every few minutes the Persian would separate a Greek from the Phalanx and the Spartan would engage three or four Persians, fighting to his death.

Again, Persian archers were called to the front, and arrows rained on the Spartan position. Another arrow struck Leonidas, this one in his thigh. His strength was beginning to wane. But he stood ever defiant. He marshaled his strength, began yelling, and hobbled toward the enemy position.

Dienekes yelled, *"Lord,"*

And followed the King into the fray. Three Persian died when another arrow struck the King. This one was directly in the center of his chest and was a killing blow. Leonidas fell to his knees and Dienekes passed him and engaged the archers. Tears rolled down Dienekes' eyes as he swung through the Persian. He knew by the fall that Leonidas, *the* son of King Anaxandridas II, and the 17th of the Agiad Line had gone to the Gods. In a moment of stillness, Dienekes smacked his forehead in mourning for his dead monarch. As Leonidas lay face down, Persians began dragging his body away. Maron and Alpheus rushed to the position, killing the Persians who were making the attempt. They pulled Leonidas back to the Greek position.

Knowing that Leonidas was a prize that would make them wealthy for life, the Persians continued to rush the corpse. Seven times the Persians dragged the body away and seven times the Greeks killed them and recaptured the body. But the Spartans were losing numbers and strength. Their spears were now all shattered, and many had multiple arrow wounds. Maron was the next to fall and when his brother knelt to grab him an arrow penetrated his neck. Both brothers had now joined their King in the land of the Gods

Dienekes stood with a band of eight other remaining Spartans. He looked at his brothers in arms and yelled, *"For valor."*

And the small group rushed the Persians. They cut their way through the first line, but were quickly overwhelmed. Dienekes was the last to fall. He stood bravely amid his fallen brothers with numerous arrows protruding from his legs and torso. Before he died, he had fallen to his knees. He had lost his sword and was preparing to defend himself with his one arm that was still in use. A Persian approached from the front and Dienekes spit at him. The Persian looked stunned at the audacity. But as he did, three swords entered Dienekes back and the man died on the spot.

Now they were all gone. Three hundred Spartans and at least twice as many Persians lay dead on the narrow Thermopylae pass. In three days, almost 20,000 Persians had died attempting to breach the Greek position. The stench of decaying bodies filled the air.

Smerdomences looked down at the fallen warriors. He was still breathing heavily from the interchange. He surveyed the now soundless scene and was too stunned into silence. He raised no sword, gave no yell of triumph. There was no immediate excitement at victory, just an overwhelming sense of emptiness. He felt no sense of gallantry or heroism as he thought he would after such a victory. He looked out over the narrow field. Body parts and blood covered the entire width of the path. His troops were ordered to mercilessly kill any wounded soldiers from either side. The instructions were explicit.

"These are brave men. End their life with honor."

He stared south. They had broken through the defense. Southern Greece was now unprotected and the road to Athens itself would be undefended laying open to their advance. Smerdomences knew that the carnage had not ended. It had just begun.

****

Themistocles and his Spartan counterpart, Eurybiadas, sat with each other contemplating what had happened and what was to follow. By incoming accounts, they had defeated the Persian navy, if the judgment centered around loss. The Persians had lost substantially more vessels than they had, yet they could ill afford the cost of the ships. After inspecting the damage, they were both buoyed by the lack of serious injury to their marred vessels. They did have to cannibalize five ships to repair the others, but the majority could be sailed. In unison they decided to walk again to the beach and see how the repairs were proceeding. A Spartan soldier approached them and bowed.

"I have news and it is not good."

Themistocles held up his hand silencing the soldier. He looked at Eurybiadas with a dejected expression. He patted the Spartan on the back then looked back at the soldier, standing dumbfounded.

"Speak man," the Athenian politician demanded in a quiet voice.

"Thermopylae has fallen."

"And the King?"

Eurybiadas asked. The man bowed his head but said nothing. The gesture was self-explanatory. After a moment the man raised his head and said, *"They are all gone, lord. There were no survivors."*

He bowed again and backed away. The Spartan looked stunned and Themistocles stared out into the bay.

"A sad day for Sparta, and a sad day for Greece."

Both men stood in silence. They both slapped their foreheads, the traditional mourning ceremony when a Spartan King had died. As they walked down the beach few words were said between them. There was little to say. The implications, beyond the death of a hero, were devastating. The irrational hope was that they could stall and possibly defeat the Persian at these two positions. Neither the pass at Thermopylae or the strait at Artemisium had served that purpose. By sheer numbers the Persians had broken both.

As his mind raced between sadness and reality, Themistocles realized certain terrifying facts. The fleet must withdraw and lick their wounds. They could not confront the Persians here again, but needed a more suitable arena. And, that withdrawal needed to happen quickly before the Persian King realized he could destroy the entire fleet with an aggressive attack. He stopped and ordered the men to prepare for the withdrawal. But Leonidas was dead. Themistocles felt a genuine pain in his heart. He could not distinguish between his fear and disappointment for Athens and Greece for his anguish for a man that he admired, and in some ways, loved. Leonidas was the bravest man he had ever known. His devotion to his people and their way of life was overwhelming to Themistocles. Themistocles knew he was a weak man. Drinking, carousing was part of him. He couldn't identify with the discipline that the King knew. When he was alone, the great Greek politician sat down on a piece of dead wood and cried.

Themistocles knew the truth was more chilling then just a naval withdrawal. Because of the fall of Thermopylae, Athens was now undefended. On his advice his beloved city had risked almost the entire male population to the navy. Only a few priests and a few older citizens remained to defend the city. The navy now seemed like a foolish and stupid strategic move. Themistocles had no doubt that the Persian King would burn the city to the ground. Themistocles also knew Spartans would not defend Athens, but would retreat to their isthmus and meet the Persians from behind a wooden wall. There would be no rescue from the Peloponnese. Having thrown everything into the navy, it would be up to what was left of Athens to engage and beat the Persians in a future battle.

Themistocles' mind flashed to the prognostications of the Delphic Oracle. It predicted Leonidas' death:

Your fate, O inhabitants of the broad fields of Sparta

Is to see your great and famous city destroyed by the sons of Perseus

Either that, or everyone with the borders of Lacedaemon

Must mourn the death of a King, sprung from the line of Heracles.

He shivered at the recollection. His mind then shifted to the prediction for Athens

This word I give you, adamant, a promise:

Everything within the borders of Attica shall fall

But the wooden wall alone, the wooden wall shall stand.

Men on horses, men on foot, sweeping they come from Asia

Divine Salamis- you will be the ruin of many a mother's son.

He stood again silent and contemplated. The wooden wall was not the wall the Spartans were building along their Peninsula. Themistocles was still convinced it was his ships. He was now more convinced than ever that his interpretation was correct. The city of Athens had to be sacrificed for the Demos, for the greater good.

Divine Salamis, that is where we will make our stand! He stopped and yelled out

"Prepare, we leave quickly. We will retreat to Salamis!"

"It is there we will make our stand," he thought. He looked up at the heavens, *"Athena, your city cries for your help."*

****

Stoically, the King of Kings sat on his golden throne. It was in a beautiful ancient cathedral handed down to him by his father, Darius. On its back were two golden unicorns with their long horns making an arch over the King's head. Their horns seemed to shine, looking like pearls in the sea. Xerxes sat in his red military outfit. His robe was a bright scarlet with a slightly lighter cape. In his left hand was a golden challis and, in his right, the magic Answerer, given to him by his mystic stepmother. The tent was quiet, and even the lioness Simeron was snoozing in the corner.

Without warning his wife Vashti entered in an unusually vile mood.

"I have no water and the food is making my stomach sick," she whined, as she marched herself toward the throne. She was indignant and had a self-righteous air about her. Her beautiful face was distorted in protest and she stomped her way across the tent.

"This is too much, too much. A Queen should not have to put up with this."

Xerxes sat still. His head slowly moved from side to side following her movement. His expression was unreadable. Finally, Vashti stopped in front of him and waved her veil. Although he sat motionless, his hands tightened on his throne.

"I wish to be sent home. These conditions do not suit me. You are my husband. First I must suffer the embarrassment of you bedding that Jewish slut, now these unspeakable conditions."

Vashti put her hands on her hips waiting for a response from her husband. But surprisingly none came. Xerxes sat staring into the distance, almost ignoring her presence. Vashti moved, trying to get in the King's field of vision. Again, she stomped.

"Do you hear me? Have you become deaf in this horrible land?"

Finally, the King rose. It was a measured movement, almost as if he was concerned about losing his balance. Instinctively the queen took a step backwards, not knowing the type of reaction her husband would show to her rage. Vashti was quite impulsive, rarely considering consequences before actions. It was a dangerous game to press this King. But in this instance The King of Kings, appeared almost over controlled. He stepped up to his wife.

"Control yourself, wife. You suffer only mild inconveniences."

"Mild inconveniences!"

Vashti protested, figuring she had picked the right time to tantrum. Seizing the moment, again Vashti stepped toward her husband. Xerxes turned to walk away, but Vashti followed and pushed him in the back. Xerxes turned, but now his face was bright red bordering on rage. The queen immediately realized that she had overplayed her hand. The King grabbed Vashti by the neck and lifted her off the ground. She began choking but didn't offer resistance. Xerxes brought her face to his.

"20,000 men have died over a two-mile pass. We mourn for their souls. But you are inconvenienced."

With a flick of his arm, Xerxes threw his wife across the room. She lye choking, as she looked and saw two black boots by her face. She raised her gaze and saw Artemisia the Warrior staring down at her.

"Ah, a real woman," Xerxes snorted, as he headed back to his throne. Vashti seemed to crawl out of the tent, with Artemisia watching her leave. She turned to Xerxes and said,

"Tell me, my King, does her beauty outweigh her temperament," *Again* the King snorted. Artemisia strode toward the throne. She stopped short and glanced back at Xerxes. Then, by surprise, she stepped up and sat in the chair. Her black outfit appeared to make the gold of the chair more luminescent. She crossed her leg and appeared content in her position.

"Stop mocking me!" Xerxes roared.

"Mocking, no, I haven't started that yet."

Xerxes looked frustrated as the Queen gloated.

"Did you come to boast?"

Xerxes said with a smirk.

"Not gloat, I came to lecture."

The Queen said rising off of the throne.

"Lecture?" Xerxes said in surprise.

"Our opportunity has passed!"

Artemisia responded. She now took a step towards the King.

"Did I not tell you that we must pursue the half beaten Greek navy? They were injured and we could have destroyed them."

"In the dark?"

Xerxes questioned, now paying attention.

"Yes, in the dark! But it is now too late, they have fled."

"Fled?" The King questioned.

"My scout ships report that their position is abandoned. They head south. The day will come when you will heed my warnings. We will now have to waste more ships and soldiers chasing them down the coast."

Xerxes looked irritated at the stern but insightful comment. Quiet followed, which was interrupted by a slave. "Lord, the general, Smerdomences, is waiting for an audience." The King waved his hand suggesting that he should be shown in. The General entered carrying a bag. He blew the King a kiss then bowed to his knee. Smerdomences then drew his sword and placed it under his own neck. Behind Xerxes Artemisia rolled her eyes at the show. Xerxes looked at his friend and gestured for him to rise.

"I have a present for you, Lord."

Smerdomences opened the bag and lifted out the head of the Spartan king, Leonidas.

The great King rose slowly at the sight. His eyes were focused on this morbid sight. Blood still dripped from the Spartan's eyes and neck. The general stood still having a confused look on his face. He expected a different response from his friend. Xerxes took two steps forward, attention absorbed on the head that dangled in from of him. There was no expression of satisfaction, just a distant gaze as the King seemed to drift away. He stood motionless for a few seconds then turned away from his general. Xerxes walked slowly to the other side of the tent. Smerdomences dropped to the ground figuring that in some way the King was disappointed in him. Xerxes ignored his friend, staring out of the back of the large tent. On his knees, Smerdomences backed out of the royal tent. Xerxes stood alone in his tent for most of the day. The head lay on the floor, but now the King ignored its presence.

The man who ruled the largest Empire on the planet, looked back at the 'thing' lying on the floor. He thought, "so this is what revenge feels like"

Xerxes called back the slave.

"Place this head on a staff. I want our entire army to view it as we ride through the pass at Thermopylae. Word will spread about the consequences for opposing the King of Kings. I want all the Greeks to tremble, for their fate is sealed, they will burn. I swear it."

****

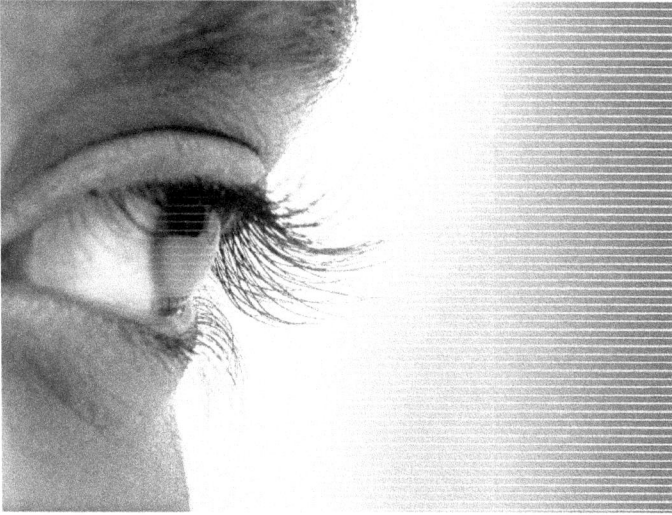

Chapter XVIII – Diaspora

Eudoxia was rushing. She was usually a quiet, almost compulsive woman, who took things slowly and deliberately. But today was a day for haste. Her children, Nikon and Zoe were both dressed and standing by the door. They shivered, not with cold but with freight. Neither had ever seen their mother in such a frantic state. Zoe was six and did not quite comprehend what was happening. She stood by the front door holding her puppy with her sack of clothes lying next to her on the ground. Her face was blank, yet her eyes were red and swollen. Nikon was the oldest. Although just 10, he was trying very hard to be brave. He watched his mother run from room to room with dizzying speed. He sympathetically placed his hand on his sister's head as she began silently weeping. With a questioning glance Zoe looked up at her brother and his eyes were tear swollen as well. She held her puppy firmly to her chest.

Zoe had been told that the dog could not come with the family. There was no room and no animals would be allowed on the boats. But she was determined in her resolute manner to stand firm. Nikon understood her pain. He had also developed a fondness for the animal. Mother kept running between rooms. Neither child knew what she was doing. At one point she stopped and looked at the children.

"Your father would be proud of both of you."

Eudoxia took a step toward Zoe.

"My love," she said with general sympathy.

"I know how much you love Yalu. But you know he cannot join us. No animals will we allowed on the boats."

Zoe stomped her foot.

"Then I will stay. I will stay with him here. He needs me. He will die without me, mother!"

Eudoxia put her hand over her heart, understanding the emotional pain that her young child was experiencing. She tried to be firm, putting her hand on her child.

"Put Yalu in the back. He will join the other dogs being left behind and they will form their own family."

Eudoxia went back into the bedroom. Zoe did not believe a word of what she heard, and she would not let go of Yalu. Nikon looked down again at his sister. He reached for his satchel and rummaged through it, taking out his special box. He took the box and walked across the room, dumping its contents in the corner behind a small table. He took a small tool from the table and began banging on the top of his box. It was a special keepsake of Nikon's. The box had been given to him by his grandfather, but he stood and continued to pound on the top until a hole appeared.

Nikon walked back to Zoe.

"Give me Yalu," he said in a demanding voice.

"Please, Nikon, please don't put him out back."

Nikon took the dog from his sister as she let out a cry of desperation. He walked to the back as Eudoxia watched out of the corner of her eye. Nikon returned with the box and put it back in his satchel. Zoe didn't quite understand and the tears flowed down her cheeks without stop. Nikon came to his sister and winked. Eudoxia appeared.

"We are ready. Where is Yalu?"

Nikon answered, *"He is in the back mother, I put him there myself."*

Eudoxia walked past her children out of the front door. Zoe and Nikon followed. Eudoxia had a big sack on her right shoulder and a larger one on her left. The children picked up their own satchels and followed. Eudoxia stopped and turned looking at their small house. Zoe asked a question she had been repeatedly asking.

"Where are we going, mother?"

Again, Eudoxia looked with compassion at her daughter.

"I don't know where we are going, my children. I only know that we cannot stay here, for the Persians are coming to burn our city."

"Why mother, why must they come?"

"I don't know love, I don't know."

Nikon asked, *"If we leave here, mother, how will father find us when he returns from the war?"*

"Father will find us. He always has."

Now it was Eudoxia's time to silently cry. Everything in her told her that Sosigenes would never return. But she could not let her fears and worries bother her children. The three began walking to the docks.

Paramonos oversaw the loading area. He counted the people and made sure that no contraband was brought on the journey. People brought many keepsakes to the loading area, none of which would be allowed on the boats. All valuables would need to be searched. As part of the evacuation, all precious metals had to be confiscated to help to pay for the navy. A big ditch had been dug and anything was deemed too bulky or unnecessary was thrown into the pit and burned. Domestic animals were not allowed either. Other transport ships were being arranged for sheep and cattle. The entire population of Athens had to be evacuated.

There was general panic amongst the populace. The rumor about the fall of Thermopylae and Artemisium had spread like wildfire. Hoplites stood by the docks. Their purpose was to quell outbreaks of panic. A story had spread through the public about the Acropolis and its existence added to the sense of alarm. It was always accepted that a great snake dwelled in the Acropolis as its protector. The snake had been positioned there by Athena herself. The priests of the temple would put out honey cake for the snake to feed. The cakes always disappeared fueling the belief that the snake partook of the bounty. But after Thermopylae, there was an unexpected change. All of a sudden, the cakes were offered but none were eaten. This ominous portent powered the belief that Athena had already abandoned her city.

Paramonos had a horrible job. An entire city, many of whom lived in this area since the beginning of remembrance were leaving, heading into the unknown. Everything they had planned for and built was now ending. People stood in a flood of tears as they waited for their turn to enter the ships.

A smallish heavyset woman approached Paramonos. She was clearly agitated. She walked up to him and shoved.

"Why?" she yelled.

"Why, are we being forced to abandon our lives?"

Paramonos had no answers left. He had been asked this question a thousand times this day and he had run out of explanation.

"What is your name, woman?"

She was snorting like an angry swine.

"My name is Phile and I have a mind to spit on you and return to my home."

"That is your choice, Phile. If that is what you choose, step out of the way and let another pass."

This quieted the woman and she went back to her place to board the boat.

****

The Goddess was beside herself. Her people were crying and her city was being evacuated. The future was already written and she could only have limited influence. She hated this feeling, this helplessness. Athena had never felt weakness or frailty before. In the millennium that proceeded this time, the Goddess had always been in control, at least partial control. For all intents and purposes, Zeus had already abandoned his power. He had turned into a sulking, withdrawn old man. All the power he wielded was now oozing from his bones, never to be regained. Their time as deities was ending and Athena knew it. And now her people were being destroyed. They would melt into other cities and countries, no longer being pure bred Athenians.

Bubo sat on her shoulder making strange grumbling noises.

"I know our time is limited, my friend. But you are right, my dear. I must help my people. I have loved them for such a long time that I cannot let this pass without my presence."

The people were crowded into the small boarding areas. Small families stood in line, as most of the male population had left joining the navy. There were those expressing anger at the current dilemma, some blaming fate and some blaming Themistocles. Then there were those looking lost, just staring out into the bay. There were many breaking down, watching everything they knew disappearing, heading into a new life and starting with nothing. The general feeling among the crowd was that the decision to take all the men into the navy was misplaced and foolish. Most believed that if the men were still in the city they could resist the Persian invasion. Themistocles believed that this was just a pipe dream. He believed that if they stayed, their fate would be much more troubling, as they would all end up in slavery in some distant land.

Pelegia stood on the side of the crowd very close to the water. A year previous, Pelegia lost her mother to sickness. Her brothers and her father were all on boats. She had not heard from them in weeks. Pelegia tried to determine what to take from their modest house, but she could only carry a certain number of things. Her mind continuously raced through her now abandoned house, wondering whether she had made the correct choices. She tried to stop the worrying, but her mind needed something to focus on rather than fear. Out of the corner of her eye she saw a friend, Syntyche. Although not a close friend, she knew somebody amongst this sea of faces. She walked over to her friend and touched her shoulder. The young woman jumped in surprise.

"Pelegia, I'm so glad to see you!"

The two-woman hugged. Both held onto each other as if their lives depended on it. It gave them each a comfort being close to a familiar face. Neither woman wanted to let go of the other, so they held on as if sisters and returned to their position on line. After taking a few steps both young women simultaneously began sobbing. Pelegia looked at Syntyche and said,

"I'm sorry, Syntyche. I feel like we're doomed. I don't want to die."

Syntyche had no reply but both began crying again. Behind them, an older woman appeared. She was taller than the two girls with long white hair. Neither girl knew this woman but her touch helped. Syntyche looked at her and noticed her bright green eyes. They seemed to shine even though her expression was blank and did not betray her thoughts. Both younger women stood speechless and stared at the older woman.

"My name is Anthousa. Why do you cry?"

"We are scared," Pelegia babbled.

"Scared, ladies? Why, you are Athenians. You should be proud."

"Proud?"

Syntyche questioned.

"We stand here waiting to board boats to leave our homeland. We might never return. There is rumor that everything we know will burn when the Persian army arrives."

"It is true, and very likely that will happen," Anthousa said.

"But remember, my children, everything has a price and freedom is the costliest of gifts. Be proud you are trading things for ideas. I promise that your new life will hold wonders that you cannot yet understand. Challenges, yes, but wonders nonetheless."

Then, by surprise, Anthousas eyes began to shine. The glow seemed to envelope the two young women. Heat flowed through their bodies. But it was more than just warmth; there was a new-found sense of vitality invigorating each cell in their muscles. Fear seemed to flow out of their bodies, down their limbs and into the ground. The fear was replaced by a new sense of strength, dedication, and resolve. Anthousa raised her arms and the glow passed over the people who were standing on the beach. It seemed to hang over the people and then disperse downward.

Eudocia and her children had reached the embarkation point. Paramonos looked at the trio and put his arm out asking to see the bags that they carried. Nikon hesitated, knowing the contraband that he carried in his special box. But as he reached for the satchel another arm grabbed his elbow. Anthousas stood behind Paramonos and the man looked strangely at the older woman. She leaned forward and whispered something into Paramonos' ear. The man looked strangely at her, staring into her eyes. Without changing his gaze, Paramonos said,

"You may pass."

Anthousas smiled and placed her hand on Paramonos' forehead.

"You have done well, my child"

****

His scouts had reported back that the road through Elatea was clear.

"And beyond?" Xerxes inquired. The scout bowed and continued his report.

"Past Elatea the road is straight to Thebes. From there it is almost a direct route to Athens itself. From everything we can ascertain, the Greeks have no standing army to offer resistance along this route. It is reported that the Greek navy is south of Athens at Piraeus, evacuating

citizens. They are being taken to the city of Troezen and the island of Salamis. The Spartans have not left the Peloponnese. They are building a wall across the Isthmus of Corinth to battle us at that point."

Xerxes dismissed the scout and turned to his assembled generals and admirals. Mardonius was the first to speak.

"Lord, once we defeat the remaining Athenian Triremes, the Spartans will be easy pickings. We will sail around the Saronic gulf and land troops behind their position."

"An adequate plan," Xerxes commented, not really appearing impressed. After a silent minute the Great King said: *"But these Greeks are tricky. I worry about the next surprise they have for us."*

Zephan, the admiral who Xerxes felt was responsible for the stalemate at Artemesium spoke next.

"Lord, our navy can sail to Piraeus and cut off their evacuation plans."

"No, No," Xerxes commented.

"Let them be. We are not here to butcher people. Let them have the illusion that they can escape. We need a few days rest to enjoy our victories."

The generals laughed and heads nodded. Smerdomences stepped forward and bowed in reverence.

"Lord, I understand that the temple at Delphi holds vast riches beyond what we can imagine. I would like to take my men and liberate it in the name of the Empire."

"You have no fear of their Gods?"

Xerxes asked. Smerdomences laughed, *"Their Gods have abandoned them. They hide in their Mount Olympus behind their clouds."*

"What about the storms that ravished our navy? On two occasions?"

"Nature, Lord, nothing but nature."

"Nature you say," The King of Kings commented. *"Do not be overconfident. Our victory at Thermopylae cost many brave men."*

The young King paced in obvious thought. *"But I am not opposed to replenishing our coffers with Greek gold. When we reach the town of Parapotamii, you can take your army to Delphi."*

"Its riches will raise you higher, my Lord"

"I hope you are right, Smerdomences. I hope you are right."

****

Two priests and three priestesses rustled through the temple. Outside, men were building a wooden wall to surround the temple. Some of the priests and priestesses had decided to evacuate with the populace, but the most conservative of the priesthood believed that the Goddess Athena would protect them against the advancing Persians. The remaining five devout leaders of the temple spent all their time together. Since the others had left, there was barely a time when any of them was alone. Although their faith was unflinching, this crisis had left them scared. Besides this hastily constructed wooden wall, the five were unprotected. A very small garrison of hoplites remained to guard the wall. Throughout their adult lives, these religious leaders had enjoyed positions of authority and respect within the city of Athens. They were untouchable, as their conduct was beyond reproach. But now, all their protection, all their standing, had vanished overnight. The people were leaving their homes, leaving their city, leaving their Gods, and the priests were dejected at the prospect. What would happen to the Gods if all the people abandoned their beliefs?

Damianos was the head priest of the temple of Athena within the Acropolis. He now prayed upwards of four hours a day, urging the green-eyed Goddess to rescue their city. He went so far as to remind the deity about the years of prayer and commitment. Everything he believed in, everything he lived every day for, was now teetering on the brink of oblivion. And Damianos knew why. Ever since the populace became seduced by this Demos, they had been forgetting about their loyalty to the Gods. This new form of government, taking the power away from the people who were trained to govern and placing faith in the farmers and tradesmen, had transformed the populace into questioners. Yes, the people still prayed, still made sacrifices to the deities, but Damianos knew that their enthusiasm had waned. They now prayed because they were trained to, not because they loved their Gods. For centuries their passion focused on pleasing the Gods. Now their time was spent in argument about laws, amendments, and constitutions. What was worse was that this Demos lead to disagreement and hesitation. Damianos considered this more than a waste of time. He thought it bordered on blasphemy. And what had it gotten them. It has gotten them deported to another city. Their beautiful city, which gave life to their fathers and their fathers, now became a slave to the desires of the masses. Their city was dedicated to the green-eyed Goddess, Athena, and now this piety had been lost. Damianos was emotionally and spiritually sick. When he prayed, he cried not for his life, which he reflected might be sacrificed when the Persians arrived, but for the loss of faith. The eyes of the people had lost their focus. No longer could the people's internal strength be rooted in the devotion to the Gods. This métier now had to come from some changeable concept of equality. Their souls had been sacrificed to their thought and misguided logic. Imagine believing in your own ill-advised thoughts, rather than follow what the Gods thought. He considered it a black day.

On this night, Damianos was preparing for an ancient ceremony. He was a pharnakos. The ceremony would expel the bad spirits that had taken over the city. Damianos was surprised at the number of people that remained behind in the city after the evacuation. He found it interesting that many were influential or wealthy people. He assumed that they were very reluctant to give up their wealth and status. He had realized that most of them were planning to attend the evening ceremony to pray to their patron deity for protection. While he prepared, all the people at the temple as well as the small garrison left behind, continued to build this 'wooden wall' around the Acropolis, believing somehow that they could stop the incoming Persian horde.

The table was set. Many domestic animals were left behind during the evacuation. If nothing else this small group of people would eat well in the next few days. Damianos had sent the priestesses out to gather the special herbs and mushrooms to make the potions that would be used in their prayers.

The remaining Athenians had sent a desperate message to Sparta, pleading for support. But the message had returned that the Spartans could not, and would not, send relief. They replied that their 30,000 ground troops had to remain on the Isthmus; Attica would just have to defend themselves.

"Betrayal, just betrayal" a farmer shouted.

"We sent our navy to Artemisium to defend all of Greece and the Spartans have refused to help us."

But through all their complaints they knew that no help would be coming. They would have to defend themselves. The special mixture of drink was consumed by everyone present. Damianos knew that most of the remaining people needed an escape and the hallucinatory mixture would serve that purpose. The priestesses began rousing the parishioners. They danced and shouted until most of the people were in a religious frenzy. Darkness had set on the Acropolis and the remaining Athenians were dancing and shouting. It was an eerie sight as the flames from the fires made the dancing appear surreal. Flickering images, changing colors, spreading their shadows on the majestic columns of the great structure. As the drink took its hold, each person began fading into their own world of images and symbols. Some of the men began stripping their clothes off as they yelled and danced without inhibition.

Suddenly a low grumbling sound seemed to vibrate through the air itself. It knocked over some, but gained the attention of all. And then a stillness settled and the fires began rising, encircling the area. The laughing stopped and crying began as the people dropped to their knees in reverence. Three men grabbed their chests and began screaming as they fell to the ground. Blood began flowing from all parts of their bodies as the life drained from them. People watched in shock as their screaming turned to gagging, then silence and then death. And then when all focus was on the bodies disintegrating in front of them, a woman appeared in the background. She raised her arms and the fire came to her like a child returning to her parent. She seemed to ingest the flames as she rose above the assembled parishioners. Her green eyes blazed through the vapor and the haze. She seemed to float over the assembly, as people turned their heads trying not to look her in the burning eyes. She stopped at certain people, placing her hands on their heads. As she did, their souls were released from their bodies, and merged with the air.

"Only I know the future. Only I know who you are. Soon you will all return home. My children, rise off your knees and face me."

The gathered men and woman all rose and shakily began walking to this peculiarity. None were quite sure what they were seeing, or whether it was the drink that had them hallucinating. As they closed on her, the aberration that was Athena raised her arms and the people were enveloped in a green mist that originated from her eyes. Many of their heads fell backwards as if they were going to faint, but none did. Some teetered, but almost floated a few inches from the ground. The fire encased the Goddess, encircling her entire body with flames. As the priests, priestesses, and parishioners gathered around the Goddess, one could almost see tears in her green eyes. She began to speak in a low ominous tone:

"My love for you is endless. The fall of your lives is upon you, so you must prepare to return home. No longer will the grass grow green. Do not mourn when the temple is razed. Both tears and blood will stain the ground. You are brave and devoted, but your reward will be returning to your master. No reward can be greater than losing your life in this service. Smile, my children, for I am here with you. Do not be afraid, my children, for your reward waits with me. I am all life, and you will return to my spirit."

She touched a few more people and their essence left the body through the Goddess's hands and floated upward. Their bodies fell lifeless to the floor as their souls left the earth. With every soul, Athena shook as if organismic. She held her arms to her chest and her ephemeral body seemed to fragment into many directions.

As she began disintegrating, the remaining Athenians heard a voice fading in the sky.

"I cannot, nor do I want to save the city. It will be reborn and achieve even greater glory. Life needs to die to live. Gods need to die to live. I will return, but my form will be changed from what you have known. I will become much more powerful once you merge with me. I will shield you from pain and from want. You will see as you have never seen, feel as you have never felt, and know the answers to all

*unanswered questions. Be strong, my children. You have been chosen
for this sacrifice. Rhapsody has arrived."*

****

It had become a cult following. The priest, Ningizzida, was now
one of the oldest living men. He rarely left his room, but even in his
infirmity, he wielded great power over the religious communities of
Babylonia, Assyria, Mesopotamia and the surrounding provinces.
Stories and myths about the priest's inhuman powers fueled his
following. The legend told of powers that rose above the earth
embraced by a light from above was only one of a thousand stories. It
was told that Ningizzida held the ability to control others and effect
rulers and governments just by his thoughts. It was believed that
Ningizzida rarely slept, but would spend the dark hours traveling into
the souls of others.

For years Ningizzida had been sought as an outlaw by the Persian
King of Kings. The priest had been a confidant of Xerxes' father,
Darius. But Ningizzida never trusted Darius' son, Xerxes. He
considered him vain, self-serving and narcissistic. Before Xerxes
became King, he and Ningizzida had had confrontations when Xerxes
was Viceroy in Babylonia. Xerxes had refused to bow to the religious
leader. Immediately after his inauguration, after his father's death,
Xerxes went to Babylonia to perform a religious ceremony. At that
ceremony, Ningizzida had surprised the young King. The ceremony
called for a symbolic beating of the King to show that even a King
bowed to the God. But Ningizzida was not symbolic; he knocked the
young King unconscious in front of all the parishioners. From that
time, Ningizzida was a wanted man. Xerxes had captured the priest,
but Ningizzida miraculously escaped from the dungeon in the bowels
of the palace at Susa. Xerxes again sent his men in search of the
renegade. At this point, Xerxes did not know if Ningizzida was alive
or dead. He had heard that the priest had died in a house fire, but the

260 · JEFFREY DONNER

King was unconvinced. Every bone in his body told him that the man
still lived. His hatred had built exponentially by the day.

Ningizzida was trained by the legendary priest, Baldigul-El, at the
Kossara Monetary. Although he was able to read the seven tablets of
creation and the Enuma Elish, Ningizzida's specialty was reading the
smoke from the spiritual candles. His forecasts were remarkably
reliable. It was not a trick, it was a true gift. Only the famous Delphic
Oracle was more accurate in its prognostic ability. Nobles and Kings
traveled as far away as Egypt to the east, and India to the west, to
listen to the prognostications of the Babylonian mystic.

Simicus was considered mad by most of the priesthood and the
religious community in general. He spent many hours in isolation in
the mountains fasting and praying. He used isolation, fasting, potions,
and hallucinatory formulas to reach religious heights. One morning he
was visited in his cave by two men claiming to be emissaries from the
great priest, Ningizzida. Simicus was very suspicious of this offer, as
he had never personally met the godlike priest and he couldn't fathom
why all of a sudden, he would be contacted. He instinctively knew it
was not because of his religious zeal.

When he arrived at the out of the way location where Ningizzida
was hiding, he found the famous old man laying covered up in the
corner of a back room. He looked more vulnerable than omnipotent.
Simicus was told by acolytes that the famous priest was close to death.
He seemed to go in and out of consciousness, at times talking in
ancient languages, saying things nobody in the room could
understand. Then there were times when Ningizzida seemed to switch
into reality. During one of those times, Simicus was called to his
bedside. The old priest was completely encased in robes. His face was
barely visible. But even in this state, Ningizzida's eyes shined like
stars. Simicus walked to the bed and sat on the floor by the great man.
He bowed his head and waited for the legendary priest to respond.

Finally Ningizzida spoke in a quiet, gravelly voice, *"What is your name, monk?"*

"Simicus, Khuda"

"Simicus, I have heard of your reputation."

"I am honored, Khuda"

Ningizzida had been referred to as Khuda many times before.

"Simicus, come closer. I have much to tell you."

The two religious men sat and spoke for hours. The next day the acolytes entered the room to find both men sleeping next to each other. Finally Simicus rose and looked at the younger men.

"The Persian army is marching from Susa. When will they arrive near Babylonia?"

One of the younger priests said, *"In two days, the beginnings of the army will arrive. It will take three weeks for the entire army to pass."*

Simicus smiled and turned away. A week and a half later Simicus joined the march out of Persia to Greece. Trailing the army were over 300,000 civilians who provided many services for the soldiers and sailors. Servants, cooks, merchants, priests, builders, weavers, bakers, and whores all followed the army on its march. One more man in this multitude of people was not recognized or even paid attention to. Simicus followed the army over the Hellespont and through northern Greece. By the time the army had reached the Thermopylae pass, Simicus had established quite an extensive following. Many times both noblemen and army brass called him in for guidance. So over time, his reputation led to a certain amount of trust from the guards.

The time had arrived for Simicus. The King was jubilant over the defeat of the Spartans and he reasoned that the security would be slackened because of the King's first real victory in this great quest.

He was right. There was a lot of drinking and dancing in the Persian camp. Simicus entered the camp with little trouble. In the dark, he slowly made his way past many checkpoints. Most of the guards knew him and had no second thoughts about letting pass. He walked closer and closer to the great King's tent. The resistance was surprisingly absent, and much less than the priest anticipated. As he walked, he found himself looking around more than he liked. He did not want to appear anxious, even though he was a little unsteady. Then suddenly the gold tent appeared. Simicus stopped for a second both surprised he had made it this far and a little stunned at the same time. Simicus turned and two armed guards were standing within breathing distance. A spear was already in the priest's chest.

"And who are you?" the guard scowled. His voice shook a little, but Simicus sputtered out.

"My name is Simicus"

The guard did not seem to recognize this, so Simicus said, *I am known as, The Monk*

The second guard smiled and said to his compatriot, *"It is ok, this man has been here before."*

The first guard did not budge. His lance remained on the priest's throat. Simicus boldly took his hand and moved the lance away from his neck. He stared at the guard and said, *"I am here to see the King. I would advise that you let me pass."*

The guard was not intimidated. He retorted, *"Wait here, Monk."*

The guard disappeared. The second guard stood silently watching the monk. Finally, the first guard reappeared, *"The great King will give you an audience, Monk."*

Simicus was a little surprised at the response, but considered that God or Ningizzida had taken a hand. He silently prayed and gave thanks. He followed the guard into the royal tent. As he walked, Simicus was slightly intimidated that he would soon be standing in front of the great King. When he entered the tent, Xerxes was prone on a bed. The Great King did not move as the priest approached. Simicus trembled as he walked, although he attempted to maintain composure. Simicus bowed when he got closer to Xerxes. There were two guards flanking the great King. Simicus knew that making any attempt on Xerxes' life would not be successful. In the blink of an eye, Simicus' strategy now changed. He swallowed deeply,

"Lord, I am here to bless your army."

The King looked disgusted. *"What makes you think priest, that I need, or want your blessing."*

Xerxes stared into space. He knew that people rarely came just to give him something. Everybody wanted something, so why did this priest come now. What was the real agenda? Xerxes raised his hand and Golnar, the Lector priestess appeared from the shadows. She approached Simicus. She looked the priest up and down and appeared unimpressed with what she saw. She walked past the priest with a sneer on her face. She came around Simicus and was face to face with him.

"I have heard of you, priest. Are you not from the heavenly city of Babylonia?"

Simicus stared into the void of Golnar's eyes.

"I grew up as a child in Babylonia."

"So,"

Golnar hummed, *"You must know the priest called Ningizzida!"*

The question made Simicus very uneasy. What did she know? Can she read my thoughts? He redoubled his effort at his own mind control.

"I know of him."

The great King moved slightly at the comment. His eyes betrayed some surprise. Without realizing it, Simicus had confirmed for the King that the renegade priest was still alive. Xerxes moved his head and two guards grabbed Simicus and held him tightly. He slowly rose from his bed and clutched his sword. He walked to Simicus and smiled as he reached him.

"You and I have a problem, priest. Before this night ends, you will tell me where I can find Ningizzida. Look closely at the floor priest, it will soon be red with your blood."

****

Chapter XIX – Old Men and Dogs

Themistocles was drunk. Although he stumbled and was slurring his words, he was still conscious. Even in this state, his Metis was still obvious. The Metis was a mystical ability that some claimed was given to mortals by the Gods. Odysseus had such a skill given to him by the Goddess Athena. He used it throughout the Trojan war, eventually utilizing it for the legendary empty horse. Themistocles believed that sometimes he needed wine to release his intuition. Of course, this was just his rationalization for his habit. And a habit it was. Themistocles struggled with his dependence. It was strange to him that during battle his desire evaporated like smoke, whereas during decision making periods when he needed all his Metis to make decisions, his need for wine grew exponentially. This was one of those times. Also, unbeknownst to anyone, the Greek politician also suffered from ongoing but intermittent depression. Although he believed he was able to anticipate the future, this skill also brought horrible insight into what he foresaw.

Themistocles had just stood on a shore and watched the evacuation of his beloved city. Tears rolled down his cheeks with the realization that all this was his doing. He did not feel like he could face any of his friends. The destruction of centuries of building and generation after generation of peoples who called this their home. And now it was disappearing. He worried that the multitude of ancestors were sitting with the Gods screaming their disgust over this strategy. And yet all of his senses, all of his logic, all of his prayers, had pointed to the efficacy of this decision. Athens was doomed. But it would burn with or without its peoples. He had once believed that the city and its beauty outweighed all else. But he came to realize that without the people there was no Demos. No growing democracy. This belief of the Demos could transfer to any place, it did not need the temples or the Pantheon. It needed the people. With every person who stepped off the soil of their ancestors and onto the Triremes, another tear fell off the great man's face.

But there was more, much more. Themistocles didn't have any illusions that Leonidas could fight the Persian to a standstill. The Spartan monarch also did not have any illusions about the conclusion of the battle. The odds were too great. Leonidas sacrificed himself for the good of Greece. But Themistocles did not believe that the Spartan would only be able to hold the Persian for three days. It scared him to face the reality that the strength of the Persian force was even more formidable than anticipated. Themistocles knew that even though they had hurt the Persians at Artemisium, they had also been wounded during the exchange.

The Peloponnesian Greeks, including the Spartans, wanted the navy to withdraw and abandon Salamis and return to the isthmus to make a stand. The Isthmus of Corinth was a thirty kilometer stretch of land that separated Attica from the Peloponnese. But Themistocles reasoned that if the Persian navy stood, then they could outflank the position at the Isthmus. The navy could land troops behind the

Spartans and destroy them as easily as they did Leonidas at Thermopylae. There was only one alternative - confront the Persian navy at Salamis with the hope of defeating them. Without the Persian navy, Xerxes would have a much more difficult task defeating the Spartans and the remainder of the Greek army.

Themistocles now had a major problem. The appointed head of the Greek navy was the Spartan, Eurybiadas. But Eurybiadas was not the typical Spartan. He often argued for the withdrawal of the Greek fleet. It happened before the confrontation at Artemisium. But now Eurybiadas had the votes of the military council on his side. Every single captain in the navy from the Peloponnese wanted to follow the instructions of the allied command, demanding the fleet abandon Salamis and return to protect the Peloponnese. Themistocles had already conned the captains to proceed to Salamis in the first place, and now he was running short on ideas of how to keep them there. He had made the argument that the navy had to go to Salamis to assist in the evacuation of the populace from Athens.

Themistocles sat on a small stump awaiting the time that he would enter the council of the captains where the direction of the navy would be decided. He continued to revisit his own deductions in his mind, but his conclusion was always the same. Salamis was the perfect place to confront the Persian navy. It was even more advantageous than Artemisium for a stance. The isthmus offered no such advantage. In fact, having to confront the Persian navy in the Peloponnese would be sure suicide. Themistocles was convinced of that.

What made Salamis perfect was the straight between Tropaia and a reef that protected the other shore. The Persians would only be able to bring three ships at a time through the straight. And then, because of the size of their navy, there would be no withdrawal. This advantage compensated for the superior number of ships that the Persian fleet would have. Themistocles was thoroughly convinced that in an equal fight the Greeks would prevail, or at least it would lessen the odds of total defeat. As he sat his leg began to shake in anticipation. Everything he had done and planned was reaching a culmination. If he could convince the captains of the various cities to stay and fight, they would have their greatest chance for success. He was ready to explode as he pondered his verbal strategy for this upcoming meeting. Couldn't they see what he saw. He didn't understand how narrow-minded these men could be.

All the captains were sitting in a large circle as Themistocles entered the council hollow. As he proceeded to his seat, he felt the weight of all eyes on him. In some he could see support, in others scorn. He also knew that he would be arguing against old jealousies between peoples. These old feuds invariably would show their ugly heads during these types of discussions, one block voting a certain way only because it was against what their traditional nemesis had voted. But this was an argument that Themistocles knew he could not lose.

Eurybiadas called the group to order. *"Gentlemen. We come to this impasse. Our first decision here will be to decide if we are to follow the orders of the allied council and retreat to the Peloponnese, or stay in this position and confront the Persians."*

By referencing the council in his opening remark, Eurybiadas was stating his preference. Withdraw to the Peloponnese.

Immediately, an Aegean named Knidose stood to speak.

"My fellows, we all fought together at Artemisium and gave the Persian a black eye."

Cries of applause and agreement filled the area, but Knidose raised his hand for silence.

"The Greek army is on the isthmus of Corinth building a 'wooden wall' to meet the Persian advance. My people have never been friends to the Athenians, but we can also not abandon them in this time. We

have evacuated their population, and if we leave, they will be slaughtered man for man by the invading Persian. It is estimated that the advance Persian troop will enter Athens within days. We cannot stop that advance, but we can also not act like children and run from it. If we run now, we will forever run."

"No, no, this is foolish,"

Adeimantos the Corinthian admiral stood and protested. He pointed at Themistocles.

"It is this man who wishes us to stay. Let him stand and speak and convince us of the need and strategic importance of staying here."

Themistocles stood. His impassioned plea lasted for quite some time. He first outlined the strategic advantages of the strait of Salamis. Adeimantos laughed at the comments, retorting,

"Yes, but as the Persians have no retreat, neither do we. The Bay of Eleusis which is our only refuse is a death trap. There is no way out for a navy. One or two ships yes, but a whole fleet, NO."

Heads bobbed up and down in agreement.

"We must retreat and defend the cities that still exist. "

Again, he pointed at Themistocles and stated, *"In the games, those who start too soon are defeated,"* implying that fighting here would be an impulsive gesture to an already dead city. Themistocles looked the man in the eye and retorted, *"Yes, Adeimantos, but those who do not act with authority are losers in the end."*

Mnesiphilos, an elder of the group, with a long white beard and fiery eyes, stood and said, *"If the ships each move from here, you won't fight for any one country anywhere. Each contingent will go off, city by city, and neither Eurybiadas nor anyone else will be able to stop them."*

There was quiet for a moment, then two men from Argos joined the discussion, also in favor of withdrawal. Themistocles responded, immediately walking toward the men. The men began squaring off when Eurybiadas jumped between them, raising his staff at the Athenian.

Another silence ensued and Themistocles looked at the Spartan and said, *"Hit me Spartan, but listen to my words. I have no fear of physical pain, but this is Armageddon."*

"Armageddon, Armageddon for who?"

A man from Eretria responded. The comment seemed to stun the group. The man's name was Egestian. He was not a well-respected member of the alliance, often shunned by even his Spartan allies. Egestian pointed at Themistocles.

"This man has no city. He chose to evacuate his city rather than fight. Who is the coward in this group? Maybe Themistocles should take his Athenians and sail to Italy, there to settle a new place. But what he wants is all of us to be destroyed, like the fate he committed Athens to. We should not defend a doomed city, one that even it's own general abandoned."

This stunning comment even shocked the Spartans into embarrassment. It suddenly became obvious to those gathered that the choice they had was to follow Egestian or Themistocles. Themistocles slowly walked to Egestian. This time he was in complete control. When he arrived at the man, the Eritrean took a step backwards, anticipating a blow. Instead, Themistocles bowed forward to whisper in the man's ear. But before he said anything, he took a step backwards and surprisingly he bowed in respect. He thought to himself, this man just taught me about discretion. He then leaned forward and whispered in Egestians ear,

"You my friend, are like a cuttlefish. You have a sword, but no heart!"

Then Themistocles addressed the entire group.

"It is true. We have indeed left our houses and our walls, not thinking it fit to become slaves for the sake of things that have no lives or souls. And yet our city is the greatest in all of Greece, consisting of two hundred galleys that are here to defend you. But if you run away and betray us, the Greeks will hear of the new city that will rise from the ashes despite the betrayal."

He then stood silently for a minute and spoke again. *"The first step towards liberty and victory is to gain courage."*

At that moment, the ground began shaking as an earthquake shook the land and sea. Eurybiadas held onto his chair as a sense of dread spread across his face. Three of the captains fell off their stoops at the strength of the shock. Egestian was thrown to the ground by the movement. Only Themistocles stood solidly on his spot. The tremor lasted only a few seconds, but everyone in the room took it as a sign.

The Greek politician looked to the sky and saw an owl flying circles overhead.

The next day, Eurybiadas ordered that a ship be sent north to Arapis and the Temple of Athena Skirias to offer sacrifice at the shrines to placate the great Goddess and thank her for their guidance.

Although the debate continued for a time, the decision had implicitly been made. The navy would make a stand at Salamis. In the end, they all stood, except for Egestian, and raised their hands to the air slowly narrowing the circle until all their hands touched in the center. Eurybiadas said.

"We are all free men, we come together to fight for that freedom. We have decided to stand together and face this peril."

That night Egestian the Eritrean was found hanging from a plank off one of his ships. There were rumors that he took his life from humiliation and shame, but in truth, Themistocles' friend Ptea the pirate, had paid a visit to his quarters not an hour before he was discovered.

****

Almost at the same time that the Greeks were hashing out their strategy, Xerxes held a conference of war with his naval commanders. The advanced Persian troops were in sight of Athens and the King himself would be arriving in the next few days. At this gathering were two Kings of Phoenician cities, Kings from the Karian dynasties, the King of Cilicia, and the King of Arvad. His own generals and admirals were also present. One of the commanders who was obviously missing was Smerdomences. Xerxes had sent him on a mission with his men to raid the temple at Delphi.

The King sat aloof from the gathering and allowed Mardonius, son of Gorbryas, and Xerxes' father's nephew, to take the lead in the discussion. Mardonius was a general in the army, although the great King didn't trust him as much as his closer associates. Xerxes sat in the background stroking the lioness, Simeron, as the men gathered in the counsel.

As the commanders spoke, it became obvious that the majority opinion was to engage the Greek navy at Salamis. They needed to learn the lesson from Artemesium and not hesitate. One of the commanders made the argument that if the fleet sent a detail around the island of Salamis to the Megarian channel, it would block any retreat for the Greeks and they would be trapped in the Bay of Eleusis. Another commander reasoned that the fleet should settle in the Greek port of Phaleron and not delay an attack.

"It is my belief, great King, that the Greeks have finally committed a fatal error. They have split their forces with their army retreating to the isthmus and their navy staying here at Salamis. Victory is ours and will be swift."

Many of the commanders nodded their heads in agreement, with one eye on the great King to gauge his inclinations. In fact, most believed that Xerxes was in favor of quick victory, and standing up to his logic could be life threatening. Their decisions, therefore, were fueled by politics, not strategy. Again, Mardonius spoke, *"We are unanimous in agreement. We will anchor at Phaleron and with all haste prepare to engage the Greek navy."*

But suddenly a voice in the background overwhelmed the meeting

"No, we are not in unanimous agreement."

A tall figure, dressed in black with a purple cape appeared from the shadows to walk to the center of the gathering. She looked at the King and spoke.

"These men do not speak their hearts or their minds. They speak what they think you want to hear, Great King. I will not stand among them in agreement. "

The Warrior Queen now strode directly towards Xerxes, stopping before him. She bowed and then reached down to put a small piece of meat in the lioness's mouth. She made eye contact with the great King. In a low voice she asked, *"Do you want to hear my true heart, or should I just agree and stand in the back?"*

Xerxes nodded slightly and Artemisia smiled. She then backed away returning to the council. She circled like a caged cat.

"We must accept certain truths. First, the Greeks have superiority over us in naval tactics."

A gasp of objection filled the room. Some of the commanders stood, reaching for their swords. The Warrior Queen did not seem concerned. She stared at them and one by one they sat. She laughed to herself.

"Sheep," she muttered, loud enough for others to hear.

"My King. I do not doubt the bravery of your troops. But we are allowing the Greeks to choose their ground for their battle. You are on the verge of capturing Athens, the original objective of this invasion. You have already won, my Lord. All of Greece is at your feet, but only if you have patience."

Artemisia slowly walked around the circular arrangement.

"I don't agree that hesitation caused us problems at Artemisium. We were baited. The Greeks made us question our resolve and drew us into a battle that did not favor us. We are there again, Great Xerxes. This is no different than Marathon."

The word was spoken. The word that drew blood to Xerxes eyes- the humiliation at Marathon. The other commanders seemed to back away at the reference.

"If only you are not in too great a hurry to fight at sea, if you keep the fleet on the coast where it now is, the, whether you stay here or advance into the Peloponnese you will easily accomplish your purpose. The Greeks will not be able to hold out against you for long. You will soon cause their forces to disperse. They will soon break up and go home. I hear they have no supplies in the island where they are now; and the Peloponnesian contingents, at least, are not likely to be very easy in their minds if you march with the army towards their country."

Again, she laughed. *"They are traditional enemies Lord. They will hardly like the idea of fighting in defense of Athens, an already defeated and abandoned city."*

Artemisia now spread her arms out. *"We have won, my comrades. Position the fleet and let the Greeks come to us. This will allow us to fight them in open water, not within a constricted strait. Majesty, the Warrior Queen is not in favor of attack, but we must wait for the snake to come to us. We must do the baiting, not be lured into a less strategic position."*

There was dead silence. The other commanders did not know whether to protest or agree. The Great King was silent. His eyes seemed to cut through the room. Many of the commanders worried if Xerxes would have the head of the Warrior Queen for voicing such a strong stance. Many looked concerned. Was this the calm before the storm? Xerxes stood and slowly walked away from his throne. He made a motion indicating that he wanted the room cleared. It did not take long for the commanders to leave. All left except for Artemisia, the Warrior Queen.

Artemisia stood without emotion. She did not seem upset or alarmed. She had not moved even a muscle. Her eyes remained fixed on the young King, as he walked around the room. Her right hand remained on her sword with her left remaining by her side. Finally, when the tent was cleared, the young King walked to the center where Artemisia stood. He then smiled.

"None of my commanders have the nerve to stand for what they think. It saddens me to believe that I cannot trust most of my commanders. Tell me Queen of Halicarnassus, what is your strategy?"

Artemisia looked seriously at the King.

"Are you sure, my Lord, that you want to hear my detailed thoughts?"

"I wouldn't have asked."

Artemisia's face suddenly changed, transforming from stoic to thoughtful.

"The Greeks are fragmented. There are reports of continuing dissention within their commanders. We must break this coalition. In order to be successful, we must attack from a number of directions."

Xerxes was intrigued by her self-assurance.

"Lord, I have been studying this situation for quite some time. When you sent me to Delphi on that ridiculous diplomatic mission, it gave me time to consider. At the time I was angry with you for wasting my time. But I realized that you had sent me with your teacher, Hamas, to learn his skills. His approach to war suggests several things in this circumstance. I suggest that you send the Egyptian fleet to block the channel so the Greeks cannot retreat. At the same time, you send part of your army to march on the Peloponnese. This move will further splinter the Greeks. The Peloponnesian boats will be pressured to abandon Salamis and return to help defend their lands."

Xerxes was paying attention. He had sat on his throne by this time and was leaning on his elbow, focusing on what Artemisia was saying. There was a silence, a break in the interchange. Xerxes was processing. Finally, he said, *"Continue."*

"Lord, we then send our boats into attack position. The Greeks will scramble to their boats. But we don't attack. We wait. Then, without warning, we withdraw."

"Withdraw?"

Responded the King, in a puzzled fashion.

"Bait, my King, bait. I want the Greeks to come out of the strait. We then set up in the small harbors and wait. If we are patient, the snake will come to us. Then as they splinter, we will pick them off and

crush them ship by ship. They are out of time. We are not. If we are patient they will dissolve and turn to mist."

Xerxes had not moved, but a small smile appeared on his face.

Artemisia walked away from Xerxes, allowing the anticipation of the last part of her plan to intrigue the King.

"Weakness, my King. The Greeks have one more area of weakness that we must exploit."

The King's curiosity was peaked. *"This Greek. This Athenian who leads the navy. He is a weak man. I have heard he overindulges in woman and wine."*

She smiled again with a devilish look.

"What he likes more than wine is gold. Let us up open a discussion with this man. We will offer him gold and amnesty for his Athenians who are now in Salamis."

This made Xerxes excited.

"It is a brilliant plan!"

"Thank you, Lord. But I must tell you, the important part of the strategy is patience. When it comes time, I will lead the attack"

****

Thantos had been through many trials and tribulations with his mentor, Themistocles. When he looked back on their association, he still did not fully understand why he decided to follow this man. When he met Themistocles, Thantos was already a wealthy man. He had made his fortune smuggling wine and other commodities throughout the Aegean. He was an adventurer, so he had no need for other thrills. Nor was Thantos a politician or a nationalist for that matter. In fact, he had spent his life avoiding political entanglements. He had no real need for this Demos, this belief in egalitarianism. In fact, he wasn't quite sure he really understood it, or why it was so important. Thantos had no love for the Persian, but he also had no real hate for them either. He had made a lot of money from their foolishness and their lust for Greek wine.

Since joining with Themistocles and his wild adventures, Thantos had lost his best friend on a mission to spy on the Persian strength. He had travelled to the city of Corinth and bartered with a local ship builder to gain the template vessels that led to the establishment of the navy. He had saved Themistocles life a few times. Thantos had never been a follower, but this Themistocles had him enchanted, maybe hypnotized. He had questioned the attraction many times, but could not figure out what the draw was. He had eventually accepted the fact that he was captivated by the Metis. Sometimes, when speaking with Themistocles, Thantos felt mesmerized, feeling as if he did not really have control over his own decisions.

This most current assignment involved returning to Delphi. Greek spies had reported that Xerxes was sending part of his army to ransack Apollo's temple. Themistocles sent Thantos to Delphi to warn the Pythia and the priests about the upcoming invasion, and more importantly, to make sure that Lasiandra was not murdered.

The Pythia was the priestess who merged with the God, Apollo, during the rapture. The God Apollo, spoke to the pilgrims through the Pythia, delivering his message in answer to their questions. It was the Pythia's job to bridge the gap between mortal man and the deity. The current Pythia was well known to Thantos. It wasn't long ago that the previous Pythia was murdered by Artemisia, the Warrior Queen. Bion had been one of the most gifted of the Pythias in a long time. Before she died, Bion had taken on a very young girl named Lasiandra as her acolyte. While challenging the Naiads, the river demons, Bion had rescued Lasiandra from death. The Naiad was able to steal Lasiandra's eyes in the confrontation. After Bion's death, Lasiandra had become the youngest Pythia in recorded memory. There were always three standing Pythias. But there was no question in the temple that Lasiandra had the approval of Apollo. When Kings or other royalties arrived at Delphi to seek direction, it was Lasiandra who merged with the God.

The garden of the temple was one of the most peaceful places in all of Greece. The temple at Delphi was almost a mile up the mountain. The temple funded many gardeners who were continually grooming the pathways that led to the temple. On this day the sun shone brightly, breaking through the early cloud cover. Streams of light cut through the clouds as if they were burning their way to the earth. Remarkably one of the streams fell directly on the Delphic garden. A stream with two small waterfalls ran through the center of the garden. Two very large trees, unusual for this area, stood proudly in the center of the garden. There were many meditation benches spread throughout the area. There was one special wooden base that was Bion's favorite. On this day it was occupied by a meditating Lasiandra. Somehow Lasiandra felt closer to her mentor Bion when she was sitting on this particular bench. Especially in times of tension, Lasiandra would come to the bench and visualize that she was sitting with Bion. She would imagine Bion sitting next to her. Lasiandra would "see" Bion in her mind. She focused on her face, studying the lines and wrinkles. With this contemplation, Lasiandra could see again. These were her favorite times.

On this day, Lasiandra had been sitting in her meditation for at least two hours. Her other senses had been heightened since losing her sight. One of the things she easily noticed was when someone was getting close to her. Before losing her sight, Lasiandra could "feel" somebody else's presence before the confrontation with the Naiade. But now, now her body had a type of radar, feeling things moving she could not see or hear. Her meditations would often get distracted because a bird flew overhead or a moth landed on a nearby flower.

Someone was approaching. The sensation came from behind her right shoulder. It was a man and Lasiandra sat up because the rhythm of the walk was unfamiliar to her. But as he approached his scent was very familiar. She jumped from her seat, *"Thantos!"*

"Lasiandra!"

The two old friends hugged. But it was more than a friendly hug, Lasiandra held on as if trying to gain strength from her friend. The captain was shocked by the familiarity of the embrace. As she held on, tears welled up in her eyes and she said, *"I'm afraid, Thantos. I have heard that the Persians have sent a large army to raid the temple. I fear they will arrive tomorrow."*

The two separated. Lasiandra smiled and looked up at her friend. Her blind eyes were red and wet.

"Tell me" Lasiandra said, *"how is Themistocles. I worry so much."*

"You don't worry about me?"

They both laughed and hugged again. Thantos said, *"Themistocles is fine. He sent me here to see you."*

"See me?"

"My mission, Lasiandra, is to bring you safely back to Salamis."

"Oh Thantos. I cannot leave Delphi. I am the Pythia."

"Well, Pythia, then I have a question. I would like you to ask the God a question."

"I will consider it, Thantos."

"No, no Lasiandra, there is no time. You must ask the God this day."

Lasiandra stared at her friend. She seemed frozen, but Thantos continued.

"Themistocles wanted me to insist that by tomorrow, midday, I will force you to leave Delphi."

Lasiandra laughed.

"My friend Themistocles would have me kidnapped."

Thantos was not flippant, *"Lasiandra, I am not joking. This is a very serious situation. The Persians have swept through northern Greece leaving death and destruction. When they arrive here they will not spare anyone. They will take the treasures of the temple and leave no Greek standing. Not the priests, not the priestesses, not the Pythia."*

Now Lasiandra became more serious.

"I am not a priest or a priestess. I am the person who merges with the great God. It is my solemn oath."

"You will die."

"Then I will die."

Lasiandra turned and forcibly walked away. She turned as she was leaving the garden and said, *"I will ask Apollo."*

It was unusual for the Pythia to make an unplanned visit to the God. There were specific days and times that the rapture was attempted, and this was not one of the days, nor the correct time. But the crisis was at hand, as the news of the Persian march to Delphi was creating panic among the populace. When the Athenians had asked the Oracle about the upcoming Persian conflict, the response from the God was specific and ominous.

O Pitiful man, why do you come here? Fly to the ends of the earth, leave your houses and wheel shaped city. Everything will fall to ruin.

Fire and Ares, God of war, destroy all. Many fortresses will be obliterated, not yours alone. Many temples will be devoured by fire, black blood dripping from their roofs, portending inevitable suffering. Leave this sanctuary and prepare yourselves with courage to meet misfortunes.

This response from the Oracle had been partially responsible for Themistocles' decision to abandon Athens and flee to Salamis. So now Thantos had come with a question for Apollo.

"With the approach of the Persians, what should the Pythia and the rest of the city do? Should they stay or abandon the temple?"

The preparation for merging with the God Apollo was prescribed. The first step involved cleansing oneself in the holy waters of the Castilian spring. It is here that the Naiad, Tu, waited to capture the soul and body of the person entering her domain. It was here that Lasiandra lost her sight to Tu. But now Tu was tamed. The fight between Lasiandra and the Naiad had always been a test of mental strength. During their first encounter, which was an impulsive and unwise act by Lasiandra, she had almost lost her life to the water nymph. She was giving into the cold of the heart when she was rescued by Bion. Lasiandra was lucky to have only lost her sight in the encounter with the nymph. The tides had now turned and Tu avoided the current Pythia. Lasiandra had gained strength from the Goddess, Demeter, who was her patron. She had joined the cult of the Eleusinian mysteries. In fact, it wasn't Bion who rescued Lasiandra from Tu, it was the Goddess, Demeter. Demeter ripped the already lost Lasiandra out of Tu's grasp seconds before it would have been too late. The nymph protested, but Demeter would not have it and vanquished Tu from the area.

After the cleaning, the Pythia drank from the holy waters of Kassotis. She was draped in her red robes, the special dress for the union with Apollo. Lasiandra held an ornamental bowl of laurel leaves next to her cup of Kassotis water. As she drank, the laurel leaves were set on fire and she inhaled the smoke from the burning. This step made the Pythia dizzy and she would rest some of weight on the two slave girls that accompanied her. The hallowed water was spread on the floor as she began to walk toward the inner sanctum of the temple where she would sit on the holy tripod. The tripod was situated above a small fissure that led to the center of the earth. The fissure emitted the fumes of trance. The Pythia sat on the tripod breathing these fumes and meditating. Slave girls surrounded her as the effects of the intoxication would, at times, render her unconscious.

This day Lasiandra was already shaky as she entered the Adyton. This inner sanctum was located about two feet below the floor, so only the top half of the Pythia was visible to the naked eye. Since Delphi was considered the center of the world, this fissure was supposed to touch every sacred site in the known world. It was told that Zeus sent two eagles to search the earth for the center of the world. The two eagles landed at Delphi.

Lasiandra began her breathing techniques to maximize her consumption of the Pneuma fumes.

The fumes were sweet to the smell. These mephitic vapors filled her nose and chest. As she breathed her trance deepened. Reality became mixed with hallucination as her head flung back in a spasmodic fashion. Then without warning, Lasiandra began seizing. Her moans and cries rose proportionally as her body violently shuddered. Waves of pain seemed to encompass her body, and the slave girls began showing signs of concern. Lasiandra would quiver and then calm almost in a recognizable pattern. Her voice was no longer recognizable, and her language was of an ancient dialect that was not understandable to any of the slaves. Lasiandra began sweating profusely, until finally her body went limp and she began falling off the tripod. Three slave girls, wide eyed, immediately responded, jumping into the Adyton to save the Pythia from falling. But even unconscious, Lasiandra's muscles tightened at the touch of the slave. She flung one of the slaves out of the Adyton with inhuman strength. As she did, a deep scream emitted from her mouth. The remaining slaves held tightly onto the Pythia, yet she did not again respond with violence.

In a very deep grizzled voice, the Pythia began chanting some unknown song. Suddenly her eyes opened but pupils were not present, only a white glow was seen now. Lasiandra now calmed. Lasiandra could see her body below her, and yet even though she knew it was her, she didn't recognize her form. She had been disembodied once before while studying the Eleusinian mysteries, but his was a different experience. Lasiandra knew she had passed from the world of the living to eternal reunion with the Gods. She felt no fear or confusion, just a peaceful recognition of what was. She had no regrets and remarkably, she could see again. She focused on the faces of all those below her. Lasiandra saw her body moving and she heard language coming from her mouth, but it was not of her doing and not of her voice. She instinctively knew that the God had taken over her essence and she was left to wait between life and death until he completed his desires. Not many Pythias in all the thousands of decades had ever achieved ecstatic rapture. But Lasiandra knew that she had achieved the highest form of rapture that was possible. Lasiandra realized that she no longer had a body, but her spirit was energy and essence, no longer corporal form. And yet in this state she felt more alive than ever before.

"Is this final truth?" She thought.

With death comes life, but life on a different plain of existence, but fuller, less constrained, and unimaginably more peaceful than before.

When he saw Lasiandra having convulsions, Thantos had to be restrained from jumping into the Adyton to retrieve her. When he heard the horrible sounds coming from her mouth, his eyes widened in shock, and his mouth opened to yell, but no sound came out. One of the priests who had helped restrain him whispered into his ear.

"Lasiandra has left us, now only the God remains."

Thantos looked at him in shock.

"Bring her back," he yelled, *"bring her back,"*

He pleaded, now on his knees. He immediately came to realize how deep his emotions were for this young girl.

Lasiandra's body rose from the tripod. Her eyes, now bright with light, searched the room. Finally, a sound engulfed the temple. It didn't come from Lasiandra but just seemed to be there for all to hear.

"I have heard your pleas. Already the black blood flows from the fields. The statues shine with dread. All my people cry with grief."

Lasiandra's body now reached out towards Thantos.

"I will not desert my heart. Give me your fear and I will transcend you. I will return the Pythia. Her life still has time."

Lasiandra's body drifted back toward the holy tripod. The slave girls reached up to greet it as it descended. Lasiandra coughed and vomited next to her chair. All eyes centered on her. She briefly opened her eyes and smiled at Thantos. But with that two priests dropped to their knees as if a heavy weight suddenly overwhelmed their legs. The voice was heard again.

"Send your bravest to meet the advance of the Medes. But they will not be needed. Apollo will defend his temple. Man cannot overcome heaven and earth. I will defend Delphi."

****

Xerxes rose from his throne in anticipation as the courier entered his tent. The courier bowed and lay as close to the floor as he could

"A message, you have a message for me?"

"Yes Lord, our advanced troops have entered Athens. They have encountered almost no resistance. Old men and dogs."

Penish, the Executioner, the King's trusted bodyguard smiled as he stood next to his master. Xerxes turned and embraced his friend.

"It has finally happened. Soon we will be able to rid our mouths of the bitter taste of Marathon."

Xerxes turned to the courier and said with urgency,

"Return to the army. I want nothing burned until I arrive in the city. Tell them to restrain themselves. I will punish any of our troops who destroy any part of the city. Is that understood?"

"Yes, lord."

"Then go and tell the generals. I want no mistakes."

"Yes, Lord, it will be done."

Penish left Xerxes' side, leaving the King of Kings alone. There were very few times that Xerxes was alone with his thoughts. He sat on a small chair which was next to his resting place. Before long the King was lost in his own thoughts. He reflected on the hardships of bringing this large army to this place. He also considered how many men had been lost in this venture. In his recapturing of Egypt years before, the Persian troops lost very few men. But this was different. He hadn't anticipated the extent of the loss. But although this was unfortunate, Xerxes did not regret his actions. What bothered him more was that he did not have an overwhelming sense of conquest. His greatest accomplishment lay at his feet, and yet he did not feel an overwhelming sense of triumph. Just the opposite, he felt empty.

Xerxes debated this anomaly in his mind. He held onto the thought that he had not yet smelled the fires of his achievement. When he saw the city burning, watched the great Acropolis being destroyed, then he would feel his completion.

The great King had been consumed with dreams. Every night he had recurring images of his ancestors crying out to him for revenge. The images were so defined that they would wake him in the middle of his sleep. They cried out to him with desperate pleas. He dreamt about his father lying in his grave crying for retribution, urging him to claim blood for blood. He foresaw that he would capture the first Athenian he encountered, and drain his blood into a flask that a slave carried. That blood would be returned to Persia, and poured over his father's grave, satisfying the spirits that haunted him. He saw the completion of this revenge many times. It was palpable in his dreams.

The next day, on a gilded, golden throne, the great King was carried into Athens. What he saw was an abandoned city. And yet the lack of people did not affect Xerxes. As he was carried, he pointed to building after building that he wanted burned. Soon the entire city was aflame, and the smoke rose in dark clouds, blocking the sun from the sky. Some structures, hundreds of years old, were laid waste as the great King wrought his vengeance on the city he hated. As he was carried, the slaves noticed smiles of satisfaction on his face. His slaves were instructed to carry him slowly so he could savor every moment of this triumph.

Finally, arriving at the Acropolis, Xerxes saw a hastily built wall surrounding the structure. His eyes had been on it as his troops carried him through the city. One could easily see the structure for it stood on a large hill in the center of Athens. It was magnificent, he thought, but it also reminded him of the defeat at Marathon. He was told that the structure was constructed to celebrate Marathon. But its glory! The Acropolis reminded him of the structural wonders of Persia. Xerxes had thought of the Greeks almost as subhuman before this venture.

But their valor and bravery at Thermopylae, their cunningness at the Artemision strait, and now this, began to convince him otherwise.

Demaratus and the psychic, Golnar, were called in front of the King. The ex-Spartan general was addressed first.

"What is the significance of this place?"

Xerxes asked upon his arrival. Demaratus thought for a second and then spoke,

"This place is held in esteem for two reasons. There stands a Temple to Athena Nike Polias- the protectress of the city. It is said that here she fought her uncle, Poseidon, for dominance of the city."

With his eyes still fixed at the structures, Xerxes sarcastically grunted. Demaratus continued *"This is also the place that the new philosophy of Demos has been worshiped."*

Xerxes stared at the ex-Spartan general.

"So this place represents this new order?"

"Yes Lord"

"Return to your men general."

After the ex-Spartan left, the Great King turned to his spiritual guide.

"Now that we have conquered this city, what is your recommendation for this Temple of Demos?"

Golnar had brought prescient rocks with her which she used to predict the future. She let out a blood- curdling scream, then threw the rocks on the ground. After staring at them for a few minutes she lifted her head to the King.

"My Lord, it is a delicate situation. The reports of the power of the Goddess Athena are legendary. You do not wish to overly offend her"

The son of Darius spit on the ground at the comment.

"Look around, priestess. Her city burns in front of her eyes. Do you not believe that she is already affronted?"

"Be careful, my Lord. Her temple on that mount is a very revered place."

The King moved away from her, disbelieving her powers and cursing to himself.

"I did not come here to tread lightly," Was his first thought.

Chapter XX – The Frozen Vapor

Damianos had been praying to the Goddess for two days. He was concerned that no signs arose. He began to question whether the great Goddess had abandoned her people. He rose from his secluded meditation and looked over the outskirts, viewing the Persian hoard for the first time. His breath caught in his throat and his knees weakened. He was ashamed that his first thought was that not even Athena could defeat this invader. But Damianos had to straighten himself. Many others were looking to him for strength. As he emerged, many stood around him with their eyes begging for hope. Damianos knew of no hope, but he assured them anyway. The old men and some of the priests stood at the wall with bows and arrows awaiting the Persian advance. It was almost funny, Damianos thought, like a fly trying to defend against a lion.

Xerxes watched with pride as his troops surrounded the poorly guarded hill. Some of his troops were sent to foray and test the strength of the defense. He was told about the dogged resistance of the priests and citizens in the temple. He couldn't help but be impressed both by the stubbornness of the opposition and the exquisite splendor of the structure they sought to defend. It's too bad that these people are so misguided, he thought.

He contemplated for quite some time as others waited. There was still some fear of the Greek Gods in his heart, although the King would not admit it out loud. His ambivalence was tangible to him. Finally, the son of Darius, and the grandson of Cyrus, rose from his throne and raised his arms into the air. He pointed the Answerer at the wall ordering a full assault on the temple. Regulars were used, not just the advanced soldiers that tested the defenses. It took only a few hours before the hopeless resistance was overcome. The soldiers had been ordered not to kill any of the priests or the priestesses of the temple.

The great King demanded that all the people in the temple be spared. His troops were to loot nothing, destroy nothing, and kill as few as possible. As the great King entered the Acropolis, three full units of the army formed a path for the King of Kings to enter. Water and flowers were spread before him and beautiful slave women proceeded the great King. It appeared a coronation, as Xerxes was dressed in his finest outfit. These days he followed the Egyptian tradition of the pharaohs wearing a white kilt being naked on the upper half of his body. But the kilt was exquisite. White with strands of gold and purple threads adorned the linen kilt. For this ceremony, Xerxes wore a false beard. It was attached to his face with thin leather straps and glue. He also wore the Nemes, the royal Egyptian headdress that covered his head and fell behind his ears making him look serpentine. Xerxes wore dark kohl eye makeup. Besides his outfit, the King of Kings wore ornamental jewelry. He held the "Answerer" in one hand and the royal axe in the other.

Xerxes was meticulous in his presentation and precise in his walk. He slowly proceeded toward the Temple of Athena Nike Polias as his troops placed their swords under their throats and threw kisses. As he entered the temple, the King stopped for a moment, allowing Athena the time to strike him down. Not to his surprise, nothing happened. The Greek Goddess had been vanquished like her city and people. Prostrate before him were over 100 people sitting on their knees surrounded by guards. Xerxes approached the gathering.

"I am Xerxes, King of lands, King of Peoples, King of Kings. I am Pharaoh of both Upper and Lower Egypt, and my Empire reaches both heaven and earth, and now Greece"

He stood silently letting the scope of his brilliance sink into those assembled. He scanned the assembled Greeks, and then walked directly to Damianos.

"By your adornments and dress, you must be the high priest of this temple."

Damianos nodded in agreement.

"You are the first Athenian that I speak with. Every Greek I have seen so far is dead. Do you wish the same fate?"

Damianos shook his head, *"no."*

"Then denounce your Gods in front of your acolytes"

The priest's eyes widened. He tried rising to speak but was thrust back down by a guard.

"Speak to me, Greek, and tell me why you cannot."

"My life has been devoted to the Goddess Lord. I cannot forsake her"

"Why? She has forsaken you,"

The King responded in an arrogant tone. He walked to Damianos and lifted him by the collar. Xerxes dragged the priest across the temple floor and to the wall. He lifted him and forced him to see the city up in flames. Xerxes then bent down to the priest's level and whispered in his ear.

"This fight is over, priest. Tomorrow my navy will crush the Greek navy and the changing of the guard will be complete. There is nothing left to defend, nothing left to pray to. Your people have discarded their city and abandoned you. You can save these people by admitting that Athena has abandoned you and this Demos is dead. It has all fallen by the wayside like a dead tree being pushed aside by new growth."

Damianos was now openly weeping. In truth the King had no intention of letting these people live, but he wanted this priest to denounce his religion. But through all the urging and threats, the Greek priest would not deprecate his belief. Over the next three hours a gruesome event unfolded. Every Greek that was captured was singularly dragged in front of Damianos and told that it was his decision to allow them to die. The cries and screams of the dying doubly terrified the remaining hostages. Some tried to themselves denounce Athena, but the King would have none of it. The slaughter continued until Damianos was the only one left. He was now in shock and out of tears from the ordeal.

Xerxes pointed to soldiers and Damianos was dragged from the temple. The King had reached the pinnacle of his blood lust obsession, and now came the final act in this brutal celebration. Damianos was taken to a nearby olive tree. A rope was fastened to his legs, and he was hung upside down from a large branch. Golnar, the Lector priestess, came and blessed his body as he squirmed and pleaded for mercy. Damianos' clothes were cut from his body. As the blessing ceremony continued, Golnar revealed a very sharp knife and with precision, castrated the priest. As she held his bloody testicles in her hand, a slave slit Damianos' throat. Beneath him was placed a large jar and his blood was slowly drained from his body filling the jar halfway up. The testicles were placed in the jar and it was sealed with hot wax in preparation for its return to Persia. Xerxes decreed that the corpse should be left in that position for the entire cycle of the moon.

Xerxes looked towards his general staff.

"Initially I thought we should spare the temple and not incur the wrath of the Greek Gods. But I have changed my mind. Burn it down."

And with that, the Great King of Lands turned his back on the Acropolis and left.

All the generals, their staffs, and traveling nobles were invited to a triumphant feast. It was held on the Acropolis itself. Many animals had been left behind by the fleeing Athenians, and everything that moved was butchered for this feast. Some of the Athenians captured in the city and hiding in the hills were chained and stripped naked during the festivity. Wine flowed like water, although their great King did not partake. Xerxes sat on his raised throne watching the others celebrate. He was as stoic as ever, appearing almost bored at the revelry.

Xerxes sat in the remains of the temple of the Greek Goddess, Athena. He had recalled his feeling when he put down the rebellion of the Egyptian priests and declared himself Pharaoh. This feeling was similar he mused, but much more potent. Once again, the Persian resolve and might had won the day. He looked across the room and found that someone was missing. He called for a slave over.

"Find me the Warrior Queen. Bring her to me!"

An hour passed until the slave returned. Behind him, by nearly ten steps, walked the Warrior Queen, Artemisia. As always, she was magnificent, and when she entered all eyes turned to watch her. Although usually dressed in black, this day the warrior from Halicarnassus wore a white gown and purple lases. Rarely was she seen not wearing her traditional black outfit. As usual, the Warrior

Queen walked slowly so her presence could be noticed and enjoyed by everyone. Time seemed to stop as she made her way down the center of the temple.

An almost unrecognizable smile was on Xerxes' face as Artemisia made her way. Finally, when she arrived at the throne, she did not bow like others, nor throw kisses to the King. She bent over Simeron and gave her a large piece of meat, which the lioness gladly took. She then walked to the King and bowed her head.

Xerxes leaned forward, *"You are impertinent,"* he said, although there did not seem to be anger in his tone.

"Did you not get my invitation for this evening?"

Artemisia quickly responded, *"I did Lord, and thank you for the compliment".*

"Then why did you not join us in celebration?"

The Queen took another step forward. She made a gesture indicating that she wanted to talk with the King outside of everyone's ears. Xerxes rose and Artemisia followed him to another area.

"I'm listening, Queen of Halicarnassus"

"It is true that Athens is in flames. An impressive accomplishment, my Lord."

"So?"

"The war is not over. The Greek navy sits in a protected port waiting for us to advance. The Spartans, the fiercest warriors in this land, sit and wait for us behind a wall at Corinth. When the Greek navy sits on the bottom of the Aegean, and Sparta burns like Athens, then will be my time to celebrate."

"The naval battle will begin tomorrow,"

Xerxes replied and continued. *"I have also sent out feelers to see the likelihood of bribing this Themistocles. What do you know of him?"*

"I have heard he drinks and revels too much, but when sober, he is a brilliant strategist."

"As good as you?" Xerxes questioned. Artemisia smiled.

"We will see, we will see."

As she turned to leave, the Queen looked back at the monarch and said, *"Do not celebrate too much my King, death lays ahead."*

And with that, Artemisia was gone. Xerxes stood in thought. After a good amount of time, a slave entered, and the King asked him to bring Golnar. She arrived quickly to find Xerxes sitting with his hands on his head. His body was covered with sweat as if he had just gone swimming. In front of him lay the "answerer" broken in pieces. This magical staff was given to Xerxes by his mother, Ho. She told him it could predict the future. Xerxes had taken it everywhere and he had felt the energy that ran through it.

Xerxes looked up at the priestess.

"A vision, Golnar. After Artemisia left I had a vision."

"Tell me, my King, and I will help you vanquish the demons."

"I'm not sure what I saw. It was unclear, like a vapor. It looked at me and I was frozen in my spot. I could not read it but I knew it was watching me. I felt naked in front of it. It was not a vision of my ancestors. It was much older, more ancient."

Golnar had never seen fear in the King's eyes.

"I could barely move, Golnar. I tried to respond to it but no sound left my body."

Xerxes pointed to the broken staff that lay before him.

"The mist took the answerer and shattered it. I thought I saw small flames leaving the magical staff. I tried protesting, but I was attached to the ground on which I stood. What does this mean, Golnar?"

The priestess stared at the young King.

"I am not sure Lord, but I will put a protective spell around you."

Golnar turned and began taking a step away from the sovereign and she fell to the floor. Xerxes watched with eyes wide as the priestess began holding her chest in pain. Mucus poured from her mouth and Golnar began choking. Xerxes, still unable to move, watched with horror as his spiritual advisor withered in convulsions. Before long it was obvious that Golnar was dead. Still unable to move the King could only watch in helplessness. As she lay at his feet, the mist again appeared, this time rising from Golnar's body. It came up and faced the young King. He began speaking, *"I am Xerxes, King of Lands, King of Peoples and King of Kings. I order you away."*

An unrecognizable face seemed to appear in the mist. It was female and stared at the King with fiery green eyes. Then, in perfect Persian, the face began to speak, *"King of Kings. You do not understand power. Your body swells with pride at the destruction of something that is hundreds of years old. You slaughtered priests and old men, King of Lands. It angers me to see such weakness in a strong man."*

Then in an instant, the image was gone. Xerxes walked over to Golnar and knew that she was clearly dead. He called for slaves to remove the body. Xerxes then returned to the temple and stood by his throne. He raised his arm, *"Tomorrow, two goats will be sacrificed at the temple of Athena. Food and gold will be left by her feet. We will thank the Greek Goddess for allowing us to enter her city."*

The earth shook slightly at the King's proclamation as if amused by the gesture.

And with another wave from Xerxes the celebration was over.

****

The scene in front of him was overwhelming. For the first time in as long as he could remember he openly wept. He was not alone, many of his Athenian fellows sat with him and cried out loud. From their vantage point at Salami, they could see the city burn. Their beloved Athens was in ruins. Although he knew that this was the only possible outcome, Themistocles chastised himself. It was his fault, his stubbornness that forced the funds to be used for a navy, and not increase the standing army; his obstinacy to evacuate the city before the incoming Persian horde.

"What have I done?" He wondered aloud. *"What have I done?"*

There was no solace for the Greek politician turned statesman, turned warrior. Nobody came to offer condolences or tell him that he had taken the correct road. No one said that if they stayed, they would have all been slaughtered by the Persian King. He sat alone with his own guilt and sorrow. At other times, Themistocles could wash his sorrow away by over indulging in wine until unconsciousness cleared his head. But not this time, although the urge was overwhelming. He was now a man without a home, but luckily not a man without hope. But even his hope, his unflinching belief that he had made the right turns, chosen the correct path in the face of invasion with overwhelming odds, could change the reality that Athens was burning. He couldn't stop the tears. Does it make sense to save the people but sacrifice everything they had built over generations? Was he wrong in the belief that the Demos, this new form of egalitarian government was worth more than the structures of his ancestors. Was the concept more important than the tangible? In his mind it was, but tell the farmers, the businessmen and the merchants, that the idea of Demos was more essential than their livelihoods. For now, they still had their

Demos, but there was nothing to protect. No government to rule, no city to defend. Just an idea. They could have easily agreed to the Persian requests for "earth and water", making Athens another Satrap in the Persian Empire. It would have been costly, but their city and all its tradition would still be standing.

At this time, besides the Persian King, Themistocles believed that he was the most despised man in Attica. He imagined that the nobles of Athens would all blame him for this, not the Persians. History would tell that Athens burned because of the pigheadedness and foolishness of one man, Themistocles.

After an hour of feeling sorry for himself, an officer of the navy approached him. The Greek politician looked deep into the man's eyes searching for resentment. But he found none. The man did not appear angry at him and this surprised even the man with Metis. The officer saluted the general and said, *"There is a man to see you. He makes some strange reports."*

The captain now leaned forward and whispered in Themistocles' ear, *"He claims to represent the Persian King."*

Themistocles turned his head in shock. This man was serious. He looked at the captain and smiled, *"Do you think he is offering to surrender?"*

They both laughed in a low tone.

"Show him to me."

A small man, dressed more like a diplomat than a soldier, came in front of Themistocles. He bowed, going down on one knee.

"My lord,"

"Stand, I am not your lord. Your lord is ruthless and blood thirsty."

"I do not mean to insult you. I come from the great King with a message for only your ears."

"My ears are listening."

"My King wants me to convey his deep respect for you and the Greek people. Rather than see more lives uselessly lost, he offers you an agreement. In return for presenting him with earth and water and pledging your allegiance to the Empire, he will grant the people of Athens an immediate return to their city with no further penalty. He will allow you any form of self-government and religious beliefs that you choose. He asks only for taxes and loyalty. He will not punish any former member of the Greek military nor make any more land demands. He will ask that you receive a Persian governor to monitor you city and its people. No Persian troops will be stationed in Attica. He also offers you three chests of gold as payment for your skill at negotiation."

The courier bowed again. Themistocles thought for a moment then said, *"Tell your King that I will consider his generous offer. In truth, many of the Allied ships are not happy with the present position. I will send a man to him in a small boat with my response. Tell your King that my messenger will carry two gold coins and will tell the King that he will bow to the Pharaoh of Egypt. Now leave and return to your master."*

Themistocles had two major problems. The first was amongst the Greek contingents of the navy. There was talk of open rebellion. Themistocles did nothing to discourage such talk, in fact he himself had started some rumors. The point was simple, Themistocles wanted the Persians to believe that the Greeks were in disarray. Most of the talk came from lower level members of the alliance. Eurybiadas and the upper level decision makers were all in agreement to the strategy. Themistocles knew that fear was contagious and if the rumors became more intense, there could in fact, be dissolution of the alliance. All the ships were needed for the upcoming engagements. If even one contingent disserted, it would dramatically lower the odds of success.

His second problem was trickier. For any chance of success, the Greeks needed the Persians to attack them in the straits. If they waited outside, the Greeks would shrivel and die without supplies. So, he needed to create a sense of urgency in the Persians. He needed to draw them into the conflict. It was especially difficult because it was against their best interests. But fate had just lent a hand. This message from Xerxes was perfectly timed. If he could make the Persian King believe that the Greeks were in chaos, he could successfully bait them. His mind raced. The guilt that had previously consumed him seemed to have vanished in the face of the upcoming crisis. The time for action was at hand. He sent a slave to fetch him Sicinnus.

****

Smerdomences and his 10,000 troops marched hard to get to Delphi. The general was torn because he wanted to be with the King as he entered Athens. This would mean that he had to overcome the temple quickly and then force march back to Xerxes. Spies had been sent to reconnoiter and they came back with generally positive news. There was only a small contingent of hoplites guarding the holy area- they guessed about 500. The path into the city was a deep valley surrounded by a large mountain on one side and a smaller, hilly area on the other. Smerdomences was skeptical of these mountain valleys and passes since Thermopylae. He was assured though that the terrain was much friendlier, and the Greek troops could not defend the road like the Spartans did. The spies also said that the Greeks in Delphi did not appear concerned about an attack from the Persians. Another twinge of discomfort swept through the general. He recalled how the Spartans combed their hair and wrestled before their advance at Thermopylae. It was as if these Greeks knew something he didn't, and it was cause for concern.

Smerdomences was a very aggressive warrior, but he would not rush headlong into a compromising situation. He decided that as they approached the city, he would personally take an advanced group of soldiers to evaluate the strategic landscape.

As the Persians advanced, Thantos was becoming more edgy. Lasiandra had refused to leave with him as Themistocles had ordered. He could not leave her here. She was a stubborn young woman. He considered kidnapping her and taking her against her will, but he quickly discarded that idea. So he had no choice. There were only 200 hoplites to defend the city and the Temple. It was an impossible task. The Temple was high up the mountain, but although defensible, 200 against 10000 was impossible. He went to the commander and offered his services for defense of the city. The man looked at him in shock.

"What we will be doing is not defense of Delphi. What we will be doing is offering our lives to the Gods at this holy place. Yes, we will fight, but we will be overcome in a matter of minutes. You would be better served my friend to leave Delphi now while you still can."

Thantos sneered, *"I will defend this city and this shrine with you."*

The commander bowed in recognition of the courageous of the man who stood in front of him.

"We will defend it together then."

The two hundred hoplites were dispersed both at the shrine and in the valley. In this situation, strategy was useless. It would be, kill as many Persians as you can before they kill you. The Greeks also had spies in the mountains monitoring the Persian advance. They would come back wide eyed and scared. The estimates of the Persian strength rose as high as 50,000 men. The Greek commander whose name was Phichious, was unmoved by the estimations. It really didn't matter how many Persians were advancing on the city. He also knew that some of the hoplites, and much of the populace had already abandoned the city and headed to the hills. He really couldn't blame them. Some would call him foolish for staying and fighting. He had heard that the entire city of Athens had abandoned in anticipation of the Persian advance. He would not abandon the Temple of Apollo.

Phichious and Thantos led a contingent of 25 men as far into the valley as they dared. He wanted to be the first of the defenders to engage the Persians. As they waited, they began hearing low rumblings of drums in the distance. The time and the slaughter were approaching. As the low frequency sound grew louder the two men could each feel their muscles tightening in anticipation. The low rhymic sound was quite ominous, and Thantos could feel sweat forming on his brow. But then something strange happened. A group of 20 Persian horsemen broke from the advancing army. They rode straight for their position as the army halted. At the head of this small group was obviously a general. He wore ornamental arm and leg plating. His subordinate, who rode next to him carried a flag with a gold top to it. Thantos recalled when he was being given a tour of the Persian army, that this sign represented the Immortals, the Ausiya troops. Xerxes had sent an Immortal contingent to conquer and loot Delphi. These were the hardest and best trained that the Persian had.

But just then, Thantos looked more closely at this general on the lead horse. He recognized him. It was Smerdomences. Smerdomences, the Persian who murdered Thantos' lifelong friend, Phecontalis. Thantos had tried to kill him once before but was restrained by the other Persians. He knew that this man had murdered his friend because he had previously noticed a bone handled knife that had belonged to Phecontalis. A whole new sense of purpose came over the sailor. He had prayed for this opportunity since this war had begun. A chance to repay Smerdomences for his murdering ways. Thantos could feel the hate rising through his bones. He now had reason to stay in this fight even if it cost him his life.

But before he could react, a strange noise filled the air. It was a melody, one that he had never heard before. It was very high pitched and getting louder by the second. Thantos and

Phichious covered their ears, as a shooting pain passed through their skulls. He fell back, his head ringing with this painful noise. It continued to grow louder and shriller. All thoughts of Smerdomences left him as he silently pleaded for an end to the noise.

But as he and the other soldiers lay on the ground with their hands to their heads another sound began taking over for the high frequency shrill. It was a low rumbling sound, as if the earth itself was trying to speak. Thantos felt the ground beginning to move, and it instantly reminded him of being on a boat as the ground rose and fell. And then an explosion. Rocks and boulders were sent flying in all directions. The mountains were protesting and tons of rock and earth began falling from the tops of the peaks. Thantos dragged himself upright, pain still ringing in his ears, to see landslides of rock falling from the slopes. The Persians were panicking with their horses bucking wildly. The rock and smoke seemed to engulf the army that was standing in wait of their mounted leader. The entire earthly diatribe lasted only 5 or 6 minutes. But when the smoke cleared, the fallen rocks had formed an impassable barrier between the army and the advanced Persian party. All the Persians were on the ground, struggling to gain their balance. Most of their horses were lying dead in the rubble. The earthquake, and the subsequent rockslide, killed many of the Immortals waiting to attack the Temple. It left many more injured.

Without thinking, Thantos stood and with a wave of his arm ordered the Greek hoplites to advance on the small Persian party that lay on their side of the rock wall. Surprisingly, the men all rose and ran towards the disoriented Persians. The Persian warriors, some still trying to maintain their balance, were no match for the advancing hoplites. The fighting was hand to hand, although the Persians began falling quickly. Thantos ran directly at Smerdomences. He held his hand up directing the hoplites away from the general. Smerdomences down on one knee, looked up at the Greek sailor and with a sneer, said, *"I know you Greek."*

Thantos smiled, *"You do know me Persian, we met before."*

Smerdomences had blood in his eyes. He asked, *"Where have we met Greek?"*

Thantos was silent for a moment and then said, *"I was a guest of your King and he showed me around your army."*

"Oh yes, you tried to attack me."

Thantos could feel his hand tighten around his sword. He pointed it at the general of the 10,000.

"You murdered my friend, Phecontalis"

"I remember, he lost his life on a boat."

"And you, my friend, will lose your life at the entrance to Delphi"

With that threat, the Greek captain impaled the Persian General. The general fell backwards, holding the sword that protruded from his chest. As he gasped for air, Thantos landed on him and removed the bone handled knife that Smerdomences had taken from his friend. He then cut the general's throat with the knife. As Smerdomences lay with the blood draining from his neck, Thantos said,

"Now, Phecontalis can rest easily."

He wiped the knife of its blood on the dead Persian general.

When he saw Lasiandra again, they hugged. The Pythia kissed the captain on the cheek. As she did, she whispered, *"I told you that Apollo could take care of himself"*

****

Chapter XX1 – The Great Shout

The small boat approached a Persian trireme that was stationed near the city of Piraeus. The small boat seemed out of place amongst the larger crafts. It bounced on the waves like a leaf in a storm. In the vessel sat a smallish man who looked more like an intellectual than either a warrior, sailor, or spy. The man struggled to keep his tiny ship from being engulfed by the raging waters. The man in the boat did not seem to be trying to be quiet. As he approached the Persian ships, he began waving and yelling at the larger vessels. The Persian guard on the boat stopped, then looked over the side of his ship to see what the commotion was about. When the Persian sailor saw the small boat he turned to his compatriots and waved, ordering archers to the front of the ship. Ten men suddenly appeared brandishing their bows. There was an immediate response with twenty eyes focused on the small man in the small craft. The guard then held up his arms, a sign to the others to hold their bows, stay their attack. The man in the boat raised his hands in a motion of surrender. The guard pointed at the small craft and demanded to know why the man was approaching the vessel. He yelled, pointing his sword at the man. The small man in the boat began yelling back in fluent Persian

"My name is Sicinnus. I have a message for the great Persian King, Xerxes."

The guard, unsure of what to do, stared at the small boat and this funny little man in disbelief. Finally, he turned to the assembled men and ordered them to detain the man and the craft. When the small man was brought aboard the Persian trireme the guard threw him to the deck. Sicinnus bent as low as he could, hoping not to receive punishment. He was not a hardened soldier and being treated harshly was frightening to him.

As he lay on the ground with the Persian soldiers standing over him with swords and other weapons, Sicinnus began to tremble uncontrollably, as he could hear the sailor's heavy breathing. He quickly realized that he was terrified. All reality disappeared for him except the possibility of his death. He was not brave, in fact the fear that rose and exploded in his mind convinced him more and more that he was a coward. He didn't know what terrifying emotion to feel as he lay on the boat. He quietly cried, convinced that his life would end this day. The guard prodded Sicinnus while shouting at the other men. He then looked at Sicinnus and said, *"Why are you here, you rat of a man?"*

He poked again. This time it took Sicinnus' breath from his body. He coughed, trying to regain the air. Now with an angrier air, the Persian sailor said, *"I spoke to you, rat man."*

Sicinnus looked up. His face was red and his speech shallow. He coughed, and when he spoke, his voice was barely a whisper.

"I am here to speak with the great King."

"The great King! Do you even know his name, rat man?"

"His name is Xerxes. He is the King of Kings. The great ruler of a great Empire."

The guard put his foot on Sicinnus' back and pushed him to the ground.

"You are close to death rat man. You will speak only if someone asks you something. If you try to disobey, we will burn your skin from your body."

The guard left two of his spearmen to guard the prostrate man. The guard disappeared, wanting to tell his general about the man in person. He knew that bringing such a discovery to his general would mean that he was being vigilant and he would be remembered. And there was always the possibility that the rat man actually had an important message.

The general, who arrived an hour later, was named Ahumim. His name was roughly translated into; "Brother of the sea." He was a very experienced sailor, although Artemisium had been his first taste of combat. Although he would never admit it, the blood and destruction made him ill. He secretly threw up when nobody was looking. He saw the excited guard approaching and could easily tell that there was important news. The guard threw himself to the ground before the general.

"I am not a lord, stand up."

The guard rose and spoke, *"General, a man has appeared. He approached our ship and we captured him. I await to hear how you would like us to deal with him."*

"Bring him to me!"

Sicinnus was dragged in front of Ahumim. The general stared at the small man. He seemed to be considering the likelihood that this man could be the person he had heard of. He signaled for the guards to leave him alone with his funny looking small man. When the room cleared Ahumim spoke, *"We have been told to expect a visitor. I hear that you have a message for the great King. Give it to me and I will make sure that the King sees it."*

Even though he was still in pain, Sicinnus spoke in low tones to the general.

"I am sorry, lord, but my master made me swear to only give the message to the King."

The general looked sternly at the man, obviously thinking about this dilemma. Finally, he waved his arm and said, *"Very well, follow me."*

Within an hour, Sicinnus was entering the tent of the King of Kings. He had never seen such opulence in the field before and it shocked him at first. Once inside, a brutish guard pushed him down on his knees before the monarch. The great King stared down on the little man who looked even smaller on the floor. The King squatted before him. It appeared he was trying to appraise the situation before he heard the man speak. He finally rose and motioned to his guards.

The guards dragged Sicinnus to his feet and began stripping his clothes off his body. Before he knew it he was standing naked in front of the King. Another guard came over and pressed Sicinnus to his knees. He then pushed Sicinnus forward and harshly stuck his hand in Sicinnus' behind, searching for a hidden weapon. Some blood dripped from his ass as he stood. One of the guards then grabbed his hands and began spreading his fingers, again looking for a hidden weapon. When none were found, Sicinnus was pushed down again, and his clothes thrown at him. He struggled to put his pants on because of the damage done to his anus. Two of the guards chuckled as they watched him labor. When he finished the Great King asked, *"Who are you?"*

As the blood slowly dripped on the floor, Sicinnus began stuttering and said, *"My name is Sicinnus, Lord."*

Xerxes paused. then continued, *"How do you come to speak such fluent Persian?"*

"I teach the children of Themistocles in their studies."

The King of Kings heard Themistocles' name and immediately pulled his sword. He moved aggressively to the tutor and placed his sword under Sicinnus' chin. His eyes flashed, *"You know this man, Themistocles?"*

Sicinnus nodded in affirmation. Xerxes pressed the sword against the tutor's neck. Sicinnus' face was now beet red and his eyes bulged in fear. Xerxes then moved his head to within whispering distance of the Greek.

"What is his secret?"

"Secret, Lord?"

"How does he know what I will do before I do? Does he speak with your Gods?"

"No, Lord."

"Then what is it? Does he have spies?"

"No, Lord, but he does have a talent, it is called Metis."

"What is this Metis- is it a potion given to him by a shaman?"

"No potion, Lord- a gift of vision given to him by the Goddess Athena."

"A gift from the Goddess?"

"Well, tutor, there is no Goddess here. You stand now in front of the King of Peoples, the King of Lands and the King of Kings. Half the world belongs to my dynasty. What message do you have for me?"

Sicinnus bowed.

"Lord, my master, Themistocles, has considered your generous offer and has decided to accept it."

Outwardly, Xerxes appeared unmoved by this information. He began to slowly pace walking before Sicinnus. For those who knew him well, this behavior meant that the great King had a weighty decision to ponder. He was so disciplined not to let any of his internal feelings become obvious to anyone. His face remained cold. He finally responded, *"Tell me something, tutor, that would convince me that you actually represent the general, Themistocles, and that this is not a ruse, not a trick."*

"My master told me of your proposal. He said all residents of Athens would be allowed to return to their city without retribution. They would be allowed to have any form of government they wished and could practice any religion."

Xerxes kept pacing with his hand on his chin.

"Anything else, tutor?"

"Yes, Lord, he wanted me to give you these two gold coins and he said he would only make an arrangement with the Pharaoh of Egypt."

"Sicinnus also reached into a pouch and poured a small amount of water on the floor. A small amount of dirt was added to it. My master, Themistocles, submits to your superiority."

This was the traditional Persian message of subservience. The offering of water and earth.

Xerxes now sat back on his throne. Sicinnus began to speak again.

"Lord there is another piece of information that my lord wants to convey to you. He said that the Greek alliance is troubled. The ships from the Peloponnese are abandoning the alliance and plan to sneak out of the strait in the night. He says he was wrong to trust the Spartan because they only have their own interests at heart. He sees now that the only solution for Athens is what the great King has offered. He sees the inevitability of the King's victory, and he does not want his people scattered in the wind. He does not want diaspora."

Xerxes kept his stare.

"Further, Lord, my master offers the following strategy. He suggests that the great King block any Greek retreat through the Megarian Channel. Some of the Greek ships will attempt to escape through the Bay of Eleusis by running north. Blocking the channel eliminates the possibility of their escape. The Persian navy should leave their security at Phaleron and attack the Greek alliance as the sun rises. When the attack commences the Athenian navy will turn on the Peloponnese and destroy them by surprise. This will effectively eliminate their ability to return to the Isthmus of Corinth and support their army stationed there. The Persian victory will be complete, destruction and surrender of the entire Greek navy in one morning."

Again, the King began pacing. Sicinnus continued, *"My master said that if you agree to this arrangement, you should give me a gold chalice as evidence of your promise."*

Xerxes turned and faced the Greek tutor. He waved his arm and two guards grabbed Sicinnus. Sicinnus could feel the fear rising through his body. Another wave by Xerxes had Sicinnus escorted out of the tent.

Sicinnus was provided with a gold chalice and ushered back to his small craft.

Before the small craft left the sight of the Persian trireme, the Warrior Queen's informants had already come into her presence and informed her about the "deal" that the young King had made. Without hesitation she grabbed her sword and stormed out of her tent. It was unusual for the Queen to leave without proper presentation. But she was incensed. This was the second time that the young senseless King had trusted the duplicitous Greeks.

"No, No,"

she protested when she heard of the arrangement that Xerxes had made with the Athenian. Artemisia stormed into Xerxes' tent unannounced. The King had been meditating and was now napping on a makeshift bed. Out of all the people in the invasion force, it was only the Warrior Queen that had the fortitude to enter the King's reign without approval. Xerxes jerked when he heard the commotion. He saw the Warrior Queen and rose to his elbow.

"Have you changed your mind and decided to join me in bed?"

The Queen stared at him with an appalled look on her face. Xerxes rose, *"I know, I know, you have female companions to keep you company."*

Artemisia stood stiffly with a piercing gaze focused on the great King. She couldn't hold her tongue anymore and she verbally lashed out at the monarch.

"We have come this long way, Lord, to defeat the Greeks and reestablish Persian superiority. Twice before the Greeks have tricked us into believing falsehoods. Datis, the unworthy general was fooled when we suffered the humiliation at Marathon. We were fooled at Artemisium and ended up fighting when it was unwarranted. And now this! This Themistocles is the master of the liars, and he is baiting you into a trap."

Xerxes rose with some anger in his voice, *"Are you comparing me to Datis?"*

Realizing the possible mistake, she had made, the Warrior Queen backed down from her irritation.

"Lord, you are the sun and the moon. Datis was a fool, and his stupidity is what has led us here."

Xerxes kept his stare then smiled, *"All of my generals and admirals are convinced of this strategy. It is only the stubbornness of the Queen from Halicarnassus that stands in the way of unanimity. Besides, we are here because of Persian destiny."*

"All your generals are fools"

"They have gotten me here, have they not? The great Greek city of Athens burns in the night."

"We are here because of the bravery and foresight of the great King, no one else."

"Flattery is ugly on you, Artemisia."

"Please, Lord; follow the strategy I have outlined. Patience, and they will come to us. If the Corinthians want to leave, let them. The splintering of their navy is in your best interest."

Suddenly serious, The King of Kings said, *"I believe that this Themistocles is a traitor. He is a weak man, he is controlled by alcohol and women."*

He moved to Artemisia and his eyes widened.

"If we attack now, we can destroy their entire navy and end this war. I grow tired, and I want to return to Susa. I have found in northern Greece that the strength and bravery of these peoples are overrated. What type of people abandon their capital and run away from their enemies? They are cowards by heart."

Artemisia's face contorted.

"They did not run at Thermopylae. They did not run at Artemisium."

Her eyes glowed, while a low rumble emerged from the Kings throat. She continued, *"They did not run at Marathon!"*

Xerxes did not back away. He glared back at the Warrior Queen. *"When we show force, they will disintegrate."*

Artemisia stomped her foot like an angry child. She turned her back, but then turned again to Xerxes.

"You trust this liar, Themistocles, or you trust me!"

A quiet came over the tent as the two stared into each other's eyes.

Artemisia began to talk but the King cut her off.

"I trust you more than anyone, but I am convinced that this message is genuine."

Artemisia bit the inside of her mouth and bowed before the King.

The King put his hand on the Queen. Xerxes then made one final demand. With a very stern voice he demanded, *"Spread the word to the admirals and captains. If one Greek ship escapes this trap, I will behead those responsible. I expect bravery. I will not settle for less."*

Artemisia turned red, but again held her temper. She bowed and left the tent. After she left she approached the first slave she could find and slashed the man's stomach. The man looked surprised as he watched his stomach and intestines fall from his body and hit the ground. Artemisia never turned but just cursed and walked away.

When the Queen arrived back at her encampment she ordered two of her finest captains to attempt to cut the Greek messenger off before he returned to the Greek lines. Unfortunately, they were not successful, as their ships were ambushed by three pirate ships during their chase. The pirate King Ptea, rescued the Greek tutor and returned him to the Greek lines.

****

Demaratus, the ex-Spartan general walked across the field. His troops were on their way to the Isthmus of Corinth to engage the Peloponnesians. He thought it fitting that he was chosen to lead the assault on the Peloponnese. He was finally returning to his home. Demaratus had almost a light-headedness as he walked. He pictured himself returning to Sparta in victory. It would be epic. He had prayed over and over for this moment and he was trying to enjoy it as much as he could. Of course, breaching the Spartan defense would not be an easy task. But Demaratus was confident that his desire for revenge was greater than their desire for defense. He would land troops behind the Spartan position and crush them from behind. As he walked, he was approached by another ex-Spartan. His name was Zent. Demaratus had known this man when he was still King of Sparta. Zent had once sat on the high counsel of the Spartan government. Demaratus had secretly contacted him almost two years earlier in anticipation of this event. The price was right and Zent became a Persian collaborator. Between the gold that had been secretly given to his family and the promise of a superior position in the new order, Zent could not resist the temptation.

Zent approached the ex-Spartan King and patted him on the shoulder.

"Well, my King, are you ready for retribution?"

Demaratus smiled but remained silent.

"This will not be an easy conquest,"

Demaratus finally remarked.

"I have confidence, my King."

Zent said, the joy leaving his voice.

"Do you have the positions for me?"

"I do, lord."

"Let me see."

Zent pulled out a papyrus. Demaratus scanned the document in a very serious manner. Before leaving the Spartan position, Zent had written down the exact locations of the Spartan defenders. He even found a weakness in the wall that the Peloponnese were building. He believed that Demaratus could exploit the weakness and overwhelm the Spartan flank.

"This is good,"

Demaratus remarked, as he reviewed the information that Zent had brought.

"But even if we can breach this wall, our success will depend on the Navy being able to land soldiers behind the Spartan position. The Navy must destroy the Greeks at Salamis"

"Yes, yes, I understand,"

Zent *observed*, the comment from Demaratus somehow diminishing his contribution to the campaign.

As the two men walked in silence, a large dust devil appeared in the distance. It swirled and rose off the ground, gyrating in its unpredictable path. Both men stopped to stare at the natural occurrence. Zent froze.

"Do you hear it, my King?"

"Hear what?"

"Listen careful, above the noise of the wind."

The Spartan King concentrated, but said, *"I hear nothing."*

"A melody," Zent said.

"Oh my," he continued.

"It is iacche!"

"What?" Demaratus queried.

"Zent. I think you are becoming old. There is no sound."

"No, lord, I can hear it. It comes from the sky. It is the song sung to worship Demeter and the Elusion mysteries."

Zent was frozen in his spot. He finally said, *"It is a portent, lord. A warning from the Gods. Heaven is turning against us. I fear for the King's navy."*

Demaratus laughed.

You are so dramatic, Zent. There is no sound, just the wind. In any case, do not let the Great King know of your fears, for it surely will cost you your head.

The two men walked on, but Demaratus now had a knot in his stomach. If the Gods had turned away from the Persian cause, he might never return to Sparta. This was the first time that Demaratus had considered such an outcome. But as he reasoned, rationality returned to his thoughts. The Persian navy was far stronger than the Greek alliance. They would crush the Greeks and then be able to support his attack to conquer Sparta.

****

Chapter XXII – Deception

The sun still had two hours before it rose. Persian sailors had spent the night on their vessels guarding the straits for what they thought was the inevitable Greek abandonment of the straits of Salamis. They had all sat in their boats holding their oars. As the sun was beginning to reach to the sky, the Persian oarsmen were exhausted. Many slumped over their seats while their superiors tried to keep them alert and vigilant. It was a losing battle for the admirals. They were suffering as well, many keeping one eye on the strait and another on the mountain overlooking their position where their King would be watching when the battle was at hand. Within the past two hours, the Persian admiralty had begun to believe that they had been duped. Even though they stayed watchful, no Greek vessels bolted to escape.

While the Persians waited, the various Greek contingencies were all gathering to hear their admirals. Unlike their adversaries, the Greek sailors were all rested. The leaders of the contingents had spent the night coordinating their efforts and reinforcing their strategy. The Corinthians were in the north of the channel. They had the honor of beginning the conflict. In the south, by the city of Salamis in Ambelaki Bay, were the Aeginetans. In the center of the Greek position, by the island of Pharmakoussae, lay the Athenians and the ships from the Peloponnese. News had come from their many spies that the Persians had sent their Egyptian contingents south then north to prevent any Greek retreat and escape from the Bay of Eleusis. The Greek fleet was now surrounded by the Persian and their allies. Themistocles' strategy was taking hold. He wanted the Persians to be overconfident and have them believe that the Greek alliance was disintegrating in front of their eyes.

The hour of reckoning was approaching. Themistocles addressed his Athenian brothers.

"So, it comes to this. We have set a trap and baited it with our lives and our fortunes. The Persian ships now have us surrounded. They will wait for us to try and slip through, but we won't. We will not run. Look to the sky my fellows. Athena watches us with a smile. Your ancestors and your families are all watching what we do here this day. Sons of Greece, strike this day for our honor and freedom.

The Persian dogs are all in place waiting for the rabbits to abandon their lair. But these Athenian rabbits have teeth. The Persian believe that they have us surrounded, but we are the ones who have set the snare. My fellow Athenians, the Persians will bleed this day. They will cry out to their God, while Athena laughs at their stupidity. Gain strength from this my fellows. The Persians have taken the bait. We will now offer them other lures to tempt them into more mistakes."

Themistocles waited. He wanted his words to sink before he continued. Now the great Greek politician/admiral turned and looked to the east. In theatrical fashion, he pointed to the horizon. One thought they could see him choke up with emotion.

"Do you see it?"

In unison, many of the sailors turned to look at what their leader pointed to.

"Our people sit in Salamis and Troezen. Our city has been burned and many of our people enslaved. The temple that we built to honor our Goddess has been destroyed. We fight not only for our fortunes, but for the generations of our relatives who cry in their graves. Our destiny awaits my Athenian brothers. We will reclaim our birthright. It starts today, here, with our spears, with our arrows, in our boats."

The Persian sailors were exhausted waiting for the Greek abandonment that never came. Many fell asleep at their positions. They had been on the ready through the night, waiting for the Greeks to begin fleeing through the strait so they were both tired and disgusted. The admirals had all kept their sailors on the alert and thusly they were as tired as their men. As the sun rose Xerxes had his throne placed on a mountain cliff near Herakleion. It would provide the clearest picture of the battle that was set to unfold.

The King of Kings had given orders that he be awakened when the Greeks began to bolt. When he awoke with the light, he was confused that no one had come to wake him. When he was told that no Greek vessel had made a run he exploded in anger. He lashed out at the bearer of the news, opening a large gash in the man's face. The man fell to his knee in pain and the young King grabbed his hair

"Why do you lie to me?"

"I am not lying, Lord. There has been no movement in the strait during the night."

Xerxes cursed and again slashed the man. He finally released the man's head and shoved him down. The man crawled out of the tent leaving the King to stew on his own. The King paced quickly around the tent. He had believed the Greek, Themistocles, and now cursed the Greek and himself for his gullibility. Xerxes stared at the sky in disbelief and then exploded slapping himself in the side of his head. In conjunction he led out a scream. Guards came running in shocked by the sound. When they realized there was no danger, they quickly departed, not wanting to incur the wrath of the young monarch. Xerxes could feel the blood burning through his veins.

As he stood, Xerxes recalled Marathon where the Persian general, Datis, was duped by the Athenians into believing that they would open the city to the invading army. Believing the Greek saboteur, Datis split his troops taking his cavalry and ships south to Athens. He left his army unprotected on the field at Marathon. The Greeks attacked the vulnerable army, defeating the far superior force. It was a strategic stroke of genius on the part of the Greek general, Miltiades. Leaving in shame, the Persian King, Darius, Xerxes' father, never forgot this disgrace, and it consumed him until his death. When his father died, Xerxes swore to his ancestors and Gods that he would revenge himself against the Greeks. And now, here he stood. He had burned Athens, and yet the flames and the smoke did not fill his heart with satisfaction. He wanted to destroy the Greeks. And yet, had he made the same mistake that Datis did? He pondered this thought. It was like a fire in his chest that he couldn't relieve. The King now fell to his knee. He looked to the heaven and pleaded to his ancestors.

"Father, I plead with you for direction. We have been betrayed by this pig, Themistocles. It makes no great matter, we are still the stronger, we are still the Persians."

The King bowed his head. He fell into a deep meditation. Twice guards came in to check on the King, and twice they left quietly without disturbing the trance in which Xerxes dwelled.

The King was giddy as daylight approached. The next number of hours would mark the destruction of the Greek navy and the subsequent end, for all intents and purposes, to the Greek escapade. Xerxes had sent troops to march on the Isthmus of Corinth where the

of metal ringing in everyone's ears. As the two men continued their engagement, it became obvious that Ariabignes was beginning to effectively take the offensive, as Ameinias was forced to block and give way under the onslaught. The Phoenician general's face was beet red, with sweat pouring down the sides as he exerted his entire energy into the blows. But as Ameinias was giving ground, suddenly the Phoenician general let out a scream. Ameinias stopped in surprise, noticing a spear point protruding from his chest. Ameinias' second in command, Socles, had killed the Phoenician marine he was engaged with, and then noticing the trouble his captain was in, skewered the general from behind. Ariabignes fell to his knees, and within seconds, fell forward. His body began convulsing in death throes. Ameinias and Socles quickly lifted the general's body and threw it overboard. The sight of this death seemed to deflate the Persian marines on the Pallenian ship and the tide quickly turned in favor of the Greeks. Many of the Persian marines jumped over the side rather than face death at the hand of the sword. The impact of the ramming had been so complete that it took the help of other Greek triremes to disengage the Pallenian vessel from the Phoenician ship, allowing it to sink to the bottom of the strait. First blood was spilled.

The loss of the Admiral confused the Phoenician advance. There was no leader to take his place and the ships were now each on their own. It led to a quick loss of discipline and a more disordered approach to the confrontation.

On his perch, watching this first encounter, Xerxes swallowed hard as bile rose in his throat and stomach.

While as the battle between the Navies began to unfold, it became obvious that the Greeks were acting in disciplined unison, whereas the Persians were more disorganized. As the Athenians ships advanced on their left, they were keeping pace with the Ageon contingents. An Ageon boat passed dangerously close to Themistocles' vessel, and the captain of the ship, a man named Polykritos yelled across to the

328 · JEFFREY DONNER

Athenian, *"Themistocles, you can take your Athenians and return to the beach. We Aeginians will take care of the Phoenicians."*

He waved and laughed as his trireme passed Themistocles' vessel. Themistocles turned to one of his captains and gave a motion. The captain raised a red flag in the air, which was responded to in kind by the other Athenian vessels. Suddenly the entire Athenian contingent sharply turned left, leaving the Aeginians to engage the Phoenician fleet first. The Phoenician vessels seemed to ignore the maneuver, concentrating their attack on the incoming Aeginians.

A smile arose on Polykritos' face as he watched the Athenians disengage and move left. Aegina and Athens had been enemies in a ten-year war. The Aeginians had the upper hand for years because of their superior sailing skills. They had embargoed the Athenian ports, making life very difficult in Athens. Ironically, when Themistocles was arguing for the building of the Athenian navy, he had used the Aeginian threat as one of the reasons to strengthen the navy. And now, the two adversaries were working in unison to defeat a common enemy.

As the Athenian boats were veering away, one of the sailors on Themistocles' vessel looked up to the sky.

"Do you hear that?"

He yelled above the sound of the battle to his right. Themistocles heard the man's calls and ordered quiet on the ship. In the background, and barely audible, the men seemed to hear singing. But it was a strange unearthly sound, seeming to arise from the heavens. The sound continued and after ten minutes, Themistocles turned again to a man next to him and gave another command, *"Raise the yellow banner!"*

And, as the yellow flag was lifted, it was answered by every Athenian vessel raising their own yellow banners. At this sight the

Athenians began turning to the right and pointing their advance back at the Phoenician flank. The Persians, now fully engaged with the Aeginians, did not notice the entire Athenian navy bearing down on their right flank. The engagement was devastating, as ship after Phoenician ship was rammed by the Athenians. Some of them had their entire side of oars sheared off in the engagement.

Polykritos began pumping his fist and shouting in glee as it became apparent that the Phoenician were beginning to withdraw. As they attempted to backwater, the Athenians and Aeginians began pushing some of the Persian vessels back, beaching them on coastlines and shattering them on hidden rocks. The fight, at this end of the strait, was turning into a romp. The Phoenicians had hoped that their flank would be protected and reinforced by the Ionian Greek vessels. Unfortunately for them, the Ionian help never materialized. And then, the disarray arrived. Because of the narrowness of the strait, the Phoenicians could not withdraw and reorganize. Their escape lanes were blocked by incoming ships, so the Greeks were able to pick off ships with impunity.

The Warrior Queen was in her element as her ship slashed through the oncoming Greek vessels. Her trireme was piloted by a man she considered an illusionist. She would bark out orders, and by artistically using the side rudders the pilot could outmaneuver any other vessel. His name was Adonia, and he had piloted the Queen's vessel for many years. Artemisia received all the credit, but many felt that if it was not for Adonia, her sailing reputation would be superior, but not at the untouchable level that it was. In truth, it was the combination of the two maestros, the man who was able to control the ship as if it was part of his body, and the Queen whose aggressiveness and strategy was unparalleled by any man, that created the deadly magic. The two formed a lethal masterpiece of death.

In these opening stages of the battle, the Warrior Queen's trireme outraced the other Persian vessels to engage the enemy from the south.

Unlike other captains, Artemisia rarely showed indecision. She had the focus of a stalking cat, quickly identifying a weak link and separating it from the herd. She passed a lead Athenian vessel then turned immediately to broadside it. Without hesitation Artemisia's ship swiveled and sheared off the side of another vessel.

Xerxes, in watching the Phoenician withdrawal stood and yelled into the air. He identified the Warrior's Queen's trireme and watched her destroy two Greek vessels. Xerxes looked at his aide and said, *"My men fight like woman and my women fight like men."*

As she overtook the second disabled Greek trireme, Artemisia happened to consider the water. What she saw shocked her. Floating past her vessel was the dead body of the Phoenician general, Ariabignes.

As Artemisia's trireme turned to focus on another victim, two Greek vessels bore down on her rear. One of the soldiers cried out and she turned to notice the impending danger she faced. She looked at Adonia with an expressionless face and tapped her hand to her forehead. Adonia made a motion and Greek flags were raised on the Queen's ship replacing the Persian flags. The vessel quickly swung and rammed a nearby Persian vessel. The two Greek vessels that were targeting the Queen noticed the Greek flags on Artemisia's craft, as well as her attack on the Persian ship. They then turned off their attack and began heading in another direction. As her trireme moved off, the Queen smiled to herself at the deception. And yet Artemisia didn't rest on her laurels. She immediately motioned to Adonia and the Greek flags were replaced with their Persian equivalents. Her boat veered off again and headed for an Aegean vessel.

Three Phoenician captains crawled up on the rocks. Their boats had been shredded on the outcrop of rocks on the shore. All three had attempted to withdraw in the face of the Athenian trap. The Phoenician fleet had expected that their flank would be guarded by the

Ionian contingency. When the Ionians were cut off, the Phoenicians were left vulnerable to the Athenian attack. Their ability to fight a defensive battle was deterred by the narrowness of the strait and the Persian vessels advancing behind them. Chaos ensued and the Phoenician vessels became trapped between the Athenians and the shore.

Unlike most of the Persians the three Phoenicians knew how to swim. Although they struggled, Tabnit, Myberalous, and Tetune all made it to the shore. The three men sat on the sharp rocks and tried catching their breath. As they lay on the rocks they could see remnants of their vessels float by. But as bad as that felt, they also watched their dead compatriots float by. The Athenian and Aegean attack had made a mockery of them. The Phoenicians had a reputation for valor and fearlessness that was laid a partial myth by this one battle. They had turned and run, and in the ensuing pandemonium had lost 40 ships, many brave men, and their reputation. Tabnit wanted to cry. He attempted to replay the morning in his mind to determine where they had gone wrong, but it was a useless endeavor. All he kept seeing was his men screaming and his ships sinking. His conclusion was an ill tasting one that they had believed too much in their own reputation. Tabnit was ashamed and dispirited.

Myberalous noticed his compatriot's mood and became a little agitated.

"This defeat was not in our hands!"

The two other men looked at him in surprise.

"The Ionians betrayed us,"

Myberalous concluded. Tetune laughed then remarked, *"The King will not accept any excuses. He had made it clear that anyone caught retreating would be punished."*

As the men sat, three of Xerxes guards appeared and ominously walked towards them. The men helped the three captains to their feet and escorted them up the mountain to where the King of Kings sat. Xerxes sat silently, but his rage was evident. Next to him stood the Executioner. Behind the King were at least twenty cavalry that were also there for protection. The guards had brought the three captains into the King's presence and forced them to their knees. A cold chill ran up Tabnit's back as the seriousness of their position was becoming obvious. Tetune was right, there would be no excuses. As the three men sat in front of the monarch, Penish walked behind them. He quietly pulled his sword and impaled Myberalous through the neck. The two other captains jumped at the quickness of the attack. Myberalous lay bleeding in front of them. Tetune began to visibly shake in anticipation of the next blow. Xerxes rose from his thrown.

"52 ships destroyed, and only 5 Athenian vessels sank."

The rage shone through his stoic demeanor. The two captains sat silently.

"The great Phoenician navy, conqueror of the world, were duped into a trap. Your job was to penetrate the Greek left. Instead, you ran like rabbits. Wasn't I clear enough that no retreat would be tolerated? You have humiliated yourself, your Gods and the Empire."

Xerxes pointed at Tetune

"Rise, general and explain."

Tetune needed help to stand, as his legs visibly trembled.

"Great King, our success was dependent on the Ionians protecting our flank. They did not arrive, so the Athenian vessels were able to ram us from the side."

Xerxes raised his hand and Tetune went silent. He took two steps toward the general. Xerxes put his hand under the general's chin and lifted his head up.

"Are you saying that the Phoenician navy was not strong enough to take the Athenian ships by themselves?"

Sweat poured down Tetune's face. He had no response to the question and he knew it. Xerxes pulled a knife from his robe and cut Tetune's tongue out of his throat. The man withered in pain, and Penish came up from behind and with a swift motion ended his life. Xerxes walked back to his throne. He summoned his guards and ordered that the heads of the two fallen Phoenician generals should be placed on staffs so all could see the price of cowardness. Xerxes now approached Tabnit.

"You are last of the cowards. What do you think would be a fitting punishment?"

Tabnit swallowed hard. His life expectancy could be counted in seconds, but he tried to straighten himself.

"There is no excuse lord. We were beaten and we ran."

Xerxes began pacing in front of the general. He looked at Tabnit and said, *"An honest man. For that you deserve some praise."*

Xerxes turned and raised his hand again. Penish swung his sword and beheaded the remaining Phoenician general.

"Do not place this man's head on a stake. At least he was honest in his cowardness."

Chapter XXIII – Aftershock

It appeared contagious. Fear is transmittable. The breakdown and collapse of the Persian right seemed to set a wave of dismay through the Persian allies. When the Phoenician contingent appeared so inconsequential against the Athenians, the remainder of the Empire is ships began to panic. The strategy to engage the Greeks in the Salamis straits was now proving disastrous. The Persian contingents could not maneuver, and attempting to withdraw left them defenseless to side attacks. And yet, within this fluid and disordered conglomeration, Artemisia, the Warrior Queen, would not retreat. As many of the other ships turned, she continued to attack. Immediately following the execution of the Phoenician captains, Xerxes rose to applaud Artemisia's next sinking. He needed some good news no matter how minor or inconsequential, regardless of the total picture.

The sun was finally setting. Xerxes himself had retreated to his camp. Considering what he had just witnessed, he was surprisingly calm. At least on the outside he was presenting an emotionless face. As he got closer to his tent, his pace and internalized anxiety increased. After spending a few hours alone, the King fell to his knees and looked to the sky.

Tears welled up in the King's eyes as he began to pray. Xerxes was confused. He was starting to doubt the strength of his God. The Greek navy had consistently out-strategized and then outfought his most experienced sailors. He was feeling abandoned. " *I cannot trust my generals or admirals, and I cannot trust my advisors. The only person I should have trusted I scorned.*" Xerxes began to silently weep at the conclusions he was reaching. Still on his knees, Xerxes again looked to the heavens.

"Father, I have burned the Greek city of Athens and revenged our dynasty against the Greeks. We have never been sailors, father. Because of this I put my faith in others that let us down. I am sorry for this, father."

My Lord, Xerxes rose from his chair and again began his pace. His bodyguard and confidant, Penish, entered the tent.

"Lord,"

The King of Kings cut the warrior off by raising his hand. Finally, with his jaw clenched the King broke down.

"Every day I spend time praying to my God. I have praised him at the highest. I believe that Abu Mazda has embraced my ancestors and my Empire. But here we stand, and my God has abandoned me. I have watched my navy beaten. Beaten by a lessor force. I have watched thousands of my troops drown and cry out in these foreign waters. My ships turned and ran. Turned and ran! I am ashamed. I saw this in Egypt but did not believe my eyes."

Penish *had* dropped to his knees as the King spoke. He remained silent, intensely listening to the pleas of the young monarch. Xerxes looked directly at the warrior. The usually stoic, ice-faced King walked to Penish and kneeled in front of him. He raised his head and saw tears in the King's eyes. But even so there was a hollowness in his stare. The look of someone who had lost their way. He had just witnessed the near obliteration of an indestructible force. Everything he knew, everything he depended on, was now called in to question. He silently wondered whether the sun would rise again the next day. And then, to Penish's amazement, Xerxes started weeping. It was not a wailing, and the sound was muffled, but he sat in front of him and cried. After a minute, Xerxes rose and turned away from Penish.

"I have let them down,"

he muttered as he walked away from the bodyguard. Suddenly, as the great King reached the end of the tent, a light seemed to appear in the center of the area. Xerxes turned sensing that something was happening. His eyes were fixed on the light, although it did not originate at the top of the tent but seemed to grow from the earthy ground. Xerxes looked at Penish and the warrior had already drawn his sword and assumed an attack position. Neither knew whether to run. Both stood frozen in place staring at the center of the tent. Suddenly the King began rubbing his eyes, feeling as though there were bugs crawling through his sockets. The light began dimming, but as it did, a mist seemed to appear in its place. There was a strange smell to the mist, almost sickly sweet, and Xerxes immediately recognized it from an earlier time. The mist became thicker as Penish began backing away. He was having some trouble clearly seeing the King who stood at the other end of the tent. Penish then screamed as he was lifted off the ground, waving his weapon. The mist engulfed him, and he floated only a foot or so off the ground. Xerxes was stunned into paralyzed fear. He dropped to his knees prostrating himself in front of this unearthly event. His mind was frozen with

338 · JEFFREY DONNER

dread. Xerxes had faced armies, warriors, lions and assassins. Through these trials, the young King never flinched, never sweated. But this, how can he protect himself from a transcendent event. Xerxes prayed with words that were as ancient as the hills. Words that he learned from his father without really knowing their specific meaning. But he was taught to return to these prayers when he could not understand the boundaries of reality. And this, this unearthly experience was beyond his grasp. As he sat on the ground Xerxes searched for his scepter which he called the Answerer. The Answerer was a magic amulet given to him by his step-mother, Ho. He instinctively reached to his right to find his staff, but while his fingers searched the ground, his eyes were fixated on the floating warrior that had saved his life numerous times. He watched as a terrified Penish wet himself while he was floating. Finally, the King realized that the amulet he was searching for had already been destroyed and he jumped in pain. His head turned and he pulled his arm back. The young King stared in disbelief. His entire world was decompensating in front of him.

Xerxes now bent in reverence to whatever was happening. His head was bent to the ground and then he heard a blood curdling scream. Penish's face had changed color. He hovered above the ground and his body began to swell. His face was now purple and it seemed to expand to three times its original size. Blood began dripping from his face as he shook uncontrollably. Suddenly, his body went limp, and it was obvious to the King that Penish was dead. As he watched, parts of his body began to vanish until only his head remained. Penish's head now began drifting toward Xerxes. A it came closer, Xerxes attempted to flatten himself and disappear into the ground, but the face kept approaching. It finally reached the King and Xerxes lifted his head to look. He was now visibly shaking. The eyes were blood red dripping onto the floor. In a low gravelly voice, the aberration began speaking:

"There is no King. This land does not belong to you. You were warned of this son, of Darius. Your ancestors cannot hear you. The decision has been made. You will return to your mountains and deserts."

The face now drifted closer and another worldliness came about it.

"You have burned my city. I will not stand for much more, Son of Darius, grandson of Cyrus."

The head began fading and lifting toward the sky. Its last words were:

"It is time, go home, go home."

And with that, Xerxes was alone again. Not believing what had happened, the great King lifted his head to the heavens. He called out to his father for help.

"Please, father, in my time of trouble, guide me through this aberration."

His head bowed and the weeping continued. The Great King was being watched, but the eyes that looked down were **bright green.**

Epilogue

After the battle of Salamis, the Greeks did not fully understand the scope of their victory. In all, the Persian allies had lost over 200 ships to the Greek 40. After realizing the importance of the battle, Themistocles gave chase, but never caught the Persian retreat. He believed that the Delphic Oracle's prediction had finally come to pass. The wooden wall had withstood the invasion and turned away the horde. Many stories arose about Athena's divine intervention and how the Metis made Themistocles invulnerable, and an Oracle, in and of himself.

After these experiences, Xerxes the King of the greatest Empire on the planet, decided to retreat back to Asia and re-establish his dynasty. He had had enough of the deception and the duplicity of the Greeks. His pride was bruised. He had avenged himself and his father for the defeat at Marathon. He also avenged the death of his teacher, Hamas (fictionalized person), by killing Leonidas in the battle at Thermopylae. He had conquered (at great loss) a King of Sparta. His further rationalization was that Athens burned in ruins, its population abandoned and its temples razed. He attributed his naval loses to other cultures in their alliance that did not have the courageous hearts of the Median warrior. After Salamis, the Persian fleet retreated to cover the King's withdrawal. The navy was sent to the Hellespont to guard against an attack that would cut the King off from Asia. Xerxes left his cousin, General Mardonius, with an army of forty thousand, both to protect his withdrawal and to subdue the remainder of the Greeks. In truth, Mardonius knew it was a suicidal mission, as without the support and supplies from the navy, his troops would eventually succumb to the land and the Greeks. Mardonius attempted to break the

Greek alliance by offering Athens a peace if they abandoned Sparta and the Peloponnese. The Athenians refused and Mardonius reconquered Athens, burning he city again. In the battle of Plataea, the Persian army was defeated and Mardonius was killed in the conflict.

In one of the greatest tragic political ironies of the time, Themistocles was honored by the Spartans after the war and rejected by many in his own city. Rumors were spread about his treason. He was eventually ostracized from Athens. Even after his ostracism, the Greek courts found him guilty of treason and tried to return him to Athens for sentencing. He ended up in Xerxes' son, Artaxerxes court, begging for asylum. So, in the mockery of life (no good deed goes unpunished), the man who set the stage for the eventual defeat of the Persian invasion was now seen not as a hero, but as a collaborator with the enemy against the city he cherished and defended. It is reported that he lived out his life as a governor of Magnesia. To my knowledge it took years until he was finally returned to his rightful place in history.

Like his father, Xerxes was murdered by poison. In my story the murderer would have been the followers of the renegade priest, Ningizzida (fictional character), but in reality, not much is known about the incident. It has been suggested that he was poisoned by a eunuch named Asperities, under the order of a man named Artabanos. Demaratus, the ex-Spartan King returned to Asia with the great King and spent his remaining years ruling a Persian province. His dream of returning as the new head of Greece never reached fruition. The great Warrior Queen disappears from history after providing escort for the Great King's family back to Asia. Her prodigy appears again in later years.

Author's Note

I hope you enjoyed the reading of this historical series. It should be remembered that this is a fictional account of this important historical story. For a more accurate rendition of history, some of the scholars in the field should be read such as, "The Greek and Persian Wars", by Philip de Souza; "Xerxes Invasion of Greece", by C. Hignett; "Persian Fire", by Tom Holland; "Persia and the Greeks", by A.R. Burn; "The Greco-Persian Wars", by Peter Green, "Themistocles", by Plutarch; "The History of the Persian Empire", by Olmstead, and of course, Herodotus', "The History". I did borrow some of their brilliant conclusions for this story.

Many of the characters in this story are fictionalized. There is a thread of truth that runs through the story as well as the major characters. The main players were all real people (Xerxes, Themistocles, Artemisia, Leonidas), but their interactions are all dramatized. This was an intriguing time in history in the sense that it was the first confrontation between these two political ideologies that continues to this day. Who knows how the evolution of the Demos would have occurred if the result had been different.

In many historical texts, the great King Xerxes is presented in many ways. Some saw him as more effeminate and others more warrior-like. I chose to use the second characterization. There was little question about Themistocles, as most renditions saw him as a drunkard, a philanderer, and a manipulator par excellence. The most intriguing character I found was the Warrior Queen. I believe presentation of the naval strategy to the Great King was an accurate rendition of history. She was a woman in a man's world, and probably the only living being who could directly question the great King and remain alive.

The other fascinating aspect of this story was the Delphic Oracle. There were many Oracles in the ancient world, but the Delphic is the most well-known and was the most successful. It lasted for over a thousand years and it is said that Plato, after bashing fortune telling in general, made an exception for the Delphic Oracle. It is an inspiring place and should be visited.

I have also gained great respect for the Persian Culture. Xerxes was one of the first (outside of the Hebrews) to believe in one God. The Persian accomplishments were staggering in math, in engineering and in aesthetic arts, as well. The descriptions of the great temples and the engineering accomplishments were almost unmatched in their time (except maybe by the Egyptians). The Persians were much more than an expanding and militaristic Empire. Their culture and history should be taught more thoroughly in our educational system.

The Phoenicians also established an illustrious culture. Their exploits as well, tend to be overlooked in Western education.

Again, I hope you enjoyed this fictionalized account of the first great confrontation between east and west, the conflict between democracy and autocracy.

End of Book IV of the Great Persian Saga

The Great Persian Saga continues
in the last book of the series …

WARRIOR WOMEN

THE RISE OF THE SHADOW

A NOVEL ABOUT THE AMAZON WOMEN

DR. JEFFREY DONNER

Warrior Women
The Rise of the Shadow

They were vicious in their treatment of enemies, they created a society based only on female virtues. They gave no quarter and took none. They were relentless and Spartan in their battlefield exploits. They were feared in the male dominated world, and their name was that of Legends. They were the Amazon Woman of southern Ukraine.

But out of them all, there was one name that sent a chill down even the fiercest of warriors. She was seductive and ruthless. Some believed she was just a myth, a fable to scare young children. But those who experienced her strength and veracity knew that she was a force of darkness. She brought both love and vengeance. She practiced retribution, both in the bedroom and in the field. If she came for you, one way or the other, your life was over.

She was known as The Shadow, and this, is her story!

www.ingramcontent.com/pod-product-compliance
Lightning Source LLC
Chambersburg PA
CBHW060000100426
42740CB00010B/1343